About the Author

Mike McCann is a well-known sports commentator with the ABC in Sydney, where he
hosts radio's popular national weekend
sports program Summer Grandstand. Away
from the studio, he's also heard calling International and Sheffield Shield cricket, AFL,
soccer, basketball and other major events.

After starting his career as a newspaper
journalist in Tasmania, Mike joined the ABC
in 1980 and has since worked on radio and
television in Western Australia, South
Australia and New South Wales, as well as
covering the Olympic Games in South Korea
and Spain, the Commonwealth Games in
Scotland, New Zealand and Canada, and the
Goodwill Games in the United States, making
him one of Australia's senior sports
journalists.

Cricket's Ultimate Ashes Test is the second
book by Mike McCann, following the success
of his 1993 work, the *ABC Sport Quiz*. Mike
lives in Sydney with his wife Louise, and
young children Kate and Benjamin.

Thanks to Patrick Eagar for assistance with photographs.

A QUEEN ANNE PRESS BOOK

First published in 1994 by
Queen Anne Press, a division of
Lennard Associates Ltd
Mackerye End, Harpenden
Herts AL5 5DR

British Library Cataloguing in Publication Data
is available

ISBN 1 85291 5633

CRICKET'S
ULTIMATE
ASHES
TEST

MIKE McCANN
Foreword by Dennis Lillee

Queen Anne Press

Bibliography

Many dozens of books and magazines were involved in the compilation of this book. However, the principal reference sources were *The Complete Who's Who of Test Cricketers* by Christopher Martin-Jenkins (Rigby Publishers, 1983), *ABC Guide to Australian Test Cricketers* by Rick Smith (ABC Books, 1993), *England v Australia Test match records 1877–1985* by David Frith (Collins Willow Books, 1986), *The Ashes, England in Australia 1990–91* by Mark Ray and Alan Lee (The Text Publishing Company Pty Ltd, 1991) and *The Wisden Book of Test Cricket, Vol. I 1877–1977,* and *Vol. II 1977–1989* compiled and edited by Bill Frindall (Macdonald Queen Anne Press, 1990).

Contents

Author's Note

Saturday, January 10, 1970. Day two of the Fourth Test at the Sydney Cricket Ground. I was a 12-year-old schoolboy listening to descriptions of an Ashes drama unfold from my home in Launceston, Tasmania, engrossed in the deeds of our flannelled national heroes. This was the series that opened my eyes to the glorious world of Australia–England Test cricket. I'd cherished each of Stacky's 207 runs at the Gabba as if they were made off my own bat; I'd wondered why Marshy should have been unkindly called 'Irongloves' in his first match; I'd willed young Greg Chappell on to his magical hundred on debut in Perth . . . a feat I had performed so many times myself in my own backyard. So by the time that Fourth Test came along, I was ready for the biggest adventure of my life.

I decided, as Dougie was making his half-century, that I wanted to be part of this match—to see my heroes in the flesh. A note was left on the kitchen bench for my disbelieving Mum, then armed with a student concession card, I spent 24 hours of plane, train and bus travel to reach my sister's home in Sydney. All in time for the resumption of the Test after the rest day.

That's how it all started for me. The Ashes. I've loved every series since. *Cricket's Ultimate Ashes Test* is my contribution to this unique sporting rivalry. Throughout the ages, arguments have abounded over this incident or that character in Ashes Tests. This book asks more than 500 questions to test your knowledge of the 280 matches between these oldest of foes. Strictly speaking, the Ashes haven't been on the line for each of those matches, but for simplicity, they're all known as Ashes Tests. To help with the answers, the book also includes a potted history of each series, outlining the highlights and the milestones.

One player central to modern-day Ashes drama is Dennis Lillee. No-one has taken more wickets in these matches than this champion Australian fast bowler, and no-one has engendered as much fear in the hearts of opposing batsmen. I was delighted when Dennis readily agreed to write a foreword for this book and I extend my sincere thanks. I must also express my gratitude to cricket statistician Ross Dundas for providing solutions to many and varied queries, to Grandstand Test commentator Jim Maxwell for his ear and advice, to ABC Radio's Head of Sport Neville Oliver for his support in this project, and to my wife Louise, and children Kate and Benjamin for their understanding and patience during this time-consuming assignment.

To lovers of cricket, I invite you to join me in reliving the magic of Australia–England Test history . . . and then, indulge yourself, in *Cricket's Ultimate Ashes Test.*

MIKE McCANN

Foreword

I'm very grateful to Mike McCann for producing this book. It's going to let me off the hook!

I couldn't estimate to the nearest hundred how many people have approached me over the years to settle a wager by answering a question about Test cricket, particularly Ashes Tests. They still do it, but from now on most of those punters won't have to take my word for it. I'll be referring them to *Cricket's Ultimate Ashes Test* quiz book.

This is a gem of a book, for sheer trivia buffs and for all those dedicated cricket fans who are fascinated by Ashes history and statistics.

Ah, the Ashes. Every young Australian cricketer progressing through the junior ranks aspires to one day play for his country. To play for his country against England is his ultimate ambition, the dream that lights a fire in his belly.

England is the traditional enemy and the 117 years of Ashes, or at least, Australia vs England Test history, are characterised by fierce rivalry born of a colony trying to prove itself against the mother country.

Ashes battles have produced the most memorable moments in all Test history. I was lucky enough, in the years spanning my first encounter with England, in Adelaide during the 1970–71 series, to my last, in Perth in November 1982, to have been involved in quite a number of them.

The old adrenalin still starts pounding again when I reflect on those moments.

Cricket's Ultimate Ashes Test is a faithful record of Anglo-Australian Test matches since their very origin. It is the last word in Ashes statistics—and the ultimate bet settler.

DENNIS LILLEE

Chapter One

19th Century

1876–77

And so it all began. In reality, these matches were not 'Australia' versus 'England', nor were they 'Ashes' Tests.

It would have come as something of a surprise to captain Dave Gregory and his teammates that their Grand Combined Melbourne and Sydney XI would later become recognised as the first Australian Test team. And that the professional outfit led by Sussex businessman James Lillywhite would become England's first Test side. As for the Ashes, they weren't created and the Test contests so named until some years later.

In what was later recognised as the first Ashes series, Australia won the first match and England the second as the series was drawn.

Charles Bannerman faced the first ball in Test cricket and scored the first run.

Bannerman scored the first Test century before retiring hurt for 165, struck on the right hand by a rising ball from Yorkshireman George Ulyett.

The first ball in Test cricket was delivered by Nottinghamshire paceman Alfred Shaw.

John Selby, of Nottingham, became the first wicketkeeper to open the batting in Test cricket. The team's regular keeper, Edward Pooley, had been gaoled in New Zealand over illicit gambling activities. The other opener, Henry Jupp, of Surrey, kept wicket from lunch on the first day of both Tests.

The first bowler to take five wickets in a Test innings was Australia's Billy Midwinter, who went on to play for England, and then Australia again.

The first brothers to play Test cricket were Dave and Edward 'Ned' Gregory.

The first duck in Test cricket was scored by Ned Gregory.

The first toss in Ashes contests was won by Australia, through Dave Gregory.

The Test umpires were CA Reid and RB Terry.

Australia's demon fast bowler Fred Spofforth missed cricket's first Test match, refusing to play unless Billy Murdoch was chosen as wicketkeeper. Instead, Victorian Jack Blackham was selected, but Spofforth played in the Second Test, with Murdoch chosen as a batsman.

1876–77 SERIES DRAWN 1–1

1 1st Test Melbourne Cricket Ground, March 15, 16, 17, 19

AUSTRALIA 245 (C Bannerman 165 ret hurt) and **104** (A Shaw 5/38)
ENGLAND 196 (H Jupp 63, WE Midwinter 5/78) and **108** (T Kendall 7/55)
CAPTAINS DW Gregory [AUST], James Lillywhite [ENG]
RESULT Australia won by 45 runs

2 2nd Test Melbourne Cricket Ground, March 31, April 2, 3, 4

AUSTRALIA 122 (A Hill 4/27) and **259** (DW Gregory 43, N Thompson 41, James Lillywhite 4/70, J Southerton 4/46)
ENGLAND 261 (A Greenwood 49, A Hill 49, T Emmett 48, T Kendall 4/82) and **6/122** (G Ulyett 63)
CAPTAINS DW Gregory [AUST] James Lillywhite [ENG]
RESULT England won by four wickets

1878–79

This was a one-off match, played at the Melbourne Cricket Ground two years after the first Test match. Some years later, this match became accepted as cricket's third Test match.

Nine England players made their Test debuts, including the Fourth Lord Harris, Francis MacKinnon (the 35th MacKinnon of Clan MacKinnon) and the extravagantly-named Rev. Vernon Peter Fanshawe Archer Royle.

Fred Spofforth achieved the first hat-trick in Test cricket, with the wickets of Royle, MacKinnon and Emmett in the first innings for figures of 6/48.

Spofforth took 7/62 in the second innings, making him the first bowler to take 10 or more wickets in a Test match.

3

Australian captain Dave Gregory assumed an interesting role, batting at number eleven for 12 not out, and yet failing to bowl.

The Test was the first for Alec Bannerman, younger brother of the first century-maker in Tests, Charles Bannerman.

1878–79 AUSTRALIA WON ONLY TEST

3 Melbourne Cricket Ground, January 2, 3, 4

ENGLAND 113 (CA Absolom 52, FR Spofforth 6/48) and **160** (FR Spofforth 7/62)
AUSTRALIA 256 (AC Bannerman 73, T Emmett 7/68) and **0/19**
CAPTAINS Lord Harris [ENG] DW Gregory [AUST]
RESULT Australia won by 10 wickets

1880

This is recognised as the first Test played in England. The match was not played at the home of cricket, Lord's, but at Kennington Oval and, in fact, was staged at the expense of a scheduled match between Australia and Sussex.

Fifteen players made their Test debuts, eight for England and seven for Australia.

The Test was the first for the great Englishman, Dr William Gilbert Grace, who'd toured Australia in 1873–74 before the birth of Test cricket.

Older brother Dr Edward Mills Grace and the younger George Frederick Grace also played in the match ... the first time three brothers played in the same Test.

WG Grace and EM Grace opened the first innings, failing by nine runs to post Test cricket's first century opening partnership.

WG Grace scored England's first century in Test cricket ... 152 in the first innings.

The first century partnership in Test cricket came in the same innings, 120 between WG and Alfred 'Bunny' Lucas for the second wicket.

George Grace, in his only Test match, became the first man to score a Test 'pair'. He died a fortnight later, after contracting a severe cold, leading to congestion of the lungs.

Billy Murdoch captained Australia for the first time, becoming the first Test captain to score a hundred (153 not out in the second innings).

England's numbers eight and nine, the Rt Hon Alfred Lyttelton and George Grace, opened the second innings, scoring 13 and 0 in a decidedly unsuccessful reshuffle.

1880 ENGLAND WON ONLY TEST

4 The Oval, London, September 6, 7, 8

ENGLAND 420 (WG Grace 152, AP Lucas 55, Lord Harris 52, AG Steel 42) and **5/57**
AUSTRALIA 149 (F Morley 5/56) and **327** (WL Murdoch 153*, PS McDonnell 43)
CAPTAINS Lord Harris [ENG] WL Murdoch [AUST]
RESULT England won by five wickets

1881–82

Back to Australia, and Test cricket as we know it started to take further shape. A second Australian venue was used for the first time, the scores were getting bigger, an England player scored a century in Australia for the first time and . . . rain washed out a day's play.

One of the umpires in each of the four Tests was James Lillywhite, the man who captained England in the first two Test matches.

Billy Midwinter, who played for Australia in the first two Tests, made his debut for England.

In the First Test, Irish-born Victorian Tom Horan and South Australian George Giffen shared Australia's first century stand . . . 107 for the fifth wicket. Horan retired in 1891 to become Australia's first great cricket writer, 'Felix' of *The Australasian*.

In the First Test, more than 1000 runs were scored in a match . . . and, also for the first time, a Test ended in a draw.

Australian George Palmer bowled more than 100 overs in each of the first two Tests, for 14 wickets, and finished with 24 for the series.

The England side toured New Zealand for seven matches between the First and Second Tests.

The Second Test was the first to be played in Sydney.

Billy Murdoch kept wicket for the entire England first innings and part of the second innings of the Second Test, despite the presence of regular 'keeper Jack Blackham.

George Coulthard played for Australia in the Second Test after umpiring an Ashes Test three years earlier . . . his sole contribution 6 not out, batting at number 11. He also umpired the Fourth Test of this series.

The last day of the Fourth Test, in Melbourne (March 14, 1882), was the first day washed out in Ashes contests.

The Fourth Test was drawn. It was to be the last drawn Test in Australia for more than 60 years.

George Ulyett's 149 in the Fourth Test was the first Test century by an Englishman in Australia.

1881–82 AUSTRALIA WON SERIES 2–0

5 1st Test Melbourne Cricket Ground, December 31, January 2, 3, 4
ENGLAND 294 (G Ulyett 87, W Bates 58, J Selby 55) and **308** (J Selby 70, WH Scotton 50*, W Bates 47, A Shaw 40, WH Cooper 6/120)
AUSTRALIA 320 (TP Horan 124) and **3/127**
CAPTAINS A Shaw [ENG] WL Murdoch [AUST]
RESULT draw

6 2nd Test Sydney Cricket Ground, February 17, 18, 20, 21
ENGLAND 133 (GE Palmer 7/68) and **232** (G Ulyett 67, RG Barlow 62, GE Palmer 4/97, TW Garrett 4/62)
AUSTRALIA 197 (HH Massie 49, JM Blackham 40, W Bates 4/52) and **5/169** (WL Murdoch 49)
CAPTAINS A Shaw [ENG] WL Murdoch [AUST]
RESULT Australia won by five wickets

7 3rd Test Sydney Cricket Ground, March 3, 4, 6, 7
ENGLAND 188 (A Shrewsbury 82, GE Palmer 5/46) and **134** (A Shrewsbury 47, TW Garrett 6/78, GE Palmer 4/44)
AUSTRALIA 260 (PS McDonnell 147, AC Bannerman 70, E Peate 5/43) and **4/66**

CAPTAINS A Shaw [ENG] WL Murdoch [AUST]
RESULT Australia won by six wickets

8 4th Test Melbourne Cricket Ground, March 10, 11, 13, 14 (no play)
ENGLAND 309 (G Ulyett 149, TW Garrett 5/80) and **2/234** (G Ulyett 64, RG Barlow 56, W Bates 52*, J Selby 48*)
AUSTRALIA 300 (WL Murdoch 85, PS McDonnell 52, WE Midwinter 4/81)
CAPTAINS A Shaw [ENG] WL Murdoch [AUST]
RESULT draw

1882

This one-off match is remembered as the Test that gave birth to the Ashes, with Australia's first victory over a full-strength England team on English soil. A mock obituary was published in The Sporting Times *newspaper, announcing that the body of English cricket was to be cremated, with the ashes taken to Australia.*

Spofforth's figures of 7/46 and 7/44 made him the first player to take 14 wickets in a Test.

The match lasted only two days, but already, Test cricket was a crowd-puller with more than 39 000 paying spectators through the gates.

Australia won the match, despite being bowled out for only 63 in their first innings.

The match aggregate of runs was only 363, with the highest innings total Australia's second effort of 122.

WG Grace effected the first of Test cricket's controversial runouts, dismissing Australian Sammy Jones who, after completing a run, left his crease to pat down the pitch.

1882 AUSTRALIA WON ONLY TEST

9 The Oval, August 28, 29
AUSTRALIA 63 (RG Barlow 5/19, E Peate 4/31) and **122** (HH Massie 55, E Peate 4/40)
ENGLAND 101 (FR Spofforth 7/46) and **77** (FR Spofforth 7/44)
CAPTAINS WL Murdoch [AUST] AN Hornby [ENG]
RESULT Australia won by seven runs

1882–83

The history of the Ashes began to evolve in this series, with a group of Melbourne ladies burning a bail after England's win in the Third Test. They sealed the ashes in an urn and presented it to the England captain, the Hon. Ivo Bligh. During this tour, Bligh met his future wife, Florence Morphy, who, upon his death in 1927, passed the urn on to the MCC. Now, snug in its embroidered velvet bag, the urn is housed at Lord's Memorial Gallery.

Bligh led England in all four Tests—and that represented his entire Test career.

In the Second Test, Billy Bates became the first English player to take a Test hat-trick. He scored 55 in the first innings and had match figures of 14/102, making him the first player to score a half-century and take 10 or more wickets in the same Test.

England won the Second Test by an innings and 27 runs—the first innings margin in Test cricket.

Two pitches were prepared for the Third Test, with each captain having the choice of pitch on which to bat.

For England, Edmund Ferdinando Sutton Tylecote scored 66 in the first innings, becoming the first wicketkeeper to score a Test half-century.

Australia was represented in the first three Tests by Billy Murdoch's 1882 touring team. The Fourth Test featured a combined Australian team.

In the Fourth Test, the captains agreed to an experiment, using a different pitch for each of the four innings.

Billy Midwinter, who played for Australia in the very first Test in 1877 and then played four matches for England, returned to the Australian side in the Fourth Test.

NSW batsman George Bonnor, in the Fourth Test, became the first Australian to be dismissed on 87 . . . his country's 'devil's number' . . . after giving eight chances along the way.

In the Fourth Test, Australia's Jack Blackham scored 57 in the first innings and 58 no out in the second—the first time a wicketkeeper had scored two half-centuries in a Test.

1882-83 SERIES DRAWN 2–2

10 1st Test Melbourne Cricket Ground, December 30, January 1, 2
AUSTRALIA 291 (GJ Bonnor 85, WL Murdoch 48, PS McDonnell 43) and **1/58**
ENGLAND 177 (GE Palmer 7/65) and **169** (G Giffen 4/38)
CAPTAINS WL Murdoch [AUST] Hon. Ivo Bligh [ENG]
RESULT Australia won by nine wickets

11 2nd Test Melbourne Cricket Ground, January 19, 20, 22
ENGLAND 294 (WW Read 75, W Bates 55, CFH Leslie 54, GE Palmer 5/103,
G Giffen 4/89)
AUSTRALIA 114 (HH Massie 43, W Bates 7/28) and **153** (W Bates 7/74)
CAPTAINS Hon. Ivo Bligh [ENG] WL Murdoch [AUST]
RESULT England won by an innings and 27 runs

12 3rd Test Sydney Cricket Ground, January 26, 27, 29, 30
ENGLAND 247 (WW Read 66, EFS Tylecote 66, FR Spofforth 4/73) and **123**
(FR Spofforth 7/44)
AUSTRALIA 218 (AC Bannerman 94, G Giffen 41, F Morley 4/47) and **83**
(RG Barlow 7/40)
CAPTAINS Hon. Ivo Bligh [ENG] WL Murdoch [AUST]
RESULT England won by 69 runs

13 4th Test Sydney Cricket Ground, February 17, 19, 20, 21
ENGLAND 263 (AG Steel 135*, CT Studd 48) and **197** (W Bates 48*)
AUSTRALIA 262 (GJ Bonnor 87, JM Blackham 57) and **6/199**
(AC Bannerman 63, JM Blackham 58*)
CAPTAINS Hon. Ivo Bligh [ENG] WL Murdoch [AUST]
RESULT Australia won by four wickets

1884

*Cricket continued to spread its wings, with this the first series . . .
as distinct from one-off Tests . . . played in England. The series
saw the birth of Lord's as a Test venue. And it was the first time
a Test was staged at Old Trafford, Manchester . . . cricket's home
of rain . . . Appropriately, the first day of that maiden Test was
washed out.*

Australian captain Billy Murdoch played a part in the Second Test
dismissal of his teammate Henry 'Tup' Scott. Murdoch substituted

in the field for England's WG Grace, who'd injured a finger, and caught Scott for 75.

Stanley Christopherson, president of the MCC from 1939–46, played in the maiden Lord's match ... his only Test.

In the Third Test, Billy Murdoch scored 211, which was the first double-century in Test cricket.

In the Third Test, Australia's 551 was the first time a team had made more than 500 runs in a Test innings.

England's Walter Read scored 117 in the first innings of the Third Test—the highest score for a number-10 batsman in Test cricket.

In the Third Test, England captain Lord Harris called on all 11 players to bowl during Australia's big first innings. This was the first instance of this in Tests. England's best bowling figures, ironically, were returned by the wicketkeeper, the Rt Hon. Alfred Lyttelton, who took 4/19 off 12 overs.

1884 ENGLAND WON SERIES 1–0

14 1st Test Old Trafford, Manchester, July 10 (no play), 11, 12
ENGLAND 95 (A Shrewsbury 43, HF Boyle 6/42, FR Spofforth 4/42) and **9/180** (GE Palmer 4/47)
AUSTRALIA 182
CAPTAINS AN Hornby [ENG] WL Murdoch [AUST]
RESULT draw

15 2nd Test Lord's, July 21, 22, 23
AUSTRALIA 229 (HJH Scott 75, G Giffen 63, E Peate 6/85) and **145** (G Ulyett 7/36)
ENGLAND 379 (AG Steel 148, GE Palmer 6/111)
CAPTAINS WL Murdoch [AUST] Lord Harris [ENG]
RESULT England won by an innings and five runs

16 3rd Test The Oval, August 11, 12, 13
AUSTRALIA 551 (WL Murdoch 211, PS McDonnell 1C3, HJH Scott 102, Hon. A Lyttelton 4/19)
ENGLAND 346 (WW Read 117, WH Scotton 90, GE Palmer 4/90) and **2/85**
CAPTAINS WL Murdoch [AUST] Lord Harris [ENG]
RESULT draw

1884–85

This was the first five-Test series, and with England taking the first two matches and Australia the third and fourth, the Ashes were on the line for the final match, in Melbourne. During this series, the beautiful Adelaide Oval became a Test venue for the first time.

Percy McDonnell, from Victoria, who'd scored 103 in the final Test of the 1884 England tour, scored 124 in the First Test in Adelaide, becoming the first batsman to make hundreds in successive Test innings.

Three umpires rather than two shared officiating duties in Adelaide.

Yorkshire's left-arm spinner Bobby Peel made his debut for England in the First Test for match analysis of 8/119, including 5/51 in the second innings.

Australia's First Test team decided on a show of strength with cricket's officialdom, demanding 50 percent of the gate-money for the Second Test, in Melbourne. Consequently, the entire team was sacked for this match, and nine players were picked to debut, with Tom Horan back as captain.

The mass sacking ended the unique sequence by wicketkeeper Jack Blackham, who'd played in each of the first 17 Tests. He was replaced by South Australian Arthur 'Affi' Jarvis, who scored 82.

The six-run margin to Australia in the Third Test, in Sydney, was the closest result in Tests until the turn of the century.

Spofforth took 10 wickets in the Third Test, including the first three England wickets in the space of four balls.

For the first time in Test cricket, in the Third Test, England's superstitious number 111 struck, with both the eighth and ninth first-innings wickets falling on that total.

Australia used four captains in the series: Billy Murdoch (First Test), Tom Horan (Second and Fifth), Hugh Massie (Third) and Jack Blackham (Fourth).

George Bonnor scored his only Test century in 100 minutes in the Fourth Test—the first time a Test century had been scored in even time.

Arthur Shrewsbury, with 105 not out in the Fifth Test, became the first England captain to score a Test hundred. Shrewsbury was revered as a 19th century Jack Hobbs ... his greatest admirer WG Grace. 'Give me Arthur' became cricket lore.

Umpires had their problems in those days also, with debut umpire JH Hodges refusing to continue after tea on the third day of the Fifth Test because of England's complaints about his performance. Australian player Tom Garrett stood in for Hodges.

Paddy McShane, umpire in the Fourth Test, played for Australia in the Fifth.

1884–85 ENGLAND WON SERIES 3–2

17 1st Test Adelaide Oval, December 12, 13, 15, 16
AUSTRALIA 243 (PS McDonnell 124, JM Blackham 66, W Bates 5/31) and **191** (PS McDonnell 83, G Giffen 47, R Peel 5/51)
ENGLAND 369 (W Barnes 134, WH Scotton 82, G Ulyett 68, GE Palmer 5/81) and **2/67**
CAPTAINS WL Murdoch [AUST] A Shrewsbury [ENG]
RESULT England won by eight wickets

18 2nd Test Melbourne Cricket Ground, January 1, 2, 3, 5
ENGLAND 401 (J Briggs 121, A Shrewsbury 72, W Barnes 58, SP Jones 4/47) and **0/7**
AUSTRALIA 279 (AH Jarvis 82, TP Horan 63, JW Trumble 59) and **126** (W Bruce 45, W Barnes 6/31)
CAPTAINS A Shrewsbury [ENG] TP Horan [AUST]
RESULT England won by 10 wickets

19 3rd Test Sydney Cricket Ground, February 20, 21, 23, 24
AUSTRALIA 181 (TW Garrett 51*, W Flowers 5/46, W Attewell 4/53 and **165** (W Bates 5/24)
ENGLAND 133 (TP Horan 6/40, FR Spofforth 4/54) and **207** (W Flowers 56, JM Read 56, FR Spofforth 6/90)
CAPTAINS HH Massie [AUST] A Shrewsbury [ENG]
RESULT Australia won by six runs

20 4th Test Sydney Cricket Ground, March 14, 16, 17
ENGLAND 269 (W Bates 64, W Barnes 50, JM Read 47, A Shrewsbury 40, G Giffen 7/117) and **77** (FR Spofforth 5/30, GE Palmer 4/32)
AUSTRALIA 309 (GJ Bonnor 128, AC Bannerman 51, SP Jones 40, W Barnes 4/61) and **2-38**
CAPTAINS A Shrewsbury [ENG] JM Blackham [AUST]
RESULT Australia won by eight wickets

21 5th Test Melbourne Cricket Ground, March 21, 23, 24, 25
AUSTRALIA 163 (FR Spofforth 50, G Ulyett 4/52) and **125**
ENGLAND 386 (A Shrewsbury 105*, W Barnes 74, W Bates 61, J Briggs 43)
CAPTAINS TP Horan [AUST] A Shrewsbury [ENG]
RESULT England won by an innings and 98 runs

1886

England, having retained the Ashes with a big win in the final match of the previous series, continued that good form in this series . . . three Tests, three wins to England.

In the Second Test at Lord's, Arthur Shrewsbury scored 164 in the first innings—then the highest Test score by an England player.

WG Grace scored 170 in the Third Test to regain the highest Test score record.

Lancashire's left-arm slow bowler Johnny Briggs was primarily responsible for Australia's Second Test demise, with 11/74.

Henry 'Tup' Scott captained Australia in this series—the first Victorian to lead his country in England.

In the Third Test, Australia's Tom Garrett bowled 99 (four-ball) overs in England's big innings of 434. His full analysis: 99-55-88-3. In all, the Australians sent down 304.1 overs for the innings.

George Lohmann, who made his England debut in the First Test, took just one wicket in the first two Tests, and then 12 in the Third, at The Oval, as the home side won by an innings and 217 runs.

1886 ENGLAND WON SERIES 3–0

22 1st Test Old Trafford, Manchester, July 5, 6, 7
AUSTRALIA 205 (SP Jones 87, AH Jarvis 45, G Ulyett 4/46) and **123** (HJH Scott 47, RG Barlow 7/44)
ENGLAND 223 (WW Read 51, FR Spofforth 4/82) and **6/107**
CAPTAINS HJH Scott [AUST] AG Steel [ENG]
RESULT England won by four wickets

23 2nd Test Lord's, July 19, 20, 21
ENGLAND 353 (A Shrewsbury 164, W Barnes 58, FR Spofforth 4/73)
AUSTRALIA 121 (J Briggs 5/29) and **126** (GE Palmer 48, J Briggs 6/45)
CAPTAINS AG Steel [ENG] HJH Scott [AUST]
RESULT England won by an innings and 106 runs

24 3rd Test The Oval, August 12, 13, 14
ENGLAND 434 (WG Grace 170, WW Read 94, J Briggs 53, A Shrewsbury 44, FR Spofforth 4/65)
AUSTRALIA 68 (GA Lohmann 7/36) and **149** (G Giffen 47, GA Lohmann 5/68)
CAPTAINS AG Steel [ENG] HJH Scott [AUST]
RESULT England won by an innings and 217 runs

1886–87

Although Australia hosted a full five-Test series two years earlier, this time England's visit involved only two matches. And England's domination continued, winning both Tests to take their sequence of victories over Australia to six.

In the First Test, Australia's Percy McDonnell became the first captain to send the opposition in to bat—a good decision given that England were bowled out for only 45 in the first innings. However, despite that all-time low score, England won the match by 13 runs.

Charles Bannerman, who had faced the first ball in Test cricket, made his debut as an umpire in the First Test, with his brother Alec on the field for Australia.

In the Second Test, George Lohmann became the first bowler to take eight wickets in an innings. He finished with 10 for the match.

Billy Gunn, who also represented Notts County and England at soccer, took on dual responsibility in the Second Test, batting at number four for England and deputising for umpire JS Swift on the final morning.

1886–87 ENGLAND WON SERIES 2–0

---

25 1st Test Sydney Cricket Ground, January 28, 29, 31
ENGLAND 45 (CTB Turner 6/15, JJ Ferris 4/27) and **184** (JJ Ferris 5/76)
AUSTRALIA 119 and **97** (W Barnes 6/28)
CAPTAINS A Shrewsbury [ENG] PS McDonnell [AUST]
RESULT England won by 13 runs

26 2nd Test Sydney Cricket Ground, February 25, 26, 28, March 1
ENGLAND 151 (JJ Ferris 5/71, CTB Turner 5/41) and **154** (RG Barlow 42*, JJ Ferris 4/69, CTB Turner 4/52)
AUSTRALIA 84 (GA Lohmann 8/35) and **150** (W Bates 4/26)
CAPTAINS A Shrewsbury [ENG] PS McDonnell [AUST]
RESULT England won by 71 runs

1887–88

England's winning sequence stretched to seven with this one-off Test played in Sydney, where rain prevented play on the scheduled second and third days of the match.

Australia's total of 42 in the first innings is its lowest in any Test in Australia.

Andrew Stoddart, a man who was to captain England in both cricket and rugby, made his debut in this match.

Charlie Turner, who took over from Spofforth the mantle of Australia's chief bowler, took 5/44 and 7/43 . . . match figures of 12/87 which still rank as the best analysis at the SCG.

1887–88 ENGLAND WON ONLY TEST

27 Sydney Cricket Ground, February 10, 11 (no play), 13 (no play), 14, 15
ENGLAND 113 (A Shrewsbury 44, CTB Turner 5/44, JJ Ferris 4/60) and **137** (CTB Turner 7/43)
AUSTRALIA 42 (GA Lohmann 5/17, R Peel 5/18) and **82** (R Peel 5/40, GA Lohmann 4/35)
CAPTAINS WW Read [ENG] PS McDonnell [AUST]
RESULT England won by 126 runs

1888

At last, England's winning streak was broken in the first match of this three-Test series. Australia won the First Test at Lord's, but England won both the Second and Third Tests by an innings to retain the Ashes.

The First Test was one of cricket's all-time low-scoring matches, with three of the four innings failing to reach 70, and WG Grace's 24 in England's second innings the highest score in the match.

Never before or since have the bowlers had it so good, with 27 wickets falling for 157 runs in just over three hours on the second day.

On a 'sticky' wicket in the Third Test, at Old Trafford, Australia lost 18 wickets in the session before lunch on the second day— the match was all over in four sessions, and the shortest completed Test in England. Total playing time: six hours 34 minutes.

In Australia's second innings at Old Trafford, the first four batsmen, Percy McDonnell, Alec Bannerman, Harry Trott and George Bonnor, were all dismissed for ducks, and the number five John Edwards scored one. At one stage Australia were 6/7.

1888 ENGLAND WON SERIES 2–1

28 1st Test Lord's, July 16, 17
AUSTRALIA 116 (R Peel 4/36) and **60** (R Peel 4/14, GA Lohmann 4/33)
ENGLAND 53 (CTB Turner 5/27) and **62** (JJ Ferris 5/26, CTB Turner 5/36)
CAPTAINS PS McDonnell [AUST] AG Steel [ENG]
RESULT Australia won by 61 runs

29 2nd Test The Oval, August 13, 14
AUSTRALIA 80 (J Briggs 5/25) and **100** (W Barnes 5/32, R Peel 4/49)
ENGLAND 317 (R Abel 70, W Barnes 62, GA Lohmann 62*, CTB Turner 6/112)
CAPTAINS PS McDonnell [AUST] WG Grace [ENG]
RESULT England won by an innings and 137 runs

30 3rd Test Old Trafford, Manchester, August 30, 31
ENGLAND 172 (CTB Turner 5/86)
AUSTRALIA 81 (R Peel 7/31) and **70** (R Peel 4/37)
CAPTAINS WG Grace [ENG] PS McDonnell [AUST]
RESULT England won by an innings and 21 runs

1890

By now, England and Australia's mortgage on Test cricket was over, with South Africa entering the fray and having played two Tests against England.

Victorian Jack Barrett played only two Tests, but in his first, the opening match of this series, he became the first player in Ashes

history to carry his bat through a completed innings, with 67 not
out, out of 176.

Tasmanian Kenny Burn played his entire Test career in this series.
He was originally selected for the tour as Australia's reserve
wicketkeeper, despite having never kept in his life. As it turned
out, he was the only player in the party not given an opportunity
behind the stumps. He batted at number 11 in the second innings
of the First Test and opened in the second innings of the Second.

Kent's left-arm medium-pacer Frederick Martin took 6/50 and 6/52
in the Second Test, at The Oval, becoming the first bowler to take
12 wickets on debut. The Oval match was his only Test against
Australia.

On a rain-affected pitch 22 wickets fell for 197 runs on the first
day of the Second Test.

1890 ENGLAND WON SERIES 2–0

31 1st Test Lord's, July 21, 22, 23
AUSTRALIA 132 (JJ Lyons 55, W Attewell 4/42) and **176** (JE Barrett 67*)
ENGLAND 173 (G Ulyett 74, JJ Lyons 5/30) and **3/137** (WG Grace 75*)
CAPTAINS WL Murdoch [AUST] WG Grace [ENG]
RESULT England won by seven wickets

32 2nd Test The Oval, August 11, 12
AUSTRALIA 92 (F Martin 6/50) and **102** (F Martin 6/52)
ENGLAND 100 (JJ Ferris 4/25) and **8/95** (JJ Ferris 5/49)
CAPTAINS WL Murdoch [AUST] WG Grace [ENG]
RESULT England won by two wickets

1891–92

*This three-Test series marked the introduction of six-ball overs in
Australia—a situation that stood for 33 years.*

In the Second Test, in Sydney, Surrey's Robert Abel became the
first England player to carry his bat, with 132 out of his team's
307.

Johnny Briggs captured a hat-trick in the Sydney Test, with the final three wickets of Australia's second innings.

Two bowlers each took 10 wickets in the Second Test ... England's George Lohmann and Australia's George Giffen.

In a remarkable turnabout, Australia came from 162 behind on the first innings to win the Second Test by 72 runs.

England's 230-run win in the Third Test in Adelaide was the biggest 'runs' margin in any of the 35 Tests to that point.

1891–92 AUSTRALIA WON SERIES 2–1

33 1st Test Melbourne Cricket Ground, January 1, 2, 4, 5, 6
AUSTRALIA 240 (W Bruce 57, AC Bannerman 45, JW Sharpe 6/84) and **236** (JJ Lyons 51, AC Bannerman 41, W Bruce 40)
ENGLAND 264 (WG Grace 50, G Bean 50, J Briggs 41, RW McLeod 5/55) and **158** (CTB Turner 5/51)
CAPTAINS JM Blackham [AUST] WG Grace [ENG]
RESULT Australia won by 54 runs

34 2nd Test Sydney Crickt Ground, January 29, 30, February 1, 2, 3
AUSTRALIA 145 (JJ Lyons 41, GA Lohmann 8/58) and **391** (JJ Lyons 134, AC Bannerman 91, W Bruce 72, G Giffen 49, J Briggs 4/69)
ENGLAND 307 (R Abel 132*, G Giffen 4/88) and **157** (AE Stoddart 69, G Giffen 6/72, CTB Turner 4/46)
CAPTAINS JM Blackham [AUST] WG Grace [ENG]
RESULT Australia won by 72 runs

35 3rd Test Adelaide Oval, March 24, 25, 26, 28
ENGLAND 499 (AE Stoddart 134, R Peel 83, WG Grace 58, W Attewell 43*)
AUSTRALIA 100 (J Briggs 6/49) and **169** (J Briggs 6/87)
CAPTAINS WG Grace [ENG] JM Blackham [AUST]
RESULT England won by an innings and 230 runs

1893

Australia–England contests had now been going for 16 years, and records of substance were being created. Arthur Shrewsbury, in the

First Test at Lord's, became the first player to score 1000 runs in Ashes Test matches.

Australia's Harry Graham joined the elite club to score a century in his first Test innings, and he did so at Lord's. England's Stanley Jackson went within nine runs of equalling the feat.

James Phillips, who'd already umpired in Australia, officiated in the First and Third Tests, at Lord's and Old Trafford respectively.

In the Second Test, Australia's Alec Bannerman joined Shrewsbury in the 1000 Test runs club—the first Australian to do so.

Stanley Jackson ... later Sir Stanley Jackson, president of the MCC, Chairman of England's selectors, and Chairman of Britain's Conservative Party ... made up for his near-miss at Lord's with 103 in the Second Test, at The Oval.

In the Third Test, at Old Trafford, WG Grace's medical skills came to the fore, repairing a dislocated finger on the hand of Australia's Charlie Turner.

England's fast bowler Tom Richardson took 10 wickets at Old Trafford to start a 14-Test and 88-wicket career.

1893 ENGLAND WON SERIES 1–0

36 1st Test Lord's, July 17, 18, 19
ENGLAND 334 (A Shrewsbury 106, FS Jackson 91, CTB Turner 6/67) and **8/234 dec** (A Shrewsbury 81, W Gunn 77, G Giffen 5/43)
AUSTRALIA 269 (H Graham 107, SE Gregory 57, WH Lockwood 6/101)
CAPTAINS AE Stoddart [ENG] JM Blackham [AUST]
RESULT draw

37 2nd Test The Oval, August 14, 15, 16
ENGLAND 483 (FS Jackson 103, AE Stoddart 83, WG Grace 68, A Shrewsbury 66, A Ward 55, WW Read 52, G Giffen 7/128)
AUSTRALIA 91 (J Briggs 5/34, WH Lockwood 4/37) and **349** (GHS Trott 92, AC Bannerman 55, G Giffen 53, H Graham 42, J Briggs 5/114, WH Lockwood 4/96)
CAPTAINS WG Grace [ENG] JM Blackham [AUST]
RESULT England won by an innings and 43 runs

38 3rd Test Old Trafford, Manchester, August 24, 25, 26
AUSTRALIA 204 (W Bruce 68, T Richardson 5/49, J Briggs 4/81) and **236** (AC Bannerman 60, T Richardson 5/107)
ENGLAND 243 (W Gunn 102*, WG Grace 40, G Giffen 4/113) and **4/118** (WG Grace 45, AE Stoddart 42)
CAPTAINS JM Blackham [AUST] WG Grace [ENG]
RESULT draw

1894–95

This was the second rubber involving five Tests, and like the first, England won the first two, Australia drew level in the Fourth . . . and in the Fifth, England prevailed.

England's narrow victory in the First Test, in Sydney, was remarkable—Australia scoring 586, and England forced to follow-on 261 runs behind. It was the first time a team had won after being forced to follow-on.

Australia's first double-century in a Test at home came in Sydney from Syd Gregory—a man who was in fact born at the SCG, where his father Ned was curator. Syd Gregory ended up playing 58 Tests, with eight tours to England, and scored more than 2000 Test runs.

In the First Test, George Giffen scored a total of 202 runs and took eight wickets in a remarkable all-round performance.

The first Sydney Test, over six days, was the first occasion a Test had gone beyond five days.

Andrew Stoddart scored 173 in the Second Test—a total that stood as the highest by an England captain in Australia for 80 years.

The Test career of Australia's Arthur Coningham was brief. He played just one Test—the Second, in Melbourne—but took a wicket with his first ball . . . the first of the match. Coningham is also remembered as the player who, in a match at Lord's in 1893, lit a fire in the outfield to keep warm.

Victorian Albert Trott made his debut in the Third Test, in Adelaide, scoring 38 not out and 72 not out batting at number 10, and taking 8/43 in the second innings. He played just three Tests for Australia, all in this series, then moved to England and played two Tests against South Africa four years later.

Harry Graham's century in the Fourth Test meant he'd scored centuries in his first Test in England, and his first in Australia.

In the Fourth Test, England's Johnny Briggs became the first player to take 100 Test wickets, and in the same match Charlie 'The Terror' Turner took his 100th Test wicket for Australia.

In one of Test cricket's worst batting performances, England were dismissed in the Fourth Test for 65 and 72 . . . losing 17 wickets in less than three hours on the third day.

1894–95 ENGLAND WON SERIES 3–2

39 1st Test Sydney Cricket Ground, December 14, 15, 17, 18, 19, 20
AUSTRALIA 586 (SE Gregory 201, G Giffen 161, JM Blackham 74,
T Richardson 5/181) and **166** (J Darling 53, G Giffen 41, R Peel 6/67)
ENGLAND 325 (A Ward 75, J Briggs 57, W Brockwell 49, G Giffen 4/75) and **437**
(A Ward 117, JT Brown 53, FGJ Ford 48, J Briggs 42, G Giffen 4/164)
CAPTAINS JM Blackham [AUST] AE Stoddart [ENG]
RESULT England won by 10 runs

40 2nd Test Melbourne Cricket Ground, December 29, 31, January 1, 2, 3
ENGLAND 75 (CTB Turner 5/32) and **475** (AE Stoddart 173, R Peel 53,
A Ward 41, G Giffen 6/155)
AUSTRALIA 123 (T Richardson 5/57) and **333** (GHS Trott 95, FA Iredale 68,
W Bruce 54, G Giffen 43, R Peel 4/77)
CAPTAINS AE Stoddart [ENG] G Giffen [AUST]
RESULT England won by 94 runs

41 3rd Test Adelaide Oval, January 11, 12, 14, 15
AUSTRALIA 238 (G Giffen 58, GHS Trott 48, ST Callaway 41, T Richardson 5/75)
and **411** (FA Iredale 140, W Bruce 80, AE Trott 72*, R Peel 4/96)
ENGLAND 124 (G Giffen 5/76, ST Callaway 5/37) and **143** (AE Trott 8/43)
CAPTAINS G Giffen [AUST] AE Stoddart [ENG]
RESULT Australia won by 382 runs

42 4th Test Sydney Cricket Ground, February 1, 2 (no play), 4
AUSTRALIA 284 (H Graham 105, AE Trott 85*, J Briggs 4/65)
ENGLAND 65 and **72** (G Giffen 5/26, CTB Turner 4/33)
CAPTAINS G Giffen [AUST] AE Stoddart [ENG]
RESULT Australia won by an innings and 147 runs

43 5th Test Melbourne Cricket Ground, March 1, 2, 4, 5, 6
AUSTRALIA 414 (J Darling 74, SE Gregory 70, G Giffen 57, JJ Lyons 55,
GHS Trott 42, R Peel 4/114) and **267** (G Giffen 51, J Darling 50, GHS Trott 42,
T Richardson 6/104)
ENGLAND 385 (AC MacLaren 120, R Peel 73, AE Stoddart 68, G Giffen 4/130,
GHS Trott 4/71 and **4/298** (JT Brown 140, A Ward 93)
CAPTAINS G Giffen [AUST] AE Stoddart [ENG]
RESULT England won by six wickets

1896

Harry Trott took over the Australian captaincy for this three-Test series. He scored a century at Lord's in his first match as captain, but England continued its domination of home series, taking the rubber 2–1.

Two wicketkeepers, 'Dick' Lilley (England) and James 'JJ' Kelly (Australia) made their debuts in the First Test. Both scored ducks in their first innings.

In the First Test, during his innings of 66, WG Grace passed the 1000 Test runs milestone.

South Australian left-hander Clem Hill, who went on to play 49 Tests including 10 as captain, made his debut in the Lord's Test.

Kumar Shri Ranjitsinhji, or 'Ranji', made a grand entrance to the Test arena at Old Trafford, with 62 and 154 not out. He became the first Indian to play Tests, and the first player to score a century before lunch in a Test.

George Giffen completed his 31-match career in the Third Test, at The Oval. In the previous match at Old Trafford, he took his 100th Test wicket, becoming the first player to score more than 1000 runs and take 100 wickets in Test cricket.

A player revolt over match payments threatened to disrupt the England team for the Third Test. Five players demanded double the 10 pounds fee offered to professionals, but only two—Billy Gunn and George Lohmann—stood their ground, and they were never to play Tests again. Lohmann's 18-Test career realised 112 wickets at the remarkable average of 10.75.

Yorkshire's Bobby Peel took eight wickets in his farewell Test, the Third, at The Oval, making it 102 wickets from 20 matches.

At The Oval, Australia were dismissed for 44 in the second innings—the top-scorer and the only player into double figures was the number-11, Tom McKibbin, with 16.

1896 ENGLAND WON SERIES 2–1

44 1st Test Lord's, June 22, 23, 24

AUSTRALIA 53 (T Richardson 6/39) and 347 (GHS Trott 143, SE Gregory 103, T Richardson 5/134, JT Hearne 5/76)
ENGLAND 292 (R Abel 94, WG Grace 66, FS Jackson 44) and 4/111
CAPTAINS GHS Trott [AUST] WG Grace [ENG]
RESULT England won by six wickets

45 2nd Test Old Trafford, Manchester, July 16, 17, 18
AUSTRALIA 412 (FA Iredale 108, G Giffen 80, GHS Trott 53, T Richardson 7/168) and 7/125 (T Richardson 6/76)
ENGLAND 231 (AFA Lilley 65*, KS Ranjitsinhji 62) and 305 (KS Ranjitsinhji 154*, AE Stoddart 41*)
CAPTAINS GHS Trott [AUST] WG Grace [ENG]
RESULT Australia won by three wickets

46 3rd Test The Oval, August 10, 11, 12
ENGLAND 145 (FS Jackson 45, H Trumble 6/59) and 84 (H Trumble 6/30)
AUSTRALIA 119 (J Darling 47, JT Hearne 6/41) and 44 (R Peel 6/23, JT Hearne 4/19)
CAPTAINS WG Grace [ENG] GHS Trott [AUST]
RESULT England won by 66 runs

1897–98

After a decade of English domination, the pendulum finally swung Australia's way in this five-Test home series. England, under Archie MacLaren's leadership, easily won the First Test, in Sydney, before the Australians won the next four.

Ranji scored a century in his maiden Test in Sydney to repeat Harry Graham's feat of hitting centuries in his first Tests in both England and Australia.

Joe Darling scored each of his three Test centuries in the series ... the first left-hander to score a century in a Test.

MacLaren's captaincy in the first two Tests came about due to the death of the incumbent Andrew Stoddart's mother. MacLaren also captained England in the Fifth Test.

Australia's Charlie McLeod discovered a novel method of dismissal in the First Test. Because of deafness, he failed to hear an umpire's call of 'no-ball' and left his crease on being bowled ... only to end up run-out.

Monty Noble, who went on to captain Australia and was one of his country's great all-rounders, made the first of his 42 Test appearances in the Second Test, in Melbourne.

In that Second Test, South Australian fast bowler Ernie Jones became the first bowler to be no-balled for throwing in a Test match. Legend has it that Jones once sent a ball through the beard of WG Grace.

Darling brought up his Third Test century with a six . . . the first six scored without overthrows in Test cricket. The rules stipulated that the ball had to be hit, not only over the boundary, but out of the ground.

Clem Hill's 188 in the Fourth Test wasn't his highest Test score (he scored 191 against South Africa in 1910–11), but it was achieved while he was just 20 years old, and remains the highest score by a batsman under 21 in Ashes Tests.

The Fifth Test marked the farewell appearance of England fast bowler Tom Richardson, who took eight wickets in the first innings and 10 for the match in his best Test performance in Australia.

1897–98 AUSTRALIA WON THE SERIES 4–1

47 1st Test Sydney Cricket Ground, December 13, 14, 15, 16, 17
ENGLAND 551 (KS Ranjitsinhji 175, AC MacLaren 109, TW Hayward 72, GH Hirst 62, W Storer 43) and **1/96** (AC MacLaren 50*)
AUSTRALIA 237 (H Trumble 70, CE McLeod 50*, SE Gregory 46, JT Hearne 5/42) and **408** (J Darling 101, C Hill 96, JJ Kelly 46*, JT Hearne 4/99)
CAPTAINS AC MacLaren [ENG] GHS Trott [AUST]
RESULT England won by nine wickets

48 2nd Test Melbourne Cricket Ground, January 1, 3, 4, 5
AUSTRALIA 520 (CE McLeod 112, FA Iredale 89, GHS Trott 79, SE Gregory 71, C Hill 58)
ENGLAND 315 (KS Ranjitsinhji 71, W Storer 51, J Briggs 46*, NF Druce 44, H Trumble 4/54) and **150** (MA Noble 6/49, H Trumble 4/53)
CAPTAINS GHS Trott [AUST] AC MacLaren [ENG]
RESULT Australia won by an innings and 55 runs

49 3rd Test Adelaide Oval, January 14, 15, 17, 18, 19
AUSTRALIA 573 (J Darling 178, FA Iredale 84, C Hill 81, SE Gregory 52, T Richardson 4/164)
ENGLAND 278 (GH Hirst 85, TW Hayward 70, WP Howell 4/70) and **282** (AC MacLaren 124, KS Ranjitsinhji 77, MA Noble 5/84, CE McLeod 5/65)
CAPTAINS GHS Trott [AUST] AE Stoddart [ENG]
RESULT Australia won by an innings and 13 runs

50 4th Test Melbourne Cricket Ground, January 29, 31, February 1, 2
AUSTRALIA 323 (C Hill 188, H Trumble 46, JT Hearne 6/98) and **2/115**
(CE McLeod 64*)
ENGLAND 174 (E Jones 4/56) and **263** (KS Ranjitsinhji 55, AC MacLaren 45)
CAPTAINS GHS Trott [AUST] AE Stoddart [ENG]
RESULT Australia won by eight wickets

51 5th Test Sydney Cricket Ground, February 26, 28, March 1, 2
ENGLAND 335 (AC MacLaren 65, NF Druce 64, E Wainwright 49,
TW Hayward 47, W Storer 44, GH Hirst 44, E Jones 6/82) and **178** (TW Hayward 43,
H Trumble 4/37)
AUSTRALIA 239 (CE McLeod 64, T Richardson 8/94) and 4/276 (J Darling 160,
J Worrall 62)
CAPTAINS AC MacLaren [ENG] GHS Trott [AUST]
RESULT Australia won by six wickets

1899

*The first five-Test series in England produced just one victory . . .
Australia convincingly taking the Second Test, at Lord's. The series
started with the end of one era and the dawning of another. The
first Test to be played at Nottingham's Trent Bridge marked the
farewell of WG Grace after 22 Tests while Wilfred Rhodes, whose
time at the top was to last as long as that of WG, was playing the
first Test of his illustrious career.*

Victor Trumper, one of Australia's greats, was included in the
touring party at the insistence of Monty Noble. He failed in his
debut, at Trent Bridge, but scored 135 not out in the Second Test,
at Lord's . . . the first of eight Test centuries in more than 3000
Test runs.

Australia's Ernie Jones, no-balled for throwing the previous series,
took career-best figures of 7/88 and 3/76 in the Second Test, at
Lord's.

The only 'Q' to play Ashes cricket, England's Willie Quaife, made
his debut, at Headingley.

In the Third Test, England's Jack Hearne took a hat-trick,
dismissing Clem Hill, Syd Gregory and Monty Noble for ducks.

Kent paceman Bill Bradley's Test career was brief, with only two matches. But in his first, at Old Trafford, he became the first England bowler to take a wicket with his first ball, in Test cricket. He took five for the innings.

Australia was forced to follow-on in the Fourth Test, with Noble the first player to score two half-centuries on the one day in what proved a match-saving performance.

1899 AUSTRALIA WON THE SERIES 1–0

52 1st Test Trent Bridge, Nottingham, June 1, 2, 3
AUSTRALIA 252 (C Hill 52, SE Gregory 48, J Darling 47, MA Noble 41, W Rhodes 4/58, JT Hearne 4/71) and **8/230 dec** (C Hill 80, MA Noble 45)
ENGLAND 193 (CB Fry 50, KS Ranjitsinhji 42, E Jones 5/88) and **7/155** (KS Ranjitsinhji 93*)
CAPTAINS J Darling [AUST] WG Grace [ENG]
RESULT draw

53 2nd Test Lord's, June 15, 16, 17
ENGLAND 206 (FS Jackson 73, GL Jessop 51, E Jones 7/88) and **240** (AC MacLaren 88*, TW Hayward 77)
AUSTRALIA 421 (C Hill 135, VT Trumper 135*, MA Noble 54) and **0/28**
CAPTAINS AC MacLaren [ENG] J Darling [AUST]
RESULT Australia won by 10 wickets

54 3rd Test Headingley, Leeds, June 29, 30, July 1 (no play)
AUSTRALIA 172 (J Worrall 76, HI Young 4/30 and **224** (H Trumble 56, F Laver 45, JT Hearne 4/50)
ENGLAND 220 (AFA Lilley 55, TW Hayward 40*, H Trumble 5/60) and **0/19**
CAPTAINS J Darling [AUST] AC MacLaren [ENG]
RESULT draw

55 4th Test Old Trafford, Manchester, July 17, 18, 19
ENGLAND 372 (TW Hayward 130, AFA Lilley 58, FS Jackson 44, HI Young 43) and **3/94** (KS Ranjitsinhji 49*)
AUSTRALIA 196 (MA Noble 60*, H Trumble 44, WM Bradley 5/67, HI Young 4/79) and **7/346 dec** (MA Noble 89, VT Trumper 63, J Worrall 53)
CAPTAINS AC MacLaren [ENG] J Darling [AUST]
RESULT draw

56 5th Test The Oval, August 14, 15, 16
ENGLAND 576 (TW Hayward 137, FS Jackson 118, CB Fry 60, KS Ranjitsinhji 54, AC MacLaren 49, E Jones 4/164)
AUSTRALIA 352 (SE Gregory 117, J Darling 71, J Worrall 55, WH Lockwood 7/71) and **5/254** (CE McLeod 77, J Worrall 75, MA Noble 69*)
CAPTAINS AC MacLaren [ENG] J Darling [AUST]
RESULT draw

19th Century
Questions 1–10

1 Charles Bannerman scored the first century in Test cricket (165). How did his innings end?

2 Who was the Australian player of the 19th century who became a leading cricket writer for *The Australasian* known as 'Felix'?

3 WG Grace captained England in the first Test match . . . true or false?

4 What was the result of the first Test match played in England?

5 The Third Test in 1888, at Old Trafford, ranks as the shortest completed match in Test history. Was the total playing time: *a*) six hours 34 minutes *b*) nine hours 41 minutes *c*) 11 hours 58 minutes

6 Who is the England bowler who took 112 Test wickets at an average of 10.75 before effectively ending his career by strike action over match payments?

7 Which player, with a surname starting with 'Q', made his England debut in the Third Test of 1899?

8 What was the milestone common to England's Johnny Briggs and Australia's Charlie Turner in the Fourth Test of 1894–95?

9 England's first Test hat-trick came in the 1882–83 series in Melbourne. The bowler was Billy . . .

10 Australia's first Test double-century came in Sydney in 1894–95. Who scored it?

Questions 11–20

11 Where was the second of the Test venues in Australia?

12 Australia used four captains in the five Tests of 1884–85. Name two of them.

13 Who won Test cricket's first five-Test rubber in Australia, in 1884–85?

14 Australian fast bowler Fred Spofforth refused to play in the first Test match. Why?

15 What was the venue of the first Test played in England?

16 Who was the Tasmanian selected as Australia's reserve wicketkeeper on the tour of 1890—despite having never kept in his life?

17 A left-arm spinner from Yorkshire, who went on to play 20 Tests and take 102 wickets, made his debut in 1884–85. What was his name?

18 Why did Archie MacLaren fill in for Andrew Stoddart as England captain in the first two Tests of 1897–98?

19 What was the name of the Australian who played the last three Tests of 1894–95, averaging 102.5, before playing for England against South Africa four years later?

20 The legendary WG Grace played his last Test in 1899. In the same match, which other England legend made his debut?

Questions 21-30

21 Which player from the first Test match umpired in each of the four Tests of 1881–82?

22 Who was the first England captain to score a Test hundred?

23 A new venue was chosen for a Test in England in 1884, but the first day of that match was washed out. Where was that venue?

24 Who was the first Victorian to captain Australia in an Ashes series in England (in the 1886 series)?

25 What were the names of the brothers of WG Grace who also played in Tests against Australia?

26 Which Australian became the first left-hander to score a Test century, in 1897–98?

27 Who was the England captain who scored 173 in Melbourne in 1894–95?

28 Who were the first brothers to play Test cricket?

29 Who is the Australian who once lit a fire in the outfield of Lord's to keep warm, and in his only Test, took a wicket with his first ball?

30 Who was the England captain presented with the ashes of a burnt bail by a group of Melbourne ladies in 1882–83?

Questions 31-40

31 One of Australia's first great all-rounders scored more than 200 runs and took eight wickets in the First Test of 1894–95. Who was that player?

32 Which player, known as 'The Little Dasher', scored a century in his first Test in both England and Australia?

33 Where was the first Test match played?

34 What is the significance of the names CA Reid and RB Terry?

35 During the 1884–85 series, the entire Australian team was sacked after the First Test following a stand against officialdom. What was behind the dispute?

36 In what year was Lord's first used as a Test venue?

37 Charles Bannerman, Test cricket's first century-maker, made his Test umpiring debut in the First Test of 1886–87 in a match involving his younger brother. What was his brother's name?

38 A player, later to be knighted, to become Chairman of Selectors, President of the MCC, and Chairman of the Conservative Party, made his England debut in 1893, scoring 91 at Lord's. Who was that player?

39 Which South Australian was no-balled for throwing in the Second Test of the 1897–98 series, in Melbourne?

40 Who was the first Australian captain to score a Test century?

Questions 41–50

41 In which London newspaper was the mock obituary printed in 1882, announcing that the body of English cricket was to be cremated and the Ashes taken to Australia?

42 Which member of Australia's side for the first Test match played for England five years later?

43 During the 1884–85 tour, a third Australian Test venue was first used. Which one?

44 The man who took over from Spofforth as Australia's number-one bowler took 12/87 at the SCG in 1887–88 ... still the best match figures in a Sydney Test. Who was that player?

45 In the 1893 series, two players became the first to score 1000 Test runs for their respective countries. Name one of them.

46 Which one of the Grace brothers scored Test cricket's first 'pair'?

47 Who faced the first ball in Test cricket?

48 An Australian bowler claimed a hat-trick in only the third match in Test history. Who was it?

49 Which later-president of the MCC made his sole Test appearance in 1884?

50 Who was the first Indian to play Test cricket for England, scoring 154 not out on debut at Old Trafford in 1896?

ANSWERS *19th Century*

1–10

1 He retired hurt
2 Tom Horan
3 False (WG Grace didn't play in the first Test match)
4 England won (by 5 wickets)
5 *a* 6 hours 34 minutes
6 George Lohmann
7 Willie Quaife
8 They took their 100th Test wicket—the first to do so
9 Billy Bates
10 Syd Gregory

11–20

11 Sydney (1881–82)
12 The four were Billy Murdoch, Tom Horan, Hugh Massie and Jack Blackham
13 England 3–2
14 Spofforth wanted Billy Murdoch chosen as wicketkeeper
15 The Oval (1880)
16 Kenny Burn
17 Bobby Peel
18 Due to the death of Stoddart's mother
19 Albert Trott
20 Wilfred Rhodes

21–30

21 James Lillywhite
22 Arthur Shrewsbury
23 Old Trafford, Manchester
24 Henry 'Tup' Scott
25 Edward and George
26 Joe Darling
27 Andrew Stoddart
28 Dave and 'Ned' Gregory
29 Arthur Coningham
30 Hon. Ivo Bligh

31–40

31 George Giffen
32 Harry Graham
33 Melbourne Cricket Ground
34 They were the umpires for the first Test match ever played
35 The players had demanded 50 percent of the gate-money for the Second Test
36 1884
37 Alec
38 Stanley Jackson
39 Ernie Jones
40 Billy Murdoch

41–50

41 *The Sporting Times*
42 Billy Midwinter
43 Adelaide Oval
44 Charlie Turner
45 The two were Arthur Shrewsbury (England) and Alec Bannerman (Australia)
46 George Grace
47 Charles Bannerman
48 Fred Spofforth
49 Stanley Christopherson
50 Kumar Shri Ranjitsinhji ('Ranji')

C h a p t e r   T w o

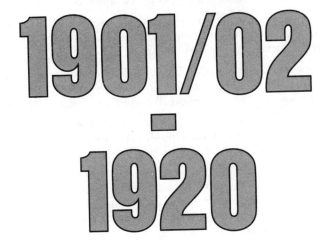

1901/02 - 1920

1901–02

The first series of the 20th century involved an Archie MacLaren-led England side visiting Australia, who once again enjoyed the home conditions. Like the previous series in Australia, in 1897–98, the Australians lost the First Test only to win the next four.

Sydney Barnes, considered by many to be the best bowler ever, made his debut in the First Test, in Sydney, taking 5/65 in Australia's first innings. He took 19 wickets in the first two Tests before a knee injury in the Third kept him out of the last two.

Another to make his England debut in Sydney was all-rounder Len Braund, who scored a half-century and took seven wickets.

MacLaren scored a century in the First Test, making him the first batsman to score four Test centuries. It was the last by an England captain in Australia for nearly 60 years.

In the Second Test, Warwick 'The Big Ship' Armstrong made the first of his 50 Test appearances. During his career, Armstrong's weight ballooned from 63.5kg (10 stone) to 140kg (22 stone).

A record 25 wickets fell on the first day of the Second Test, in Melbourne on a rain-affected pitch, with England dismissed for 61 in just 68 minutes in their first innings.

The first of Clem Hill's series of missed hundreds during the series came in the Second Test, when he became the first Test batsman out for 99. He then scored 98 and 97 in the Third Test and went on to become the first player to score 500 runs in a rubber without a century.

In the Second Test, Australia's Reggie Duff batted at number 10 in the second innings of his Test debut, scored a century, and by the Fourth Test, was opening the innings. He's the only Australian to score a century against England batting at 10.

Victorian off-spinner Hugh Trumble, who had been a key player for over a decade, completed Australia's Second Test victory by taking a hat-trick. Trumble captained Australia in the final two Tests.

Victorian left-armer John Saunders played in only one Test of the series, the Fourth, in Sydney, where he took nine wickets on debut. He missed the final Test with a fractured collarbone.

JJ Kelly took eight catches in the Fourth Test—the first Test wicketkeeper to do so, and a record for more than 50 years until Gil Langley made nine dismissals at Lord's in 1956.

1901–02 AUSTRALIA WON SERIES 4–1

57 1st Test Sydney Cricket Ground, December 13, 14, 16
ENGLAND 464 (AC MacLaren 116, AFA Lilley 84, TW Hayward 69, LC Braund 58, CE McLeod 4/84)
AUSTRALIA 168 (SE Gregory 48, C Hill 46, SF Barnes 5/65) and **172** (SE Gregory 43, LC Braund 5/61, C Blythe 4/30)
CAPTAINS AC MacLaren [ENG] J Darling [AUST]
RESULT England won by an innings and 124 runs

58 2nd Test Melbourne Cricket Ground, January 1, 2, 3, 4
AUSTRALIA 112 (SF Barnes 6/42, C Blythe 4/64) and **353** (RA Duff 104, C Hill 99, WW Armstrong 45*, SF Barnes 7/121)
ENGLAND 61 (MA Noble 7/17) and **175** (JT Tyldesley 66, MA Noble 6/60, H Trumble 4/49)
CAPTAINS J Darling [AUST] AC MacLaren [ENG]
RESULT Australia won by 229 runs

59 3rd Test Adelaide Oval, January 17, 18, 20, 21, 22, 23
ENGLAND 388 (LC Braund 103*, TW Hayward 90, WG Quaife 68, AC MacLaren 67) and **247** (TW Hayward 47, AC MacLaren 44, WG Quaife 44, H Trumble 6/74)
AUSTRALIA 321 (C Hill 98, VT Trumper 65, SE Gregory 55, RA Duff 43, JR Gunn 5/76) and **6/315** (C Hill 97, J Darling 69, H Trumble 62*)
CAPTAINS AC MacLaren [ENG] J Darling [AUST]
RESULT Australia won by four wickets

60 4th Test Sydney Cricket Ground, February 14, 15, 17, 18
ENGLAND 317 (AC MacLaren 92, JT Tyldesley 79, TW Hayward 41, AFA Lilley 40, JV Saunders 4/119) and **99** (MA Noble 5/54, JV Saunders 5/43)
AUSTRALIA 299 (MA Noble 56, WW Armstrong 55, AJY Hopkins 43, LC Braund 4/118, GL Jessop 4/68) and **3/121** (RA Duff 51*)
CAPTAINS AC MacLaren [ENG] H Trumble [AUST]
RESULT Australia won by seven wickets

61 5th Test Melbourne Cricket Ground, February 28, March 1, 3, 4
AUSTRALIA 144 (TW Hayward 4/22, JR Gunn 4/38) and **255** (C Hill 87, SE Gregory 41, LC Braund 5/95)
ENGLAND 189 (AFA Lilley 41, H Trumble 5/62) and **178** (AC MacLaren 49, MA Noble 6/98)
CAPTAINS H Trumble [AUST] AC MacLaren [ENG]
RESULT Australia won by 32 runs

1902

The Australians, having dominated the home series a few months earlier, travelled to England where they won yet again. The 2–1 result meant Australia had won four successive Ashes rubbers. This series began with the first Test to be staged at Edgbaston in Birmingham.

The First Test is a black one in Australia's history, with the first innings total of 36 the country's lowest on record. Trumper top-scored with 18.

The drawn Second Test was reduced to 105 minutes, all on day one, because of constant rain.

The third match was the only Test ever played at Bramall Lane— the home of Sheffield United Football Club.

Australia's Clem Hill is in the record books as the only player to have scored a Test century at Bramall Lane, while Monty Noble took 11 wickets.

At Old Trafford in the Fourth Test, Trumper became the first player to score a century before lunch on the first day of a Test. Charlie Macartney and Don Bradman are among the few to have equalled the feat in almost a century of cricket since.

The Australian captain, Joe Darling, who hit Test cricket's first six in Adelaide four years earlier, hit another two sixes in his half-century at Old Trafford—the first sixes in Tests in England.

Australia won the Old Trafford Test by just three runs—the closest runs margin in Ashes Tests, though equalled by England at the MCG in 1982–83.

Sussex off-spinner Fred Tate paid the ultimate penalty for the Fourth Test defeat. Dismissed with just four runs required for victory, and having dropped a vital catch off second innings top-scorer Darling, Tate was dropped—never to play for England again after just one Test appearance.

England's win at The Oval was the first one-wicket result in Test cricket. Needing 263 for victory, they were 5/48 before Gilbert Jessop scored a century in 75 minutes, then the fastest on record in Test cricket.

Hugh Trumble took 8/65 and 4/108 in the Fifth Test, becoming the first Australian to score a 50 and take 10 wickets in the same Test.

1902 AUSTRALIA WON SERIES 2–1

62 1st Test Edgbaston, Birmingham, May 29, 30, 31
ENGLAND 9/376 dec (JT Tyldesley 138, Hon FS Jackson 53, WH Lockwood 52*, GH Hirst 48)
AUSTRALIA 36 (W Rhodes 7/17) and **2/46**
CAPTAINS AC MacLaren [ENG] J Darling [AUST]
RESULT draw

63 2nd Test Lord's, June 12, 13 (no play), 14 (no play)
ENGLAND 2/102 (Hon FS Jackson 55*, AC MacLaren 47*)
AUSTRALIA did not bat
CAPTAINS AC MacLaren [ENG] J Darling [AUST]
RESULT draw

64 3rd Test Bramall Lane, Sheffield, July 3, 4, 5
AUSTRALIA 194 (MA Noble 47, SF Barnes 6/49) and **289** (C Hill 119, VT Trumper 62, AJY Hopkins 40*, W Rhodes 5/63)
ENGLAND 145 (JV Saunders 5/50, MA Noble 5/51) and **195** (AC MacLaren 63, GL Jessop 55, MA Noble 6/52, H Trumble 4/49)
CAPTAINS J Darling [AUST] AC MacLaren [ENG]
RESULT Australia won by 143 runs

65 4th Test Old Trafford, Manchester, July 24, 25, 26
AUSTRALIA 299 (VT Trumper 104, C Hill 65, RA Duff 54, J Darling 51, WH Lockwood 6/48, W Rhodes 4/104) and **86** (WH Lockwood 5/28)
ENGLAND 262 (Hon FS Jackson 128, LC Braund 65, H Trumble 4/75) and **120** (H Trumble 6/53, JV Saunders 4/52)
CAPTAINS J Darling [AUST] AC MacLaren [ENG]
RESULT Australia won by three runs.

66 5th Test The Oval, August 11, 12, 13
AUSTRALIA 324 (H Trumble 64*, MA Noble 52, VT Trumper 42, AJY Hopkins 40, GH Hirst 5/77) and **121** (WH Lockwood 5/45)
ENGLAND 183 (GH Hirst 43, H Trumble 8/65) and **9/263** (GL Jessop 104, GH Hirst 58*, Hon FS Jackson 49, H Trumble 4/108, JV Saunders 4/105)
CAPTAINS J Darling [AUST] AC MacLaren [ENG]
RESULT England won by one wicket

1903–04

The England side for this series was the first to be selected and managed by the Marylebone Cricket Club. Pelham 'Plum' Warner,

who was to become a central figure in the Bodyline series almost 30
years later, was the England captain. And, after losing the previous
four rubbers, his country won this series 3–2.

Ted Arnold, on debut for England, captured Trumper's wicket
with the first ball he bowled in Test cricket. He took 18 for the
series—second only to Wilfred Rhodes.

Noble captained Australia for the first time in the First Test, and
scored his only Test century.

Reginal 'Tip' Foster scored 287 on debut for England in the First
Test, in Sydney, setting a string of records including the highest
score in Test cricket, and the highest by a player on debut (which
still stands). Tip Foster went on to become the only man to
captain England at both cricket and soccer.

In the Second Test, Rhodes took an England record 15 wickets—
despite having eight catches dropped from his bowling.

Clem Hill struggled throughout the series, averaging only 27, but
during the Third Test, became the first batsman to reach 2000
Test runs.

In Adelaide, Trumper and Syd Gregory became the first players
to score four Test centuries against England.

England regained the Ashes by winning the Fourth Test, in
Sydney, thanks largely to the inventor of the 'googly', Bernard
Bosanquet, who took 6/51 in Australia's second innings.

Albert 'Tibby' Cotter, an early century 'slinger' in the mould of
Jeff Thomson, first played (aged 19) in the Fourth Test and took
eight wickets in the final Test.

Hugh Trumble's career came to an end in the Fifth Test, when
he took 7/28 in the second innings, including the second hat-
trick of his Test career.

The final Test was a milestone for Noble, who reached the Test
double of 1000 runs and 100 wickets, as George Giffen had done
seven years earlier.

1903–04 ENGLAND WON SERIES 3–2

67 1st Test Sydney Cricket Ground, December 11, 12, 14, 15, 16, 17
AUSTRALIA 285 (MA Noble 133, WW Armstrong 48, EG Arnold 4/76) and **485**

(VT Trumper 185*, RA Duff 84, C Hill 51, SE Gregory 43, W Rhodes 5/94)
ENGLAND 577 (RE Foster 287, LC Braund 102, JT Tyldesley 53, W Rhodes 40*)
and **5/194** (TW Hayward 91, GH Hirst 60*)
CAPTAINS MA Noble [AUST] PF Warner [ENG]
RESULT England won by five wickets

68 2nd Test Melbourne Cricket Ground, January 1, 2, 4, 5
ENGLAND 315 (JT Tyldesley 97, PF Warner 68, TW Hayward 58, RE Foster 49
ret ill, H Trumble 4/107, WP Howell 4/43) and **103** (JT Tyldesley 62, H Trumble
5/34)
AUSTRALIA 122 (VT Trumper 74, W Rhodes 7/56) and **111** (W Rhodes 8/68)
CAPTAINS PF Warner [ENG] MA Noble [AUST]
RESULT England won by 185 runs

69 3rd Test Adelaide Oval, January 15, 16, 18, 19, 20
AUSTRALIA 388 (VT Trumper 113, C Hill 88, RA Duff 79, MA Noble 59) and **351**
(SE Gregory 112, MA Noble 65, VT Trumper 59, BJT Bosanquet 4/73)
ENGLAND 245 (GH Hirst 58, PF Warner 48) and **278** (PF Warner 79,
TW Hayward 67, GH Hirst 44, AJY Hopkins 4/81)
CAPTAINS MA Noble [AUST] PF Warner [ENG]
RESULT Australia won by 216 runs

70 4th Test Sydney Cricket Ground, February 26, 27, 29 (no play), March 1, 2, 3
ENGLAND 249 (AE Knight 70*, MA Noble 7/100) and **210** (TW Hayward 52)
AUSTRALIA 131 (RA Duff 47, W Rhodes 4/33, EG Arnold 4/28) and **171**
(MA Noble 53*, BJT Bosanquet 6/51)
CAPTAINS PF Warner [ENG] MA Noble [AUST]
RESULT England won by 157 runs

71 5th Test Melbourne Cricket Ground, March 5, 7, 8
AUSTRALIA 247 (VT Trumper 88, LC Braund 8/81) and **133** (GH Hirst 5/48)
ENGLAND 61 (A Cotter 6/40, MA Noble 4/19) and **101** (H Trumble 7/28)
CAPTAINS MA Noble [AUST] PF Warner [ENG]
RESULT Australia won by 218 runs

1905

*This became known as 'Jackson's year', with FS (Stanley) Jackson
leading England to victory in the series. He won the toss in each
of the five Tests, headed the batting averages with 70.28 and the
bowling averages with 15.46. As they said, Jackson's Year.
Ironically, FS Jackson was born on the same day as the Australian
captain of the series, Joe Darling.*

For the second time in three Ashes encounters, Bernard

Bosanquet struck with his googly, taking eight wickets in the second innings of the First Test to give England victory. Bosanquet played only seven Tests and this was his finest performance.

In the First Test, MacLaren, the former England captain, scored a record fifth Test-century—the first in a Nottingham Test.

In the Third Test, Jackson scored the first Test century at Headingley. He scored another century in the Fourth Test, at Old Trafford, making him the first to score five Test hundreds in England.

Derbyshire seamer Arnold Warren made his Test debut, at the age of 30, at Headingley. He took six wickets, with his scalps including Trumper (twice), Noble, Armstrong and Darling, and yet this was his only Test appearance.

The Oval Test was to be the last for Australian opener Reggie Duff, whose 146 gave him the distinction of being the first player to score a century in both his first and last Tests between Australia and England.

At The Oval, Arthur Jones substituted for England as wicketkeeper—the first time a substitute has kept wicket in a Test.

1905 ENGLAND WON SERIES 2–0

72 1st Test Trent Bridge, Nottingham, May 29, 30, 31
ENGLAND 196 (JT Tyldesley 56, F Laver 7/64) and **5/426 dec** (AC MacLaren 140, Hon. FS Jackson 82*, JT Tyldesley 61, TW Hayward 47)
AUSTRALIA 221 (C Hill 54, MA Noble, 50, A Cotter 45, Hon. FS Jackson 5/52) and **188** (SE Gregory 51, J Darling 40, BJT Bosanquet 8/107)
CAPTAINS Hon. FS Jackson [ENG] J Darling [AUST]
RESULT England won by 213 runs

73 2nd Test Lord's, June 15, 16, 17 (no play)
ENGLAND 282 (CB Fry 73, AC MacLaren 56, JT Tyldesley 43) and **5/151** (AC MacLaren 79)
AUSTRALIA 181 (J Darling 41, Hon. FS Jackson 4/50)
CAPTAINS Hon. FS Jackson [ENG] J Darling [AUST]
RESULT draw

74 3rd Test Headingley, Leeds, July 3, 4, 5
ENGLAND 301 (Hon. FS Jackson 144*) and **5/295 dec** (JT Tyldesley 100, TW Hayward 60, GH Hirst 40*, WW Armstrong 5/122)
AUSTRALIA 195 (WW Armstrong 66, RA Duff 48, AR Warren 5/57) and **7/224** (MA Noble 62)
CAPTAINS Hon. FS Jackson [ENG] J Darling [AUST]
RESULT draw

75 4th Test Old Trafford, Manchester, July 24, 25, 26
ENGLAND 446 (Hon. FS Jackson 113, TW Hayward 82, RH Spooner 52, CE McLeod 5/125)
AUSTRALIA 197 (J Darling 73, W Brearley 4/72) and **169** (RA Duff 60, W Brearley 4/54)
CAPTAINS Hon. FS Jackson [ENG] J Darling [AUST]
RESULT England won by an innings and 80 runs

76 5th Test The Oval, August 14, 15, 16
ENGLAND 430 (CB Fry 144, Hon. FS Jackson 76, TW Hayward 59, EG Arnold 40, A Cotter 7/148) and **6/261 dec** (JT Tyldesley 112*, RH Spooner 79)
AUSTRALIA 363 (RA Duff 146, J Darling 57, JJ Kelly 42, W Brearley 5/110) and **4/124.**
CAPTAINS Hon. FS Jackson [ENG] J Darling [AUST]
RESULT draw

1907–08

England were unsettled in this series by captaincy problems, with the appointed captain, Nottinghamshire's Arthur Jones, missing the first three Tests after falling ill in Brisbane. In his absence, opening batsman Frederick Fane took over the leadership, becoming the first Essex player to captain England.

Due to Jones' illness, another Nottinghamshire batsman, George Gunn, made an unexpected debut, although not an official member of the touring party. Gunn made the most of his opportunity in the First Test, top-scoring with 119 and 74. He played in all five Tests, heading the averages at 51.33, with another century in the Fifth Test in Sydney.

Set 275 to win the First Test, Australia was 8/219 before 'Tibby' Cotter and Gerry Hazlitt, on debut at 19, added the 56 required for a two-wicket victory.

Charlie Macartney, who became known as the 'Governor-General', made the first of his 35 appearances in the First Test, in Sydney. He played in all five Tests, occupying six different batting positions during the series.

The Second Test marked the debut of an England icon, Jack Hobbs, who went on to play 41 Tests against Australia (the last in 1930) and score 3636 runs, including 12 centuries.

England won the Second Test by only one wicket. The match would have been tied but for a missed run-out attempt as the winning run was taken.

Roger Hartigan, originally from NSW, moved to Queensland before being picked for the Third Test, where he became the fourth Australian to score a century on debut. Hartigan later became a leading administrator, playing a significant role in Queensland being admitted to the Sheffield Shield.

Clem Hill dropped down the batting order in the second innings of the Third Test because of influenza and his 160 is the highest score for anyone batting at number nine in a Test.

England's hopes of retaining the Ashes were washed away with a rain-affected wicket on day two of the Fourth Test, leaving the visitors 105 all out in their first innings. Eventually they needed 495 to win, but made only 186.

Victor Trumper scored 166 in the second innings of the Fifth Test ... his fifth Test century against England.

1907–08 AUSTRALIA WON SERIES 4–1

77 1st Test Sydney Cricket Ground, December 13, 14, 16, 17, 18 (no play)
ENGLAND 273 (G Gunn 119, KL Hutchings 42, A Cotter 6/101) and **300**
(G Gunn 74, J Hardstaff sr 63, JV Saunders 4/68)
AUSTRALIA 300 (C Hill 87, VT Trumper 43, A Fielder 6/82) and **8/275**
(H Carter 61, WW Armstrong 44, PA McAlister 41)
CAPTAINS FL Fane [ENG] MA Noble [AUST]
RESULT Australia won by two wickets

78 2nd Test Melbourne Cricket Ground, January 1, 2, 3, 4, 6, 7
AUSTRALIA 266 (MA Noble 61, VT Trumper 49, JN Crawford 5/79) and **397**
(WW Armstrong 77, MA Noble 64, VT Trumper 63, CG Macartney 54,
H Carter 53, SF Barnes 5/72)
ENGLAND 382 (KL Hutchings 126, JB Hobbs 83, LC Braund 49, A Cotter 5/142)
and **9/282** (FL Fane 50)
CAPTAINS MA Noble [AUST] FL Fane [ENG]
RESULT England won by one wicket

79 3rd Test Adelaide Oval, January 10, 11, 13, 14, 15, 16
AUSTRALIA 285 (CG Macartney 75, RJ Hartigan 48, VS Ransford 44,
A Fielder 4/80) and **506** (C Hill 160, RJ Hartigan 116, MA Noble 65)
ENGLAND 363 (G Gunn 65, JN Crawford 62, J Hardstaff sr 61, FL Fane 48) and
183 (J Hardstaff sr 72, LC Braund 47, JV Saunders 5/65, JDA O'Connor 5/40)
CAPTAINS MA Noble [AUST] FL Fane [ENG]
RESULT Australia won by 245 runs

80 4th Test Melbourne Cricket Ground, February 7, 8, 10, 11
AUSTRALIA 214 (VS Ransford 51, MA Noble 48, JN Crawford 5/48, A Fielder 4/54)
and **385** (WW Armstrong 133*, H Carter 66, VS Ransford 54, A Fielder 4/91)
ENGLAND 105 (JB Hobbs 57, JV Saunders 5/28) and **186** (G Gunn 43,
JV Saunders 4/76)
CAPTAINS MA Noble [AUST] AO Jones [ENG]
RESULT Australia won by 308 runs

81 5th Test Sydney Cricket Ground, February 21, 22, 24, 25, 26, 27
AUSTRALIA 137 (SE Gregory 44, SF Barnes 7/60) and **422** (VT Trumper 166,
SE Gregory 56, C Hill 44, JN Crawford 5/141, W Rhodes 4/102)
ENGLAND 281 (G Gunn 122*, JB Hobbs 72) and **229** (W Rhodes 69,
FL Fane 46, JV Saunders 5/82)
CAPTAINS MA Noble [AUST] AO Jones [ENG]
RESULT Australia won by 49 runs

1909

*In 1989 a total of 29 players were chosen for England in the home
Ashes rubber against Australia. That, however, wasn't entirely new,
for here in 1909, the precedent was set with 25 players selected over
the five Tests.*

All of the 20 Australian wickets in the First Test at Edgbaston fell
to left-armers. Seamer George Hirst took nine wickets and slow
left-armer Charlie Blythe took 11.

England won the First Test by 10 wickets, with Jack Hobbs and
CB Fry sharing an unbroken stand of 105 in the second innings.
In the first innings, both went first ball to Charlie Macartney. Fry
was the ultimate all-round achiever, holding the world long-jump
record for 21 years, and playing soccer for England and for
Southampton in an FA Cup final.

Warren Bardsley, on the first of four tours to England, made his
debut in the First Test, at Birmingham, and in the Fifth Test, at
The Oval, and became the first player to score centuries in each
innings of a Test. In all, he scored six Test centuries but, after
the 'twin-century' match, he had to wait another 17 years before
he scored another ton in England.

John King, a 38-year-old left-hand batsman from Leicestershire, top-scored with 60 in the first innings of the Second Test, at Lord's. It was to be his only Test.

The leg-spin of Warwick Armstrong set up Australia's nine-wicket victory in the Second Test. His figures of 6/35 were his best in Test cricket.

At the age of 39, Victorian medium-pacer Frank Laver—chosen on the tour as player/manager—took 8/31 off 18.2 overs in England's first innings of the Fourth Test . . . the best figures for a tourist in England. Players called for Laver to again fill the role of player/manager in 1912, however the Australian Board refused, and six leading players declined to tour.

The Fifth Test, at The Oval, marked the debut of Frank Woolley, who went on to become one of England's great all-rounders.

Noble won the toss for Australia in each of the five Tests—just as Jackson had for England in 1905.

1909 AUSTRALIA WON SERIES 2–1

---

82 1st Test Edgbaston, Birmingham, May 27, 28, 29
AUSTRALIA 74 (C Blythe 6/44, GH Hirst 4/28) and **151** (SE Gregory 43, VS Ransford 43, C Blythe 5/58, GH Hirst 5/58)
ENGLAND 121 (WW Armstrong 5/27) and **0/105** (JB Hobbs 62*)
CAPTAINS MA Noble [AUST] AC MacLaren [ENG]
RESULT England won by 10 wickets

83 2nd Test Lord's, June 14, 15, 16
ENGLAND 269 (JH King 60, AFA Lilley 47, JT Tyldesley 46, A Cotter 4/80) and **121** (WW Armstrong 6/35)
AUSTRALIA 350 (VS Ransford 143*, W Bardsley 46, AE Relf, 5/85) and **1/41**
CAPTAINS AC MacLaren [ENG] MA Noble [AUST]
RESULT Australia won by nine wickets

84 3rd Test Headingley, Leeds, July 1, 2, 3
AUSTRALIA 188 (SE Gregory 46, VS Ransford 45, W Rhodes 4/38) and **207** (WW Armstrong 45, SF Barnes 6/63)
ENGLAND 182 (J Sharp 61, JT Tyldesley 55, CG Macartney 7/58) and **87** (A Cotter 5/38, CG Macartney 4/27)
CAPTAINS MA Noble [AUST] AC MacLaren [ENG]
RESULT Australia won by 126 runs

85 4th Test Old Trafford, Manchester, July 26, 27, 28
AUSTRALIA 147 (SF Barnes 5/56, C Blythe 5/63) and **9/279 dec** (VS Ransford 54*, CG Macartney 51, VT Trumper 48, W Rhodes 5/83)
ENGLAND 119 (F Laver 8/31) and **3/108** (RH Spooner 58)
CAPTAINS MA Noble [AUST] AC MacLaren [ENG]
RESULT draw

86 5th Test The Oval, August 9, 10, 11
AUSTRALIA 325 (W Bardsley 136, VT Trumper 73, CG Macartney 50,
DW Carr 5/146) and **5/339 dec** (W Bardsley 130, SE Gregory 74, MA Noble 55)
ENGLAND 352 (J Sharp 105, W Rhodes 66, CB Fry 62, KL Hutchings 59,
A Cotter 6/95) and **3/104** (W Rhodes 54)
CAPTAINS MA Noble [AUST] AC MacLaren [ENG]
RESULT draw

1911–12

*England's appointed captain Plum Warner fell ill early in the tour,
and JWHT 'Johnny Won't Hit Today' Douglas led the side
throughout the rubber, including in his debut First Test, in Sydney.
Three years earlier, Douglas had won an Olympic Games gold
medal as a middleweight boxer. He led England to a 4–1 victory
to regain the Ashes.*

Trumper scored his eighth Test century in the First Test. It was
his sixth against England—more than any other player to that
time.

Leg-spinner Herbert 'Ranji' Hordern, who toured England with
an American side known as 'The Gentlemen of Philadelphia' in
1907, was the first Australian to develop the googly. He took 12
wickets in the First Test (his first against England), 10 in the Fifth
(his last), and 32 for the series.

Wicketkeeper Ernest 'Tiger' Smith, who went on to become a Test
umpire and for some time was the oldest-living Test cricketer,
made his debut for England in the Second Test, in Melbourne.

Sydney Barnes gave England a remarkable start to the Second
Test, with 5/6 in his first spell, setting up England's victory.

Hobbs scored the first of his 12 centuries against Australia with
his 126 not out in the Second Test. He also scored 187—his
highest against Australia—in the Third Test. That score remains
England's highest in Adelaide.

Sussex all-rounder Joseph Vine was first selected for England in
the Fourth Test, but he'd already made his mark in the previous

Test, catching teammate Tiger Smith while substituting for Trumper.

England's openers Hobbs and Rhodes scored 178 and 179 respectively in the Fourth Test—their partnership of 323 remains England's best for any wicket in Australia. It was also the best opening partnership for either country in Ashes Tests until Geoff Marsh and Mark Taylor posted 329 at Trent Bridge in 1989.

For two Australian greats, Hill and Trumper, the Fifth Test was the last of their careers. They were Australia's two most prolific Test runscorers—Hill 3,412 (with five scores in the 90s) and Trumper 3,163.

Frank Woolley's 133 not out in the Fifth Test was the first century by an England left-hander in Australia.

1911–12 ENGLAND WON SERIES 4–1

87 1st Test Sydney Cricket Ground, December 15, 16, 18, 19, 20, 21
AUSTRALIA 447 (VS Trumper 113, RB Minnett 90, WW Armstrong 60, C Hill 46) and **308** (C Kelleway 70, C Hill 65, FR Foster 5/92, JWHT Douglas 4/50)
ENGLAND 318 (JW Hearne 76, JB Hobbs 63, FR Foster 56, W Rhodes 41, HV Hordern 5/85) and **291** (G Gunn 62, JW Hearne 43, HV Hordern 7/90)
CAPTAINS C Hill [AUST] JWHT Douglas [ENG]
RESULT Australia won by 146 runs

88 2nd Test Melbourne Cricket Ground, December 30, January 1, 2, 3
AUSTRALIA 184 (HV Hordern 49*, VS Ransford 43, SF Barnes 5/44) and **299** (WW Armstrong 90, A Cotter 41, FR Foster 6/91)
ENGLAND 265 (JW Hearne 114, W Rhodes 61, A Cotter 4/73, HV Hordern 4/66) and **2/219** (JB Hobbs 126*, G Gunn 43)
CAPTAINS C Hill [AUST] JWHT Douglas [ENG]
RESULT England won by eight wickets

89 3rd Test Adelaide Oval, January 12, 13, 15, 16, 17
AUSTRALIA 133 (FR Foster 5/36) and **476** (C Hill 98, H Carter 72, W Bardsley 63, TJ Matthews 53, SF Barnes 5/105)
ENGLAND 501 (JB Hobbs 187, FR Foster 71, W Rhodes 59, CP Mead 46, A Cotter 4/125) and **3/112** (W Rhodes 57*, G Gunn 45)
CAPTAINS C Hill [AUST] JWHT Douglas [ENG]
RESULT England won by seven wickets

90 4th Test Melbourne Cricket Ground, February 9, 10, 12, 13
AUSTRALIA 191 (RB Minnett 56, SF Barnes 5/74, FR Foster 4/77) and **173** (JWHT Douglas 5/46)
ENGLAND 589 (W Rhodes 179, JB Hobbs 178, G Gunn 75, FE Woolley 56, FR Foster 50)
CAPTAINS C Hill [AUST] JWHT Douglas [ENG]
RESULT England won by an innings and 225 runs

91 5th Test Sydney Cricket Ground, February 23, 24, 26 (no play), 27, 28, 29 (no play) March 1
ENGLAND 324 (FE Woolley 133*, G Gunn 52, HV Hordern 5/95) and **214** (G Gunn 61, JB Hobbs 45, HV Hordern 5/66)
AUSTRALIA 176 and **292** (RB Minnett 61, VT Trumper 50, SE Gregory 40, FR Foster 4/43, SF Barnes 4/106)
CAPTAINS JWHT Douglas [ENG] C Hill [AUST]
RESULT England won by 70 runs

1912

These three matches were played in England as part of a triangular tournament with South Africa. The overall result of the tournament hinged on the Third Test ... match nine of the tournament ... at The Oval, and to ensure a result, the encounter was declared a 'timeless Test'—the first to be staged in England. England won the match and the tournament with four victories and two draws. Australia won two, lost one and drew three, and South Africa lost five and drew one.

Rain ruined the drawn First Test, although Hobbs managed to add another century to his record book, and Macartney missed completing another Test hundred by just one run.

Rain also hit the Second Test, at Old Trafford, with a total of just 300 minutes play on the first two days, and not a ball bowled on the third.

England set up their Third Test victory with a 134-run lead on the first innings, with Australia bowled out for 111—thanks to Barnes' 5/30 and Woolley's 5/29. In an inglorious second innings, Australia was dismissed for 65—losing 9/19—with Woolley taking 5/20. He also scored 62, becoming the third player to score a half-century and take 10 wickets in an Ashes Test.

1912 ENGLAND WON SERIES 1–0

92 1st Test Lord's, June 24, 25, 26
ENGLAND 7/310 dec (JB Hobbs 107, W Rhodes 59, CB Fry 42)

AUSTRALIA 7/282 (CG Macartney 99, C Kelleway 61)
CAPTAINS CB Fry [ENG] SE Gregory [AUST]
RESULT draw

93 2nd Test Old Trafford, Manchester, July 29, 30, 31 (no play)
ENGLAND 203 (W Rhodes 92, GR Hazlitt 4/77, WJ Whitty 4/43)
AUSTRALIA 0/14
CAPTAINS CB Fry [ENG] SE Gregory [AUST]
RESULT draw

94 3rd Test The Oval, August 19, 20, 21, 22
ENGLAND 245 (JB Hobbs 66, FE Woolley 62, W Rhodes 49, WJ Whitty 4/69, RB Minnett 4/34) and **175** (CB Fry 79, GR Hazlitt 7/25)
AUSTRALIA 111 (C Kelleway 43, SF Barnes 5/30, FE Woolley 5/29) and **65** (FE Woolley 5/20, H Dean 4/19)
CAPTAINS CB Fry [ENG] SE Gregory [AUST]
RESULT England won by 244 runs

1901–1920
Questions 1–10

1 Which now-traditional venue was used for Test cricket in 1902 for the first time?

2 This player, who scored a century on debut for Australia in 1907–08, was later to become a leading administrator, helping with Queensland's admission to the Sheffield Shield. What was his name?

3 Who's the Victorian medium-pacer who, on the 1909 tour, was not only a player, but Australia's manager as well?

4 The highest score by an England batsman in Adelaide is 187, scored by which outstanding player back in the 1911–12 series?

5 The England captain for the 1903–04 series had for his nickname, a fruit . . . who was that player?

6 The South Australian George Giffen was the first Australian to achieve the 1,000 runs/100 wickets double. Who was the second Australian to reach that double, in the 1903–04 series?

7 Which Australian player was dismissed for 99, 98 and 97— scoring more than 500 runs in the 1901–02 series without a century?

8 Which third country made up the 1912 triangular tournament with England and Australia?

9 Thirty-eight Ashes Tests were played in the time from 1901 till the First World War. Which country had the most wins?

10 Which outstanding Australian batsman died of Bright's Disease in 1915, aged 37, forcing news of the War off the front pages?

Questions 11–20

11 A century in his final Test in 1905 made this Australian opener the first player to score a century in his first and last Ashes Tests. Who was he?

12 Which country won the triangular tournament of 1912?

13 The longest Test up until the First World War was the Fifth Test in Sydney in 1911–12. How long did it last?

14 The home of which leading soccer club hosted a Test for the only time in 1902?

15 Who was the Victorian off-spinner who took a hat-trick to complete Australia's victory in the Second Test of 1901–02?

16 The 1905 series was known as ' . . . 's Year', with that player heading the England batting averages with 70.28 and the bowling averages at 15.46. Whose year was it?

17 An England player scored 287 in his first Test, during the 1903–04 tour. Who was that player?

18 When Australia's Mark Taylor and Geoff Marsh had an opening partnership of 329 at Trent Bridge in 1989, they broke the record for the highest first-wicket stand in Ashes Tests, set by England's Jack Hobbs and . . . in Melbourne in the 1911-12 series.

19 Which Kent all-rounder made the first of his 32 Ashes appearances at The Oval in 1909?

20 England's selectors called on a then-record number of players for the 1909 rubber. Did they use:
a) 21 players
b) 25 players
c) 31 players

Questions 21–30

21 Australia's victory at Old Trafford in 1902 was its narrowest runs margin in Ashes contests. Was the margin:
a) one run
b) three runs
c) four runs

22 In the first three Tests of the 1907–08 series, Frederick Fane became the first Essex player to captain England. Who was the regular captain who missed the matches through illness?

23 In the Adelaide Test of 1903–04, Victor Trumper and which Gregory became the first players to have scored four centuries against England?

24 Who's the Australian who scored a century batting at number 10 in 1901–02?

25 Which legendary England batsman and all-round sportsman of the early 1900s was offered the Kingdom of Albania?

26 JWHT Douglas captained England in the 1911–12 series. What nick-name, or phrase, was often attached to the 'JWHT' initials?

27 Australian greats Clem Hill and Victor Trumper both retired after the 1911–12 series. Who scored more Test runs?

28 Who was the bowler who, while playing in the Lancashire League, impressed the England captain Archie MacLaren in the Old Trafford nets, and was subsequently invited to tour Australia in 1901–02?

29 At which venue was the first timeless Test played in England?

30 Who held the Ashes at the start of World War I?

Questions 31–40

31 Len Darling captained Australia in 18 Ashes Tests between 1899 and 1905 ... true or false?

32 Which future Australian captain played the first of his 50 Tests during the 1901–02 series?

33 Who was the first England left-hander to score a Test century in Australia?

34 Syd Gregory captained Australia in the triangular tournament of 1912. He was the son of which former Test cricketer?

35 By which other name was the Australian leg-spinner Herbert Hordern known?

36 Who's the Australian who, in England in 1909, became the first player to score centuries in each innings of a Test, but then waited another 17 years to score another on English soil?

37 Which England bowler was known as the inventor of the 'googly'?

38 Which NSW all-rounder led Australia in the 1903–04 series, scoring his only Test century in the First Test, in Sydney?

39 Which Australian batsman was known as the Governor-General?

40 Clem Hill hailed from which Australian State?

Questions 41–50

41 As a bowler, Warwick Armstrong was:
a) A paceman
b) An off-spinner
c) A leg-spinner
d) Slow-medium

42 Which legendary Surrey batsman made his England debut in Melbourne in 1907–08?

43 Which Australian batsman hit the first sixes in Tests?

44 Who was the early century Australian bowler known as a 'slinger', like Jeff Thomson?

45 England's wicketkeeper for the last four Tests of the 1911–12 series went on to become a Test umpire. Who was he?

46 Six of Australia's leading players refused to tour England in 1912, after a dispute with Australian authorities over what issue?

47 Australia's captain for the 1911–12 series was involved in a fist-fight over the make-up of a Test team. Who was the captain?

48 Wilfred Rhodes was the first Lancashire left-arm slow-bowler to play for England ... true or false?

49 Who took over as Australian captain for the final two Tests of the 1901–02 series?

50 Who captained England on the 1901–02 tour, becoming the first batsman to score four Test centuries with 116 in the First Test in Sydney.

ANSWERS *1901/02–1920*

1–10

1 Edgbaston, Birmingham
2 Roger Hartigan
3 Frank Laver
4 Jack Hobbs
5 Pelham 'Plum' Warner
6 Monty Noble
7 Clem Hill
8 South Africa
9 Australia (15 wins, England 14)
10 Victor Trumper

11–20

11 Reggie Duff
12 England
13 Seven days (although rain washed out the third and sixth days)
14 Sheffield United (Bramall Lane)
15 Hugh Trumble
16 FS (Stanley) Jackson's year
17 Reginald 'Tip' Foster
18 Wilfred Rhodes
19 Frank Woolley
20 b) 25 players

21–30

21 b) three runs
22 Arthur Jones
23 Syd Gregory
24 Reggie Duff
25 CB Fry (he declined the offer)
26 'Johnny Won't Hit Today' Douglas
27 Hill (3412 runs, Trumper 3163)
28 Syd Barnes
29 The Oval
30 England

31–40

31 False (Joe Darling captained Australia in 18 Tests)
32 Warwick Armstrong
33 Frank Woolley
34 'Ned' Gregory
35 'Ranji' Hordern
36 Warren Bardsley
37 Bernard Bosanquet
38 Monty Noble
39 Charlie Macartney
40 South Australia

41–50

41 c) Leg-spinner
42 Jack Hobbs
43 Joe Darling
44 Albert Cotter
45 Ernest 'Tiger' Smith
46 The players wanted Frank Laver to tour as player-manager, as he had in 1905 and 1909, but the Board disagreed
47 Clem Hill
48 False (Rhodes was from Yorkshire)
49 Hugh Trumble
50 Archie MacLaren

Photo Quiz

Answers to photo quiz p. 215

1 Who are these batsmen?

2 **Greg Chappell and Tony Greig opposed each other as captains only once in Tests. When?**

3 a) **The touring team from which country?** b) **What year?** c) **Who was the captain of the team?** d) **What was the series scoreline?**

A

B

C

D

4 Who are these bowlers?

5 a) **Who is this England player? b) Where was the match and when? c) What triggered the incident? d) How did the England captain react?**

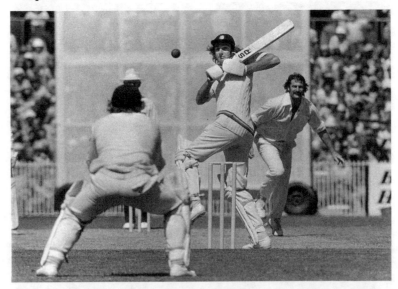

6 **Caught Marsh bowled Lillee. a) Who was the victim this time? b) How many times did Marsh and Lillee combine for dismissals in Tests against England?**

7 **Great wicketkeepers Rod Marsh and Alan Knott. Who:**
a) **Made the most dismissals in Australia–England Tests?**
b) **Played the most Ashes Tests?**
c) **Scored the most runs in Ashes Tests?**
d) **Made the most Ashes centuries?**

8 Who are these Ashes captains?

Chapter Three

1920/21 - 1938

1920–21

This was the first time Australia and England had met since before the outbreak of the First World War. Due to the long period between Tests, a total of 18 players—nine from each side—made their debuts during the five Tests.

Among the Australians to debut in the First Test were wicketkeeper Bert Oldfield, leg-spinner Arthur Mailey, batsman Herbie Collins and all-rounders Jack Gregory (nephew of Dave and Ned Gregory) and Jack Ryder ... arguably the most impressive quintet to debut together for Australia.

Collins scored 70 and 104 in the First Test—at 31, becoming the oldest Australian to score a century on debut.

Australia's First Test victory provided the springboard for eight successive wins, with Warwick Armstrong scoring a century (158) in his first match as captain.

For England the Cockney, Patsy Hendren, was making the first of three tours to Australia, playing in each of the five Tests and passing 50 in each of the first three.

During the First Test, Wilfred Rhodes passed the 2000 Test runs milestone to add to his 100 wickets—the first player to achieve that double.

Harry Makepeace, another talented all-round sportsman who won an FA Cup winner's medal with Everton, played his four-Test career in this series, scoring a century in Melbourne. At 39, he's the oldest player to score a maiden Test hundred.

For Australia, Victorian batsman Roy Park was selected for the Second Test. The story goes that his wife was knitting as Roy went out to bat. She bent down to pick up her wool ... Roy was bowled first ball ... and she'd missed her husband's entire Test career.

Jack Gregory and 'Nip' Pellew, among the newcomers in Sydney, scored maiden Test centuries in the Second Test, in Melbourne. Gregory also took eight wickets in this match.

Hobbs scored one of his 15 Test centuries in the Second Test— his third century in three innings in Melbourne.

England lost batsman John 'Young Jack' Hearne for the remainder of the series when he fell ill during the Second Test. It was the second of his three tours to Australia.

The Third Test in Adelaide was the highest-scoring of all Ashes Tests with a total of 1753 runs. Six centuries were scored—four by Australians and two by Englishmen.

The charismatic Percy Fender made the first of his 13 England appearances in the Third Test in Adelaide. He took five wickets in the first innings of both the Fourth and Fifth Tests. Some years later he settled in Australia, and at 84, he was the oldest player to travel to the Centenary Test in Melbourne in 1977.

Mailey, who'd taken 10 wickets in the Third Test, then took 13 in the Fourth, including Australia's all-time best analysis of 9/121 off 47 overs in England's second innings. He took 36 wickets in the series, which remains an Australian record for a five-Test Ashes rubber.

Armstrong scored hundreds in successive innings—in the second innings of the Third Test, and then, after an attack of malaria, in the first innings of the Fourth Test.

Yorkshire wicketkeeper Arthur Dolphin became a one-Test wonder, playing in the Fourth Test for figures of 1 and 0, and one catch. Another one-Test player to emerge in the series was England slow bowler Rockley Wilson, who scored 5 and 5 and took 3/36 in the Fifth Test.

Australia's nine-wicket win in the final Test completed an unprecedented 5–0 cleansweep of an Ashes rubber.

1920–21 AUSTRALIA WON SERIES 5–0

95 1st Test Sydney Cricket Ground, December 17, 18, 20, 21, 22
AUSTRALIA 267 (HL Collins 70) and **581** WW Armstrong 158, HL Collins 104, C Kelleway 78, CG Macartney 69, W Bardsley 57, JM Taylor 51)
ENGLAND 190 (FE Woolley 52, JB Hobbs 49) and **281** (JB Hobbs 59, JW Hearne 57, EH Hendren 56, W Rhodes 45)
CAPTAINS WW Armstrong [AUST] JWHT Douglas [ENG]
RESULT Australia won by 377 runs

96 2nd Test Melbourne Cricket Ground, December 31, January 1, 3, 4
AUSTRALIA 499 (CE Pellew 116, JM Gregory 100, JM Taylor 68, HL Collins 64, W Bardsley 51)
ENGLAND 251 (JB Hobbs 122, EH Hendren 67, JM Gregory 7/69) and **157**

(FE Woolley 50, WW Armstrong 4/26)
CAPTAINS WW Armstrong [AUST] JWHT Douglas [ENG]
RESULT Australia won by an innings and 91 runs

97 3rd Test Adelaide Oval, January 14, 15, 17, 18, 19, 20
AUSTRALIA 354 (HL Collins 162, WAS Oldfield 50, J Ryder 44, CH Parkin 5/60) and **582** (C Kelleway 147, WW Armstrong 121, CE Pellew 104, JM Gregory 78*, H Howell 4/115)
ENGLAND 447 (CAG Russell 135*, FE Woolley 79, JWH Makepeace 60, JWHT Douglas 60, AA Mailey 5/160) and **370** (JB Hobbs 123, CAG Russell 59, EH Hendren 51, PGH Fender 42, AA Mailey 5/142)
CAPTAINS WW Armstrong [AUST] JWHT Douglas [ENG]
RESULT Australia won by 119 runs

98 4th Test Melbourne Cricket Ground, February 11, 12, 14, 15, 16
ENGLAND 284 (JWH Makepeace 117, JWHT Douglas 50, AA Mailey 4/115) and **315** (W Rhodes 73, JWHT Douglas 60, PGH Fender 59, JWH Makepeace 54, AA Mailey 9/121)
AUSTRALIA 389 (WW Armstrong 123*, JM Gregory 77, HL Collins 59, W Bardsley 56, PGH Fender 5/122) and **2/211** (JM Gregory 76*, J Ryder 52*)
CAPTAINS JWHT Douglas [ENG] WW Armstrong [AUST]
RESULT Australia won by eight wickets

99 5th Test Sydney Cricket Ground, February 25, 26, 28, March 1
ENGLAND 204 (FE Woolley 53, JB Hobbs 40, C Kelleway 4/27) and **280** (JWHT Douglas 68, PGH Fender 40, AA Mailey 5/119)
AUSTRALIA 392 (CG Macartney 170, JM Gregory 93, PGH Fender 5/90) and **1/93** (W Bardsley 50*)
CAPTAINS JWHT Douglas [ENG] WW Armstrong [AUST]
RESULT Australia won by nine wickets

1921

Australia, having won the previous series 5–0, continued their post-war domination with victory in the first three Tests of this series to retain the Ashes. The series started at Trent Bridge in what was the 100th Test match between England and Australia.

The rebuilding of England's post-war side continued in this series. After blooding nine players in the previous series in Australia, England's selectors chose another 16 new players over the five Tests, using a record 30 players in the series.

The First Test was dominated by Jack Gregory, who took eight wickets, including three wickets in four balls in England's first innings. Fellow new-ball bowler, Tasmanian-born Ted McDonald, also took eight wickets for the match, and together they created Test cricket's first dual speed attack.

England's eight-wicket loss in the Second Test was their seventh defeat in a row—despite the efforts of Frank Woolley, who scored 90s in both innings.

Despite Australia's domination of the series, there was only one century of the rubber for the visitors. That came at Leeds in the Third Test, with Macartney's 115. It was the first hundred by an Australian in a Headingley Test.

Former Etonian Lionel (Third Baron) Tennyson was handed the England captaincy for the Third Test—just in time for England to equal South Africa's record of eight successive defeats. That record stood for another 63 years.

Somerset slow left-arm bowler Jack White made his debut in the Third Test, taking 3/107. He was then 30, and played just that one Test before waiting seven years to add the second in a 15-Test career.

Two others to debut in the Third Test were Kent's Wally Hardinge and Surrey's Andy Ducat, who both lasted just one match. And both were soccer internationals—Hardinge a centre-forward against Scotland in 1910, and Ducat a half-back who played six matches for England and led Aston Villa to victory in the 1920 Cup final.

The first day of the Fourth Test was yet another washout at Old Trafford.

Play was held up for 25 minutes on the second day of the Fourth Test while the Australian captain Armstrong successfully disputed an attempted England declaration under the two-day playing rules. Amid the confusion, when play resumed, Armstrong bowled the first over, having also bowled the last before the break.

The top six batsmen had a hit in England's first innings of 4/362 dec at Old Trafford. In the 13 overs required to bat out the match, England continued the original batting order, opening with numbers seven and eight, with number nine at first drop.

Andy Sandham, the Surrey opener who was to become the first batsman to score a triple-century in a Test, made his debut in the Fifth Test, at The Oval.

Phil Mead scored 182 not out at The Oval, with a century in the first session of the second day.

1921 AUSTRALIA WON SERIES 3–0

100 1st Test Trent Bridge, Nottingham, May 28, 30
ENGLAND 112 (JM Gregory 6/58) and **147** (EA McDonald 5/32)
AUSTRALIA 232 (W Bardsley 66) and **0/30**
CAPTAINS JWHT Douglas [ENG] WW Armstrong [AUST]
RESULT Australia won by 10 wickets

101 2nd Test Lord's, June 11, 13, 14
ENGLAND 187 (FE Woolley 95, EA McDonald 4/58, AA Mailey 4/55) and **283** (FE Woolley 93, Hon LH Tennyson 74*, AE Dipper 40, JM Gregory 4/76, EA McDonald 4/89)
AUSTRALIA 342 (W Bardsley 88, JM Gregory 52, H Carter 46, CE Pellew 43, FJ Durston 4/102) and **2/131** (W Bardsley 63*, TJE Andrews 49)
CAPTAINS JWHT Douglas [ENG] WW Armstrong [AUST]
RESULT Australia won by eight wickets

102 3rd Test Headingley, Leeds, July 2, 4, 5
AUSTRALIA 407 (CG Macartney 115, WW Armstrong 77, CE Pellew 52, JM Taylor 50, CH Parkin 4/106) and **7/273 dec** (TJE Andrews 92, H Carter 47)
ENGLAND 259 (JWHT Douglas 75, Hon LH Tennyson 63, G Brown 57, EA McDonald 4/105) and **202** (G Brown 46)
CAPTAINS WW Armstrong [AUST] Hon LH Tennyson [ENG]
RESULT Australia won by 219 runs

103 4th Test Old Trafford, Manchester, July 23 (no play), 25, 26
ENGLAND 4/362 dec (CAG Russell 101, GE Tyldesley 78*, CP Mead 47, PGH Fender 44*, FE Woolley 41) and **1/44**
AUSTRALIA 175 (HL Collins 40, CWL Parkin 5/38)
CAPTAINS Hon LH Tennyson [ENG] WW Armstrong [AUST]
RESULT draw

104 5th Test The Oval, August 13, 15, 16
ENGLAND 8/403 dec (CP Mead 182*, Hon LH Tennyson 51, EA McDonald 5/143) and **2/244** (CAG Russell 102*, G Brown 84, JW Hitch 51*)
AUSTRALIA 389 (TJE Andrews 94, JM Taylor 75, CG Macartney 61)
CAPTAINS Hon LH Tennyson [ENG] WW Armstrong [AUST]
RESULT draw

1924–25

Since Test cricket's beginning, the number of balls per over had varied from four to five, and then six in England ... and from four to six in Australia. In this series, Australia's authorities switched to eight-ball overs. Herbie Collins, a bookmaker by profession, assumed the Australian captaincy following Armstrong's retirement, and after leading Australia against South Africa, this was his first series in charge against England.

Two Australian greats made their debuts in the First Test . . . Bill Ponsford and Vic Richardson. Ponsford, batting at number three, became the third Australian to score a century in his first Test innings. He also scored a century in his second Test—the first player to score hundreds in his first two Test matches.

The other Australian to debut in the first Sydney Test was Arthur Richardson, a South Australian all-rounder, but not related to Vic. He made 98 in the second innings, and later went on to become a Test umpire.

England's great openers, Jack Hobbs and Herbert Sutcliffe, were first paired against Australia in the First Test. They had stands of 157 and 110, both scoring centuries . . . Hobbs 115 and 57, and Sutcliffe 59 and 115. They then shared an opening partnership of 283 in the first innings of the Second Test.

Johnny Taylor, who was the idol of a teenage Don Bradman, scored his only Test century in the First Test and his partnership of 127 with Arthur Mailey remains an Ashes last-wicket record for Australia.

In the Second Test, Hobbs and Sutcliffe became the first pair to bat through an entire day of a Test. They put on 283 on the third day, and Hobbs was out without addition for 154 on day four.

Sutcliffe, who'd scored 115 in the second innings of the First Test, followed up with 176 and 127 in the Second, becoming the first England player to score hundreds in both innings against Australia, and also the first player to score three successive Test hundreds. With the century in the Fourth Test, he was the first player to score four centuries in one series, finishing the five Tests with 734 runs at 81.55.

For the first time in Tests, a team reached 600 runs in an innings (Australia, in the Second Test, in Melbourne).

Victorian leg-spinner Albert Hartkopf made his one and only Test appearance in the second match in Melbourne, taking only one wicket but scoring a quick 80 at number eight and sharing a 100-run partnership with Oldfield for the ninth-wicket.

Australia were in trouble at 6/119 in the first innings of the Adelaide Test before Jack Ryder scored 201 not out, equalling Syd Gregory's then record score against England in Australia, and helping Australia recover to 489.

England's batting order underwent a major reshuffle in the Third Test, with every player switching positions in the second innings. In the first, Hobbs and Sutcliffe—despite their domination of the Australian new-ball attack—batted at five and six respectively.

The first three Tests were all played over seven days.

Oldfield affected four stumpings and five dismissals in total in England's only innings of the Fourth Test, becoming the first keeper to achieve either in a Test innings.

England's Fourth Test win, in Melbourne, was their first over Australia in over 12 years . . . Australia having won 11 of the past 13.

New Zealand-born Clarrie Grimmett, 'The Gnome', at age 33, made his Test debut in the final match, in Sydney, taking 11/82.

The great England paceman Maurice Tate took 38 wickets in the series, which remains the most by an England bowler in a series in Australia. Tate had match figures of 11/228 in the First Test, but sent down 89 eight-ball overs for his reward.

1924–25 AUSTRALIA WON SERIES 4–1

105 1st Test Sydney Cricket Ground, December 19, 20, 22, 23, 24, 26, 27
AUSTRALIA 450 (HL Collins 114, WH Ponsford 110, JM Taylor 43, VY Richardson 42, MW Tate 6/130) and **452** (JM Taylor 108, AJ Richardson 98, HL Collins 60, AA Mailey 46*, MW Tate 5/98)
ENGLAND 298 (JB Hobbs 115, EH Hendren 74*, H Sutcliffe 59, JM Gregory 5/111, AA Mailey 4/129) and **411** (FE Woolley 123, H Sutcliffe 115, JB Hobbs 57, AP Freeman 50*, APF Chapman 44)
CAPTAINS HL Collins [AUST] AER Gilligan [ENG]
RESULT Australia won by 193 runs

106 2nd Test Melbourne Cricket Ground, January 1, 2, 3, 5, 6, 7, 8
AUSTRALIA 600 (VY Richardson 138, WH Ponsford 128, AEV Hartkopf 80, JM Taylor 72, JM Gregory 44) and **250** (JM Taylor 90, MW Tate 6/99)
ENGLAND 479 (H Sutcliffe 176, JB Hobbs 154) and **290** (H Sutcliffe 127, FE Woolley 50, AA Mailey 5/92, JM Gregory 4/87)
CAPTAINS HL Collins [AUST] AER Gilligan [ENG]
RESULT Australia won by 81 runs

107 3rd Test Adelaide Oval, January 16, 17, 19, 20, 21, 22, 23
AUSTRALIA 489 (J Ryder 201*, TJE Andrews 72, AJ Richardson 69,

WAS Oldfield 47, R Kilner 4/127) and **250** (J Ryder 88, WH Ponsford 43,
FE Woolley 4/77, R Kilner 4/51)
ENGLAND 365 (JB Hobbs 119, EH Hendren 92) and **363** (WW Whysall 75,
H Sutcliffe 59, APF Chapman 58)
CAPTAINS HL Collins [AUST] AER Gilligan [ENG]
RESULT Australia won by 11 runs

108 4th Test Melbourne Cricket Ground, February 13, 14, 16, 17, 18
ENGLAND 548 (H Sutcliffe 143, WW Whysall 76, JB Hobbs 66,
EH Hendren 65, JW Hearne 44, FE Woolley 40, AA Mailey 4/186)
AUSTRALIA 269 (JM Taylor 86) and **250** (JM Taylor 68, JM Gregory 45,
C Kelleway 42, MW Tate 5/75)
CAPTAINS AER Gilligan [ENG] HL Collins [AUST]
RESULT England won by an innings and 29 runs

109 5th Test Sydney Cricket Ground, February 27, 28, March 2, 3, 4
AUSTRALIA 295 (WH Ponsford 80, AF Kippax 42, MW Tate 4/92, R Kilner 4/97)
and **325** (TJE Andrews 80, C Kelleway 73, WAS Oldfield 65*, MW Tate 5/115)
ENGLAND 167 (FE Woolley 47, CV Grimmett 5/45) and **146** CV Grimmett 6/37)
CAPTAINS HL Collins [AUST] AER Gilligan [ENG]
RESULT Australia won by 307 runs

1926

*After the heavy run-scoring and seven-day Tests of the previous tour
in Australia, this series got underway with rain—and plenty of it
with just 50 minutes play on the first day and none thereafter at
Trent Bridge. England's captain for the first four Tests was Arthur
Carr, who was to emerge a key figure in the Bodyline debate six and
a half years later. His unswerving support of Harold Larwood and
Bill Voce effectively brought to an end his career as a player and
administrator.*

In the rain-ruined First Test, Bill Woodfull, who'd be captain
when Australia next toured England, made his debut . . . in the
field for just 17.2 overs. So, too, did England spinner Fred Root,
although, with England batting and Australia failing to take a
wicket, he spent his entire maiden Test as a spectator.

Twenty-one-year-old Nottinghamshire fast bowler Harold
Larwood made his debut in the Second Test at Lord's, taking
three wickets and giving no clue of the impact he was to have on
the 1932–33 tour of Australia.

Warren Bardsley, by now 43 and on his fourth tour of England, scored 193 not out in the Second Test to become the oldest Australian to score a century against England, and the oldest to carry his bat through a Test innings. He averaged over 50 on his last three tours of England.

Sutcliffe and Hobbs continued to dominate, putting on 182 for the first wicket at Lord's. Hobbs became the first player to pass 4000 Test runs on his way to 119.

Four batsmen scored centuries in the Second Test, and amazingly the youngest was England's Patsy Hendren, aged 37. (Hobbs 44, Bardsley 43, Macartney 40).

Bardsley assumed the Australian captaincy for the Third Test when Collins fell ill, but made an inglorious start . . . losing the toss, then being dismissed first ball of the match.

Macartney scored a century before lunch on the first day of the Third Test, 112 in 116 minutes. He was finally out for 151. He also scored 109 in the Fourth Test, making it three centuries in three innings.

The records continued for Hobbs, who in the Leeds Test, passed Clem Hill's record aggregate of 2660 runs in Ashes Tests.

Grimmett, having been overlooked for the First and Second Tests, took seven wickets in the Third.

The first day at Old Trafford wasn't washed out—but almost, with just 10 balls bowled and Australia finishing the day at 0/6.

Percy Chapman took over the England captaincy in the Fifth Test, after Carr was dropped.

England regained the Ashes with victory at The Oval, thanks to second innings centuries by Hobbs and Sutcliffe, and six wickets by Rhodes, who'd been recalled to the England side at the age of 48.

1926 ENGLAND WON SERIES 1–0

110 1st Test Trent Bridge, Nottingham, June 12, 14 (no play), 15 (no play)
ENGLAND 0/32
AUSTRALIA did not bat
CAPTAINS AW Carr [ENG] HL Collins [AUST]
RESULT draw

111 2nd Test Lord's, June 26, 28, 29
AUSTRALIA 383 (W Bardsley 193, R Kilner 4/70) and **5/194** (CG Macartney 133*)

ENGLAND 3/475 dec (EH Hendren 127*, JB Hobbs 119, FE Woolley 87, H Sutcliffe 82, APF Chapman 50*)
CAPTAINS HL Collins [AUST] AW Carr [ENG]
RESULT draw

112 3rd Test Headingley, Leeds, July 10, 12, 13
AUSTRALIA 494 (CG Macartney 151, WM Woodfull 141, AJ Richardson 100, J Ryder 42, MW Tate 4/99)
ENGLAND 294 (CG Macaulay 76, JB Hobbs 49, CV Grimmett 5/88) and **3/254** (H Sutcliffe 94, JB Hobbs 88, APF Chapman 42*)
CAPTAINS W Bardsley [AUST] AW Carr [ENG]
RESULT draw

113 4th Test Old Trafford, Manchester, July 24, 26, 27
AUSTRALIA 335 (WM Woodfull 117, CG Macartney 109, CF Root 4/84)
ENGLAND 5/305 (GE Tyldesley 81, JB Hobbs 74, FE Woolley 58)
CAPTAINS W Bardsley [AUST] AW Carr [ENG]
RESULT draw

114 5th Test The Oval, August 14, 16, 17, 18
ENGLAND 280 (H Sutcliffe 76, APF Chapman 49, AA Mailey 6/138) and **436** (H Sutcliffe 161, JB Hobbs 100)
AUSTRALIA 302 (JM Gregory 73, HL Collins 61) and **125** (W Rhodes 4/44)
CAPTAINS APF Chapman [ENG] HL Collins [AUST]
RESULT England won by 289 runs

1928–29

Little did the people of Brisbane realise just how significant a place in history would their maiden Test match occupy. Staged at the Exhibition Ground, it marked the debut of the greatest batsman of all-time, Don Bradman. And his First Test rivals included one Douglas Jardine, and Harold Larwood . . . the trio so pivotal to the Bodyline series of 1932–33.

Bradman's maiden Test appearance was unspectacular, scoring 18 in the first innings at number seven, and 1 in the second at six. He was dropped for the Second Test, replaced by Queensland all-rounder Otto Nothling, who played his sole Test.

Although Larwood took six wickets in Australia's first innings, the first bowler to dismiss Bradman in a Test was Maurice Tate (LBW). In total, Larwood took 8/62 and scored 107 runs—the best all-round performance of his career.

Australia lost two players during the match. Jack Gregory sustained a serious knee injury that was to end his career, and didn't bat in either innings. And Charles Kelleway contracted food poisoning, and was unable to bat in the second innings in what turned out to be the last of his 26 Tests.

The First Test saw the first declaration of an innings in a Test in Australia, with Percy Chapman closing England's second innings at 8/342, setting Australia 742 for victory. Australia was bowled out for 66, giving England a record victory margin of 675 runs.

The series developed into something of a benefit for England's Walter Hammond, who after a relatively subdued First Test (44 and 28), then scored 251 in the Second, 200 and 32 in the Third, 119 and 177 in the Fourth, and 38 and 16 in the Fifth . . . in total 905 runs at an average of 113.12. He became the first player to score double-centuries in successive Test innings.

England amassed a Test record 636 in Sydney.

Australia's selectors, clearly not embracing a youth policy, picked off-spinner Don Blackie, aged 46 and 253 days, for his Test debut in Sydney. In the previous Test, Blackie's Victorian spinning partner Bert Ironmonger, aged 46 and 237 days, was chosen for his maiden Test. Blackie took 14 wickets in his three-Test career during the series, including 6/94 in England's first innings of the Third Test, in Melbourne. Ironmonger went on to play 14 Tests—his last at the age of 50 years and 327 days.

Twenty-year-old Bradman scored his first century in the Third Test—his second—in Melbourne (112 in the second innings).

Sutcliffe scored 135 in England's second innings of the Third Test, giving him four centuries in five innings in Melbourne.

England's Jack White bowled more than 100 six-ball overs in both the Third and Fourth Tests . . . his analysis in Melbourne 113.5/50/171/6, and in Adelaide 124.5/37/256/13.

Archie Jackson, rated by some to be in the Bradman class, was included in the Australian side for the Fourth Test, and scored 164 in his maiden Test innings aged just 19. He was, and remains, the youngest to score an Ashes Test century. He played just seven Tests before he died of tuberculosis at 23.

The Fifth Test, in Melbourne, was played over eight days.

Hobbs crowned his last appearance in Melbourne with yet another century—his fifth at the MCG in a career total of 15. At

46 and 82 days, he was the oldest player to score a Test century, and on his way to 142 became the first player to reach 5000 Test runs.

White captained England in the final Test, bowling 75.3 overs in Australia's first innings. But, as if to avoid accusations of overbowling himself, he asked George Geary to bowl 81 overs in the same innings.

1928-29 ENGLAND WON SERIES 4-1

115 1st Test Exhibition Ground, Brisbane, November 30, December 1, 3, 4, 5
ENGLAND 521 (EH Hendren 169, H Larwood 70, APF Chapman 50, JB Hobbs 49, WR Hammond 44) and **8/342 dec** (CP Mead 73, DR Jardine 65, EH Hendren 45, CV Grimmett 6/131)
AUSTRALIA 122 (H Larwood 6/32) and **66** (JC White 4/7)
CAPTAINS APF Chapman [ENG] J Ryder [AUST]
RESULT England won by 675 runs

116 2nd Test Sydney Cricket Ground, December 14, 15, 17, 18, 19, 20
AUSTRALIA 253 (WM Woodfull 68, WAS Oldfield 41*, G Geary 5/35) and **397** (HSTL Hendry 112, WM Woodfull 111, J Ryder 79, OE Nothling 44, MW Tate 4/99)
ENGLAND 636 (WR Hammond 251, EH Hendren 74, G Geary 66, H Larwood 43, JB Hobbs 40, DD Blackie 4/148) and **2/16**
CAPTAINS J Ryder [AUST] APF Chapman [ENG]
RESULT England won by eight wickets

117 3rd Test Melbourne Cricket Ground, December 29, 31, January 1, 2, 3, 4, 5
AUSTRALIA 397 (J Ryder 112, AF Kippax 100, DG Bradman 79, EL a'Beckett 41) and **351** (DG Bradman 112, WM Woodfull 107, AF Kippax 41, JC White 5/107)
ENGLAND 417 (WR Hammond 200, DR Jardine 62, H Sutcliffe 58, DD Blackie 6/94) and **7/332** (H Sutcliffe 135, JB Hobbs 49, EH Hendren 45)
CAPTAINS J Ryder [AUST] APF Chapman [ENG]
RESULT England won by three wickets

118 4th Test Adelaide Oval, February 1, 2, 4, 5, 6, 7, 8
ENGLAND 334 (WR Hammond 119*, JB Hobbs 74, H Sutcliffe 64, CV Grimmett 5/102) and **383** (WR Hammond 177, DR Jardine 98, MW Tate 47, Oxenham 4/67)
AUSTRALIA 369 (AA Jackson 164, J Ryder 63, DG Bradman 40, JC White 5/130, MW Tate 4/77) and **336** (J Ryder 87, DG Bradman 58, AF Kippax 51, JC White 8/126)
CAPTAINS APF Chapman [ENG] J Ryder [AUST]
RESULT England won by 12 runs

119 5th Test Melbourne Cricket Ground, March 8, 9, 11, 12, 13, 14, 15, 16
ENGLAND 519 (JB Hobbs 142, M Leyland 137, EH Hendren 95) and **257** (JB Hobbs 65, MW Tate 54, M Leyland 53*, TW Wall 5/66)
AUSTRALIA 491 (DG Bradman 123, WM Woodfull 102, AG Fairfax 65, G Geary 5/105) and **5/287** (J Ryder 57*, WAS Oldfield 48, AA Jackson 46)
CAPTAINS JC White [ENG] J Ryder [AUST]
RESULT Australia won by five wickets

1930

Rivalry between England and Australia was particularly intense around this time, with Hobbs, Sutcliffe, Hammond, Woolley, Tate and Larwood the backbone of the England side. Australia, with Woodfull and Ponsford at the top of the order, also boasted the mercurial leg-spin of Grimmett, and the batting genius of Bradman, who was on his first tour to England.

Another batting star of the '30s had his first taste of Test cricket in this series. Stan McCabe, who turned 20 during the series, played in all five Tests, passing 50 only once, but signalling he'd be a star of the future.

The First Test was Bradman's first in England, and immediately he entered the record books. His second innings century was Australia's first at Trent Bridge.

In the Second Test, at Lord's, Bradman scored 254 and the captain Woodfull 155 in Australia's 6/729 declared—still the highest individual and team score in any Ashes Test at the home of cricket.

England captain Chapman also scored a century in the Second Test—the first time rival skippers had both scored centuries in the same Ashes Test.

Australian-born 'Gubby' Allen, whose uncle Reginald Allen played one Test for Australia in 1887, made the first of his 25 England appearances in the Second Test—appropriately at Lord's, which became his second home in later life. Allen was to become England's Chairman of Selectors, and president of the MCC.

Playing at Lord's in his first match against Australia, Kumar Shri Duleepsinhji scored a century (173), emulating the feat of his uncle, Ranji, in his first Test against Australia 34 years earlier.

Bradman's Third Test 334 included 309 on the first day, which remains an all-Test record. He scored a century in each of the first two sessions and 89 in the third. Along the way, in his 13th Test innings, he passed the 1000-run milestone—all still at the age of 21.

Hammond scored 113 in the first innings of the Third Test, almost matching Bradman's effort with 1000 runs—but in his 14th Test innings.

Another Test at Old Trafford and more rain, with all but 45 minutes lost on the third day and the entire fourth day washed out.

The Fourth Test was notable for a 108-run opening partnership between Hobbs and Sutcliffe, which was their 11th and last century opening stand against Australia.

Australia won the Fifth Test—a timeless Test—to regain the Ashes on captain Woodfull's 33rd birthday.

At The Oval, Bradman scored 232 to take his series aggregate to 974 (at an average of 139.14) which remains an all-Test record.

At 47, Hobbs retired from Test cricket after the Fifth Test, having scored 3636 runs in 41 Ashes Tests.

Leg-spinner Ian Peebles returned his best innings figures of 6/204 at The Oval, having bowled 71 overs.

1930 AUSTRALIA WON SERIES 2–1

120 1st Test Trent Bridge, Nottingham, June 13, 14, 16, 17
ENGLAND 270 (JB Hobbs 78, APF Chapman 52, RWV Robins 50,
CV Grimmett 5/107) and **302** (JB Hobbs 74, EH Hendren 72,
H Sutcliffe 58 retired hurt, CV Grimmett 5/94)
AUSTRALIA 144 (AF Kippax 64*, RWV Robins 4/51) and **335** (DG Bradman 131,
SJ McCabe 49)
CAPTAINS APF Chapman [ENG] WM Woodfull [AUST]
RESULT England won by 93 runs

121 2nd Test Lord's, June 27, 28, 30, July 1
ENGLAND 425 (KS Duleepsinhji 173, MW Tate 54, EH Hendren 48,
FE Woolley 41, AG Fairfax 4/101) and **375** (APF Chapman 121,
GOB Allen 57, KS Duleepsinhji 48, CV Grimmett 6/167)
AUSTRALIA 6/729 dec (DG Bradman 254, WM Woodfull 155, AF Kippax 83,
WH Ponsford 81, SJ McCabe 44, WAS Oldfield 43*) and **3/72**
CAPTAINS APF Chapman [ENG] WM Woodfull [AUST]
RESULT Australia won by seven wickets

122 3rd Test Headingley, Leeds, July 11, 12, 14, 15
AUSTRALIA 566 (DG Bradman 334, AF Kippax 77, WM Woodfull 50,
MW Tate 5/124)
ENGLAND 391 (WR Hammond 113, APF Chapman 45, M Leyland 44,
CV Grimmett 5/135) and **3/95**
CAPTAINS WM Woodfull [AUST] APF Chapman [ENG]
RESULT draw

123 4th Test Old Trafford, Manchester, July 25, 26, 28, 29 (no play)
AUSTRALIA 345 (WH Ponsford 83, WM Woodfull 54, AF Kippax 51, CV Grimmett 50, AG Fairfax 49)
ENGLAND 8/251 (H Sutcliffe 74, KS Duleepsinhji 54, SJ McCabe 4/41)
CAPTAINS WM Woodfull [AUST] APF Chapman [ENG]
RESULT draw

124 5th Test The Oval, August 16, 18, 19, 20, 21 (no play), 22
ENGLAND 405 (H Sutcliffe 161, RES Wyatt 64, KS Duleepsinhji 50, JB Hobbs 47, CV Grimmett 4/135) and **251** (WR Hammond 60, H Sutcliffe 54, KS Duleepsinhji 46, PM Hornibrook 7/92)
AUSTRALIA 695 (DG Bradman 232, WH Ponsford 110, AA Jackson 73, WM Woodfull 54, SJ McCabe 54, AG Fairfax 53*, IAR Peebles 6/204)
CAPTAINS RES Wyatt [ENG] WM Woodfull [AUST]
RESULT Australia won by an innings and 39 runs

1932–33

And so to Bodyline. Don Bradman, by now aged 24 and virtually unstoppable, was the target of England captain Douglas Jardine, who devised the counterplan to become known as bodyline, or fast-leg theory . . . short fast bowling aimed at the body with a ring of fieldsmen in close on the leg side. When the furore exploded in the Third Test, in Adelaide, the future of the tour was threatened as forthright and bitter cables were exchanged between the respective governing bodies.

McCabe's unbeaten 187 in the First Test is regarded as one of the greatest innings ever played. He arrived at the wicket with Australia in trouble at 3/82 against the ferocious pace of Larwood and left-armer Voce, and promptly hooked Larwood to the boundary off the first ball he faced.

Like Ranji and Duleep before him, a third Indian prince, Nawab Iftikhar Ali of Pataudi, lined up for England, and like his predecessors, scored a century in his first Test against Australia.

Hammond and Sutcliffe also scored hundreds for England—for the latter, it was the last of his 16 Test centuries, and his eighth against Australia.

Bradman, who missed the First Test due to illness, was out to the first ball he faced in the Bodyline series—not to Larwood or Voce, but to Yorkshireman Bill Bowes, playing on while trying to hook. It was Bowes' only wicket of the series, while Bradman scored an unbeaten century in the second innings.

England's concentration on speed and the leg-theory was such that no specialist slow bowler was included for the Second Test. The move backfired, as leg-spinner O'Reilly took 10 wickets for the first of three times in Tests, bowling Australia to victory.

It was in the Third Test that Woodfull was hit above the heart and Oldfield suffered a fractured skull while trying to hook. It was after these incidents that Woodfull made the famous remark to the MCC manager Plum Warner: "There are two teams out there, but only one of them is playing cricket."

In the second innings in Adelaide, Woodfull carried his bat through an innings, for 73 not out, for the second time in Tests.

'Hammy' Love, of NSW, was called into the Australian side for the Fourth Test to fill in for the injured Oldfield. It was his only Test appearance.

For England, all but debutant number-11 Tommy Mitchell reached double figures in the first innings of the Fourth Test, in Brisbane.

England, leading 2–1 after the first three Tests, regained the Ashes in the Fourth, thanks in part to Eddie Paynter's first innings 83 while suffering acute tonsillitis.

Although Bradman scored only one century for the series, he still made 396 runs at 56, finishing with 48 and 71 in the Fifth Test, in Sydney.

Victor Richardson, who went on to captain Australia in South Africa in 1935–36, made his farewell appearance against England in Sydney, scoring a pair.

The Fifth Test turned out to be the last for Larwood, and sent in at number four as a nightwatchman, he reached his best Test score of 98 in England's first innings.

Fittingly, the series was completed by Hammond, whose second century of the series came in the first innings. He followed up with 75 not out in the second—and ended the game with a six to give England a 4–1 victory.

1932-33 ENGLAND WON SERIES 4-1

125 1st Test Sydney Cricket Ground, December 2, 3, 5, 6, 7
AUSTRALIA 360 (SJ McCabe 187*, VY Richardson, 49, H Larwood 5/96,
W Voce 4/110) and **164** (JHW Fingleton 40, H Larwood 5/28)
ENGLAND 524 (H Sutcliffe 194, WR Hammond 112, Nawab of Pataudi Sr 102)
and **0/1**
CAPTAINS WM Woodfull [AUST] DR Jardine [ENG]
RESULT England won by 10 wickets

126 2nd Test Melbourne Cricket Ground, December 30, 31, January 2, 3
AUSTRALIA 228 (JHW Fingleton 83) and **191** (DG Bradman 103*)
ENGLAND 169 (H Sutcliffe 52, WJ O'Reilly 5/63, TW Wall 4/52) and **139**
(WJ O'Reilly 5/66, H Ironmonger 4/26)
CAPTAINS WM Woodfull [AUST] DR Jardine [ENG]
RESULT Australia won by 111 runs

127 3rd Test Adelaide Oval, January 13, 14, 16, 17, 18, 19
ENGLAND 341 (M Leyland 83, RES Wyatt 78, E Paynter 77, H Verity 45,
TW Wall 5/72) and **412** (WR Hammond 85, LEG Ames 69, DR Jardine 56,
RES Wyatt 49, M Leyland 42, H Verity 40, WJ O'Reilly 4/79)
AUSTRALIA 222 (WH Ponsford 85, WAS Oldfield 41 retired hurt, GOB Allen 4/71)
and **193** (WM Woodfull 73*, DG Bradman 66, H Larwood 4/71, GOB Allen 4/50)
CAPTAINS DR Jardine [ENG] WM Woodfull [AUST]
RESULT England won by 338 runs

128 4th Test Woolloongabba, Brisbane, February 10, 11, 13, 14, 15, 16
AUSTRALIA 340 (VY Richardson 83, DG Bradman 76, WM Woodfull 67,
H Larwood 4/101) and **175**
ENGLAND 356 (H Sutcliffe 86, E Paynter 83, DR Jardine 46, WJ O'Reilly 4/120)
and **4/162** (M Leyland 86)
CAPTAINS WM Woodfull [AUST] DR Jardine [ENG]
RESULT England won by six wickets

129 5th Test Sydney Cricket Ground, February 23, 24, 25, 27, 28
AUSTRALIA 435 (LS Darling 85, SJ McCabe 73, LPJ O'Brien 61,
WAS Oldfield 52, DG Bradman 48, PK Lee 42, H Larwood 4/98) and **182**
(DG Bradman 71, WM Woodfull 67, H Verity 5/33)
ENGLAND 454 (WR Hammond 101, H Larwood 98, H Sutcliffe 56,
RES Wyatt 51, GOB Allen 48, M Leyland 42, PK Lee 4/111) and **2/168**
(WR Hammond 75*, RES Wyatt 61*)
CAPTAINS WM Woodfull [AUST] DR Jardine [ENG]
RESULT England won by eight wickets

1934

*With feelings still high after Bodyline, Woodfull's Australians
journeyed to England for a five-Test series. But the England side*

awaiting the contest was without three key Bodyline protagonists—
the captain Jardine, and his strike weapons Larwood and Voce.

Arthur Chipperfield had played only three first-class innings before being chosen to make this tour. Although he may have been unknown beforehand, he soon captured the headlines, playing in the First Test, at Trent Bridge, and becoming the first player to score 99 on debut.

The giant Essex fast bowler Ken Farnes made his debut in the First Test, taking five wickets in each innings for match figures of 10/179.

Australia's First Test victory was achieved primarily through its leg-spinning pair of Grimmett and O'Reilly, who bowled 183.7 overs between them and took 19 of England's 20 wickets: O'Reilly 11/129 and Grimmett 8/120.

Bradman had scores of 29 and 25 in that Trent Bridge win, which was the only time Australia defeated England from 1928 to 1938 without a century from Bradman.

Bob Wyatt, who'd replaced Chapman as England skipper for the final Test of 1930 and was Jardine's deputy in Australia, was appointed captain for the series. However, he was injured and missed the First Test when Cyril Walters led the side.

Wicketkeeper Les Ames scored 120 for England in the Second Test—the first time a keeper had scored a century in Australia-England Tests.

The Lord's Test was dominated by Yorkshire's left-arm spinner Hedley Verity, who took 15/104, including 14/80 on the third day. No-one has taken more wickets in a day's play in Ashes Tests.

Queenslander Bill Brown, playing his second Test at the age of 21, scored his maiden Test century at Lord's. Four years later he was to carry his bat for 206 on the same ground.

In the Third Test, at Old Trafford, England scored a massive 9/627 dec, with seven batsmen passing 50. The two century-makers were Maurice Leyland, who'd also made a century at Lord's and finished with three for the rubber, and 45-year-old Patsy Hendren.

Bill O'Reilly's 7/189 in England's first innings included a sequence of three wickets in four balls.

Walter Keeton, who also played soccer for Sunderland and

Nottingham Forest, played his only Ashes Test at Headingley, opening with Walters.

The Fourth Test was remarkable for the feat of one man—Bradman. For the second time in successive Ashes Tests at Leeds, he scored a triple century (304), and shared a 388-run partnership with Ponsford (181) that remains a fourth-wicket record in Ashes Tests.

Bowes took six wickets in Australia's only innings at Leeds—five of them, including Bradman, bowled.

Victorian Hans Ebeling, who organised the Centenary Test in Melbourne some 42 years later, made his sole appearance in Test cricket in the Fifth Test, at The Oval.

Australia's victory margin of 562 runs at The Oval is still in the record books as their biggest in terms of runs. It was set up by double centuries from Ponsford (266) and Bradman (244) in a second-wicket partnership of 451 in 316 minutes.

The Fifth Test win, on August 22, meant that Australia regained the Ashes—and for the second time on successive England tours the Ashes were secured on skipper Woodfull's birthday.

Frank Woolley returned to the England side for the final Test at the age of 47, in what turned out to be the last Test appearance by a pre-World War I player. His career finished ingloriously, with innings of four and a duck, and a world record 37 byes conceded when he took the gloves from the injured Les Ames in Australia's second innings.

1934 AUSTRALIA WON SERIES 2–1

130 1st Test Trent Bridge, Nottingham, June 8, 9, 11, 12
AUSTRALIA 374 (AG Chipperfield 99, SJ McCabe 65, WH Ponsford 53, K Farnes 5/102) and **8/273 dec** (SJ McCabe 88, WA Brown 73, K Farnes 5/77)
ENGLAND 268 (EH Hendren 79, H Sutcliffe 62, G Geary 53, CV Grimmett 5/81, WJ O'Reilly 4/75) and **141** (CF Walters 46, WJ O'Reilly 7/54)
CAPTAINS WM Woodfull [AUST] CF Walters [ENG]
RESULT Australia won by 238 runs

131 2nd Test Lord's, June 22, 23, 25
ENGLAND 440 (LEG Ames 120, M Leyland 109, CF Walters 82, TW Wall 4/108)
AUSTRALIA 284 (WA Brown 105, H Verity 7/61) and **118** (WM Woodfull 43, H Verity 8/43)
CAPTAINS RES Wyatt [ENG] WM Woodfull [AUST]
RESULT England won by an innings and 38 runs

132 3rd Test Old Trafford, Manchester, July 6, 7, 9, 10
ENGLAND 9/627 dec (M Leyland 153, EH Hendren 132, LEG Ames 72, H Sutcliffe 63, GOB Allen 61, H Verity 60*, CF Walters 52, WJ O'Reilly 7/189) and **0/123 dec** (H Sutcliffe 69*, CF Walters 50*)
AUSTRALIA 491 (SJ McCabe 137, WM Woodfull 73, WA Brown 72, H Verity 4/78) and **1/66**
CAPTAINS RES Wyatt [ENG] WM Woodfull [AUST]
RESULT draw

133 4th Test Headingley, Leeds, July 20, 21, 23, 24
ENGLAND 200 (CF Walters 44, CV Grimmett 4/57) and **6/229** (M Leyland 49*, CF Walters 45, RES Wyatt 44, EH Hendren 42)
AUSTRALIA 584 (DG Bradman 304, WH Ponsford 181, WE Bowes 6/142)
CAPTAINS RES Wyatt [ENG] WM Woodfull [AUST]
RESULT draw

134 5th Test The Oval, August 18, 20, 21, 22
AUSTRALIA 701 (WH Ponsford 266, DG Bradman 244, WM Woodfull 49, WAS Oldfield 42*, WE Bowes 4/164, GOB Allen 4/170) and **327** (DG Bradman 77, SJ McCabe 70, HI Ebeling 41, WE Bowes 5/55, EW Clark 5/98)
ENGLAND 321 (M Leyland 110, CF Walters 64) and **145** (WR Hammond 43, CV Grimmett 5/64)
CAPTAINS WM Woodfull [AUST] RES Wyatt [ENG]
RESULT Australia won by 562 runs

1936–37

Bradman's career took on a further dimension when he was appointed Australian captain. This was his first series in charge, and although his side suffered big defeats in the first two Tests (when Bradman was dismissed for two successive ducks), Australia recovered to win the series (with Bradman's scores including 270, 212 and 169 in the last three Tests). It was the first time a country had won a series after losing the first two Tests.

Bradman's Test captaincy initiation was one he'd rather forget, with Australia bowled out for 58 in just 12.3 overs in the second innings of the First Test, giving England a big victory. The match, though, started well for Australia with England's Stan Worthington dismissed off the first ball of the match.

Jack Fingleton's 100 in the first innings in Brisbane made him the first player to score centuries in four successive Test innings . . . then he was out for a first-ball duck in the second innings.

Hammond, who'd had so much success on Australian wickets on the previous two tours, started this rubber with a duck, but made amends in the Second Test with 231 not out—his third double-century against Australia. His average in Sydney now stood at 256.

Australia's hopes in the Second Test were dashed with rain on the third day. In reply to England's 6/426 dec Australia made 80.

On a sticky wicket, Bradman decided to open Australia's second innings of the Third Test with his tailenders, Bill O'Reilly and Chuck Fleetwood-Smith. The move, late on the second day, was successful because, despite Australia losing both makeshift openers for only three, it meant the recognised batsmen had better conditions the next day. Fingleton, at six, scored 136 and Bradman, at seven, 270 (they put on 346 for the sixth wicket) to help Australia recover from 5/97 to 564 all out.

270 is the highest second innings score in Australia-England Tests, and is the world record for a batsman at number seven.

aggregate crowd of more than 350,000 watched the Third Test, and it wasn't for another 45 years that this record figure was surpassed, in an India-England Test in Calcutta.

Maurice Leyland's 111 not out in Melbourne was his second century of the rubber. In all, there were seven Australian scores of 100 or more in the series (Bradman three, Fingleton two, McCabe, Badcock) and four for England (Leyland two, Hammond, Barnett)

Bradman's Fourth Test 212 was the second time he'd scored double-centuries in back-to-back Tests. It was his 17th Test century, passing the mark of 16 hundreds held by Sutcliffe and Hammond, whose 16th had come in the Second Test.

In the Fourth Test, in Adelaide, yet another Gregory made his debut for Australia. This time it was Victorian Ross Gregory, who scored a 50 in his first Test and 80 in his second, the Fifth, at the MCG. He played only those two Tests, was overlooked for the 1938 tour of England, and died aged 26 in the second World War.

The slow bowlers, Fleetwood-Smith and O'Reilly, took 15 wickets between them in Adelaide—left-armer Fleetwood-Smith, who was known to make birdcalls as he ran in to bowl, taking the only 10-wicket haul of his 10-Test career.

Charlie Barnett's 129 in Adelaide was the first of two centuries he'd score against Australia in a 20-Test career.

Three Australians scored centuries in Australia's innings of 604 in the Fifth Test in Sydney—Bradman (169), McCabe (112) and Jack Badcock (118). It was the only century of Tasmanian-born Badcock's seven-Test career.

For Bradman, his 12th century against England took his aggregate for the rubber to 810 at 90, which is a record for a Test captain.

Farnes took 6/96 in Australia's only innings of the final Test— the best performance of his Test career.

1936–37 AUSTRALIA WON SERIES 3–2

135 1st Test Woolloongabba, Brisbane, December 4, 5, 7, 8, 9
ENGLAND 358 (M Leyland 126, CJ Barnett 69, J Hardstaff, jr 43, WJ O'Reilly 5/102) and **256** (GOB Allen 68, FA Ward 6/102)
AUSTRALIA 234 (JHW Fingleton 100, SJ McCabe 51, W Voce 6/41) and **58** (GOB Allen 5/36, W Voce 4/16)
CAPTAINS GOB Allen [ENG] DG Bradman [AUST]
RESULT England won by 322 runs

136 2nd Test Sydney Cricket Ground, December 18, 19, 21, 22
ENGLAND 6/426 dec (WR Hammond 231*, CJ Barnett 57, M Leyland 42)
AUSTRALIA 80 (W Voce 4/10) and **324** (SJ McCabe 93, DG Bradman 82, JHW Fingleton 73)
CAPTAINS GOB Allen [ENG] DG Bradman [AUST]
RESULT England won by an innings and 22 runs

137 3rd Test Melbourne Cricket Ground, January 1, 2, 4, 5, 6, 7
AUSTRALIA 9/200 dec (SJ McCabe 63) and **564** (DG Bradman 270, JHW Fingleton 136, KE Rigg 47)
ENGLAND 9/76 dec (MW Sievers 5/21) and **323** (M Leyland 111*, RWV Robins 61, WR Hammond 51, LO'B Fleetwood-Smith 5/124)
CAPTAINS DG Bradman [AUST] GOB Allen [ENG]
RESULT Australia won by 365 runs

138 4th Test Adelaide Oval, January 29, 30, February 1, 2, 3, 4
AUSTRALIA 288 (SJ McCabe 88, AG Chipperfield 57*, WA Brown 42) and **433** (DG Bradman 212, SJ McCabe 55, RG Gregory 50, WR Hammond 5/57)
ENGLAND 330 (CJ Barnett 129, LEG Ames 52, M Leyland 45, LO'B Fleetwood-Smith 4/129, WJ O'Reilly 4/51) and **243** (RES Wyatt 50, J Hardstaff, jr 43, LO'B Fleetwood-Smith 6/110)
CAPTAINS DG Bradman [AUST] GOB Allen [ENG]
RESULT Australia won by 148 runs

139 5th Test Melbourne Cricket Ground, February 26, 27, March 1, 2, 3
AUSTRALIA 604 (DG Bradman 169, CL Badcock 118, SJ McCabe 112, RG Gregory 80, K Farnes 6/96)
ENGLAND 239 (J Hardstaff, jr 83, TS Worthington 44, WJ O'Reilly 5/51, LJ Nash 4/70) and **165** (WR Hammond 56, CJ Barnett 41)
CAPTAINS DG Bradman [AUST] GOB Allen [ENG]
RESULT Australia won by an innings and 200 runs

1938

This five-Test series was reduced to four matches with the Manchester rain striking again—this time resulting in the Third Test, at Old Trafford, being abandoned without a ball being bowled. It was a contest between two talented teams, led by two of the all-time batting greats, Don Bradman and Walter Hammond, who was leading England for the first time. It was to be the last Ashes rubber before the outbreak of World War II.

Included in the strong England batting line-up for his Test debut at Trent Bridge was Bill Edrich, who went on to become a fine player with a Test average of 40. However, in this series he failed with just 67 runs in four matches.

Another to debut for England in the First Test was Kent leg-spinner Doug Wright, who was the master of the hat-trick, completing that feat a record seven times in first-class cricket.

Future Australian captain Lindsay Hassett also made his debut in the First Test. He scored only 1 and 2 in that match, but averaged over 50 on tour. Hassett ended up playing 43 Tests and scoring more than 3,000 runs, despite missing probably his best cricketing years due to the war.

At Trent Bridge, for the first time in Tests, four batsmen scored centuries in the same innings in England's 8/658 dec (Barnett 126, Hutton 100, Paynter 216 not out, Compton 102). For Len Hutton and Denis Compton, who'd both made their Test debuts against New Zealand 12 months earlier, the centuries came in their first Test against Australia.

Compton was only 20 years and 19 days—still the youngest to score a century for England. He was the first of cricket's glamour players, advertising's original 'Brylcream Boy'.

Eddie Paynter's 216 not out was one of his four Test hundreds. He averaged over 100 for this series, and 84.42 against Australia overall.

The three Australian centuries in the First Test took the match tally to a record seven (McCabe 232, Brown 133 and Bradman 144 not out). It was Bradman's 13th hundred against England, setting a new record in Australia-England Tests.

England's Reg Sinfield played only one Test match—the First Test. But the first of his two Test wickets was one to remember: DG Bradman.

Hammond's 240 in the Second Test is the highest score against Australia at Lord's and the biggest score by an England captain in Ashes Tests.

Brown carried his bat through Australia's first innings of the Second Test with 206, his highest score and Australia's 100th century against England.

Bradman's unbeaten 102 at Lord's was the 200th century in Australia-England Tests, and during that innings he passed Hobbs as the highest scorer in Ashes Tests.

Bradman then scored 103 in the Fourth Test—the sixth Test in a row in which he'd scored a century. It was also his third hundred in successive Test innings at Headingley.

Amid all the batting hundreds was a bowling 'hundred'. In the Fourth Test, O'Reilly had a 10-wicket match for the third time against England—5/66 and 5/56.

England used three keepers in the series. Ames played in the First Test and injured a finger in the Second. Fred Price, of Middlesex, made his sole Test appearance in the Fourth, and Arthur Wood, of Yorkshire, played in the Fifth.

Sid Barnes, the brilliant NSW batsman who in later years was to take the Australian Cricket Board of Control to court over his non-selection, made his Test debut in the final Test, at The Oval, scoring 41 and 33. He'd missed the earlier Tests because of a broken wrist.

Victorian Ben Barnett was chosen to tour as wicketkeeper ahead of Oldfield. In the Fifth Test, he missed a stumping chance against Hutton when the Yorkshireman was 40. Hutton went on to score 364 in England's all-Test record of 7/903 dec. Hutton's score was England's 100th century against Australia and remains England's highest score in all Tests.

England's massive innings in the Fifth Test, with Leyland also scoring a career-high 187 and Hardstaff 169 not out, set the home side up for a record all-Test victory margin of an innings and 579 runs.

The Fifth Test was the last for Leyland, making him the first Englishman to score centuries in his first and last innings against Australia.

Australia's bowlers sent down 335.2 overs in England's Fifth Test innings—Fleetwood-Smith's analysis: 87/11/298/1.

Australia's cause at The Oval wasn't helped by injuries to key batsmen Bradman and Fingleton, who were both hurt while in the field. Neither batted in either innings.

Despite England's huge win at The Oval, Australia retained the Ashes.

1938 SERIES DRAWN 1-ALL

140 1st Test Trent Bridge, Nottingham, June 10, 11, 13, 14
ENGLAND 8/658 dec (E Paynter 216*, CJ Barnett 126, DCS Compton 102, L Hutton 100, LEG Ames 46, LO'B Fleetwood-Smith 4/153)
AUSTRALIA 411 (SJ McCabe 232, DG Bradman 51, WA Brown 48, K Farnes 4/106, DVP Wright 4/153) and **6/427 dec** (DG Bradman 144*, WA Brown 133, JHW Fingleton 40)
CAPTAINS WR Hammond [ENG] DG Bradman [AUST]
RESULT draw

141 2nd Test Lord's, June 24, 25, 27, 28
ENGLAND 494 (WR Hammond 240, E Paynter 99, LEG Ames 83, EL McCormick 4/101, WJ O'Reilly 4/93) and **8/242 dec** (DCS Compton 76*, E Paynter 43)
AUSTRALIA 422 (WA Brown 206, AL Hassett 56, WJ O'Reilly 42) and **6/204** (DG Bradman 102*, AL Hassett 42)
CAPTAINS WR Hammond [ENG] DG Bradman [AUST]
RESULT draw

* The 3rd Test was set down for Old Trafford, Manchester, but was abandoned without a ball being bowled.

142 4th Test Headingley, Leeds, July 22, 23, 25
ENGLAND 223 (WR Hammond 76, WJ O'Reilly 5/66) and **123** (WJ O'Reilly 5/56, LO'B Fleetwood-Smith 4/34)
AUSTRALIA 242 (DG Bradman 103, BA Barnett 57, K Farnes 4/77) and **5/107**
CAPTAINS WR Hammond [ENG] DG Bradman [AUST]
RESULT Australia won by five wickets

143 5th Test The Oval, August 20, 22, 23, 24
ENGLAND 7/903 dec (L Hutton 364, M Leyland 187, J Hardstaff, jr 169*, WR Hammond 59, A Wood 53)
AUSTRALIA 201 (WA Brown 69, AL Hassett 42, SG Barnes 41, WE Bowes 5/49) and **123** (BA Barnett 46, K Farnes 4/63)
CAPTAINS WR Hammond [ENG] DG Bradman [AUST]
RESULT England won by an innings and 579 runs

1920–1938
Questions 1–10

1 Who was the Australian wicketkeeper who started his 54-match career in the First Test, in Sydney, in 1920–21?

2 Who was the MCC manager on the 1932–33 Bodyline tour?

3 What was Don Bradman's score in the Third Test at Headingley in 1930?

4 Who was the England player known as 'Patsy' who made three tours to Australia in the 1920s?

5 Yet another Gregory was selected for Australia after World War I, scoring a century and taking eight wickets in his second Test. What was his christian name?

6 Who replaced JWHT Douglas as England captain for the last three Tests of the 1921 series?

7 On the 1938 tour of England, one Test was abandoned without a ball being bowled. At which venue?

8 Two Richardsons played for Australia in the 1920s, Arthur and Vic. Which of them went on to become a Test umpire?

9 In Bradman's first Test, England completed victory by a record margin of:
a) 419 runs
b) 522 runs
c) 675 runs

10 Which 47-year-old returned to the England side for the final Test of 1934, in the last Test appearance by a player who'd made his debut before the first World War?

Questions 11–20

11 An Australian leg-spinner who first came into Test cricket after the War, took 36 wickets in the 1920–21 series, including 9/121 in the second innings of the Fourth Test, in Melbourne. Who was that bowler?

12 Who was the Surrey batsman, who was later to score Test cricket's first triple-century, who made his Test debut at The Oval in 1921?

13 The first three Tests of the 1924–25 series were all played over seven days . . . true or false?

14 Who was the Yorkshireman who, with Jack Hobbs, formed one of cricket's all-time great opening partnerships?

15 In the Second Test of 1926, Hobbs and Hendren for England, and Bardsley and Macartney for Australia, all scored centuries. The oldest of these players was 44, and the youngest 37. Who was the youngest?

16 Which outstanding player was recalled to England's side for the final Test of 1926 at the age of 48, taking six wickets?

17 Who were the two 46-year-old Victorian spinners who made their Test debuts in the 1928–29 series?

18 Australia regained the Ashes in England in both 1930 and 1934 on:
a) Captain Bill Woodfull's birthday
b) The King's birthday
c) Harold Larwood's birthday

19 What was the other name for Bodyline?

20 By what margin did Australia win the five-Test series in 1920–21 under Warwick Armstrong?

Questions 21–30

21 Where in England was the 100th Ashes Test match played?

22 Who was the Sussex bowler, nicknamed 'Chub', who took 11/228 off 89 overs in Sydney in 1924–25?

23 In which Australian city did Don Bradman make his Test debut in the 1928–29 series?

24 Who was the England bowler who took 13/256, bowling 124.5 overs, in the Adelaide Test of 1928–29?

25 Who made this famous remark during the Bodyline series: "There are two teams out there, but only one of them is playing cricket."

26 Who was the left-arm spinner from Yorkshire who took 15 wickets at Lord's in 1934?

27 Which Australian bowler, known as 'The Gnome', took 11 wickets on debut in 1924–25?

28 Lancashire batsman Harry Makepeace is the oldest player to score his maiden Test century. When he did so, in Melbourne in 1920–21, was Makepeace:
a) 34
b) 39
c) 41

29 Who was the Australian captain in the first series after World War I?

30 Who was the Queensland opener who scored his maiden Test century at Lord's in 1934, and four years later carried his bat for 206 at the same ground?

Questions 31–40

31 In which country was the first Ashes series after the First World War?

32 Which England batsman had scored five Test centuries at the MCG by the end of his final Australian tour in 1928–29?

33 The Third Test in Adelaide in 1920–21 remains the highest-scoring of all Ashes Tests. Was the match aggregate:
a) 1,673 runs
b) 1,753 runs
c) 1,811 runs

34 Which great Australian opening batsman made his debut in the 1924–25 series, becoming the first player to score hundreds in his first two Tests?

35 What was unusual about the Test debut of England spinner Fred Root at Trent Bridge in 1926?

36 At what position in the batting order was Don Bradman in his maiden Test innings?

37 The England captain for the 1920–21 series had also led England on an Australian tour almost a decade earlier. Who was that captain?

38 Who's the Victorian all-rounder who captained Australia for a short time in the 1920s, and later became a long-serving Test selector?

39 Who was the England nightwatchman who scored 98 in the final Test of the Bodyline series of 1932–33?

40 For the 1924–25 season, Australian authorities decided to change the number of balls per over. What did they switch to?

Questions 41–50

41 Herbie Collins scored a century in his Test debut for Australia in 1920–21, and scored 557 runs for the series. Collins was a bookmaker and his nickname was associated with the racing industry. What was that name?

42 South Australian brothers Vic and Arthur Richardson made their Test debuts in 1924–25. Is that statement true or false?

43 Which top-order batsman scored Australia's first Test hundred in a Headingley Test—the only Test century by an Australian on the 1921 tour?

44 Which 43-year-old scored 193 not out in the Lord's Test of 1926, becoming the oldest Australian to score an Ashes century, and the oldest to carry his bat through a Test innings?

45 Which England batsman scored successive double centuries while amassing 905 runs at 113.12 in the 1928–29 series?

46 Kumar Shri Duleepsinhji scored 173 in his Test debut in 1930. What relation was Kumar to the man known as 'Ranji', who'd also scored an Ashes century on debut, in 1896?

47 After the first World War a host of new players made their debuts in the 1920–21 series. Did the number of new players total:
a) seven   b) 12   c) 18

48 What was the margin of England's victory in the Bodyline series of 1932–33?

49 Bill O'Reilly and Chuck Fleetwood-Smith opening the batting for Australia during the 1936–37 series ... true or false?

50 Which charismatic Englishman, who made his England debut in 1920–21, later settled in Australia to run a wine business in Horsham?

ANSWERS *1920/21–1938*

1–10

1 Bert Oldfield
2 Pelham 'Plum' Warner
3 334
4 Patsy Hendren
5 Jack Gregory
6 Hon Lionel Tennyson
7 Old Trafford
8 Arthur
9 c) 675 runs
10 Frank Woolley

11–20

11 Arthur Mailey
12 Andy Sandham
13 True
14 Herbert Sutcliffe
15 Patsy Hendren
16 Wilfred Rhodes
17 Don Blackie and
Bert Ironmonger
18 a) Bill Woodfull's birthday (33 in 1930 and 37 in 1934)
19 Fast leg-theory
20 5–0

21–30

21 Trent Bridge
22 Maurice Tate
23 Brisbane
24 Jack White
25 Australian captain Bill Woodfull
26 Hedley Verity
27 Clarrie Grimmett
28 b) 39
29 Warwick Armstrong
30 Bill Brown

31–40

31 Australia
32 Jack Hobbs
33 b) 1,753 runs
34 Bill Ponsford
35 Fred Root didn't take the field in his Test debut, with rain restricting the match to just 50 minutes, with England batting
36 Number seven
37 JWHT Douglas
38 Jack Ryder
39 Harold Larwood
40 eight

41–50

41 'Horseshoe' Collins
42 False (Vic and Arthur Richardson were unrelated)
43 Charlie Macartney
44 Warren Bardsley
45 Walter Hammond
46 Kumar was Ranji's nephew
47 c) 18
48 4–1
49 True, in the second innings of the Third Test in Melbourne when Bradman changed the batting order because of a sticky wicket
50 Percy Fender

Chapter Four

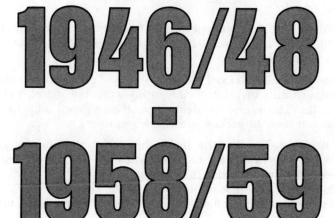

1946–47

The first Ashes rubber after the Second World War, and eight years on, the names and faces had changed considerably for both countries. Barnes, Bradman and Hassett were the only Australians in the First Test side who'd also played in the final Test of the 1938 series, at The Oval. England had Hutton, Edrich, Compton and Hammond, although Wright had played in the earlier Tests of that series and Voce's Test career dated back to 1930.

Left-handed opener Arthur Morris played his maiden Test when the series started at the Gabba, starting a successful Test opening partnership with Barnes. He scored only 2, but later in the series scored a century in the Third Test and a century in each innings of the Fourth.

Australia's First Test centuries came from captain Bradman (187) and his newly-appointed deputy Hassett (128). They added 276 for the third wicket.

All-rounder Colin McCool, playing his first Test against England, missed a century by just five runs in Brisbane, but scored 104 not out in the Third Test in Melbourne. He averaged 54.5 for the series, and took 18 wickets with his leg-spinners.

The Brisbane Test was the first Ashes encounter for the great Australian all-rounder Keith Miller, whose 55-Test career reaped almost 3,000 runs and 170 wickets. He scored 79 and then wrecked England's first innings with 7/60. The Englishmen had earlier seen Miller's talents in the 1945 Victory Tests under Hassett's captaincy.

Miller took nine wickets in the First Test, as did left-arm medium-pacer Ernie Toshak, who took 6/82 in England's second innings to complete their demise.

England's First Test hopes were set back by heavy rain, bringing with it hail and galeforce winds. England lost 15 wickets in less than four hours on the final day.

Edrich had a fine double of 71 and 119 in the Second Test, but the match was otherwise dominated by the Australian batsmen.

Australia's Second Test 8/659 dec was due mainly to a record fifth-wicket partnership of 405 between Barnes and Bradman, who both scored 234.

The Second Test was the first against Australia for the champion and extrovert England wicketkeeper Godfrey Evans. He demonstrated why he'd go on to play 91 Tests and make 219 dismissals by not conceding a single bye during Australia's big innings.

The Second Test was the only one for Victorian Fred Freer. He took three wickets—the first of them with only his fourth ball in Test cricket.

The Third Test was the first drawn Test in Australia for 65 years.

Ray Lindwall, one of the greatest fast bowlers to play for Australia, was in his first series against England. His initial impact was with the bat, scoring the first of his two Test centuries in the Third Test after coming in at number nine. In the Fifth Test, he took seven wickets in England's first innings.

The Fourth Test, in Adelaide, signalled the end of the outstanding career of Walter Hammond. In the eight innings he'd failed to reach 40—a disappointing end after such a distinguished 33-match Ashes career, which had realised 2,852 runs with nine centuries. Norman Yardley took over the captaincy for the final Test.

Morris wasn't the only player to score a century in each innings in Adelaide. For England, Compton did the same—the first instance of two players each scoring two centuries in the same Test.

Miller's first hundred against England came in the Adelaide Test where, batting at number five, he scored 141 not out. All up, he made seven Test centuries during his career.

Evans, who was to later narrowly miss scoring a century in a session in a Test against India, took 97 minutes to get off the mark in England's second innings of the Fourth Test. He shared an unbroken ninth-wicket partnership of 85 with Compton, scoring only 10 but helping Compton get his century.

Hutton narrowly missed a century in the Fourth Test, then scored 122 in the Fifth before retiring ill, after being admitted to hospital suffering tonsillitis. He didn't bat in England's second innings.

1946-47 AUSTRALIA WON SERIES 3-0

144 1st Test Woolloongabba, Brisbane, November 29, 30, December 2, 3, 4
AUSTRALIA 645 (DG Bradman 187, AL Hassett 128, CL McCool 95,
KR Miller 79, IW Johnson 47, DVP Wright 5/167)
ENGLAND 141 (KR Miller 7/60) and **172** (ERH Toshack 6/82)
CAPTAINS DG Bradman [AUST] WR Hammond [ENG]
RESULT Australia won by an innings and 332 runs

145 2nd Test Sydney Cricket Ground, December 13, 14, 16, 17, 18, 19
ENGLAND 255 (WJ Edrich 71, JT Ikin 60, IW Johnson 6/42) and **371**
(WJ Edrich 119, DCS Compton 54, C Washbrook 41, CL McCool 5/109)
AUSTRALIA 8/659 dec (DG Bradman 234, SG Barnes 234, KR Miller 40)
CAPTAINS WR Hammond [ENG] DG Bradman [AUST]
RESULT Australia won by an innings and 33 runs

146 3rd Test Melbourne Cricket Ground, January 1, 2, 3, 4, 6, 7
AUSTRALIA 365 (CL McCool 104*, DG Bradman 79, SG Barnes 45) and **536**
(AR Morris 155, RR Lindwall 100, D Tallon 92, DG Bradman 49, CL McCool 43)
ENGLAND 351 (WJ Edrich 89, C Washbrook 62, NWD Yardley 61, JT Ikin 48,
B Dooland 4/69) and **7/310** (C Washbrook 112, NWD Yardley 53*, L Hutton 40)
CAPTAINS DG Bradman [AUST] WR Hammond [ENG]
RESULT draw

147 4th Test Adelaide Oval, January 31, February 1, 3, 4, 5, 6
ENGLAND 460 (DCS Compton 147, L Hutton 94, J Hardstaff, jr 67,
C Washbrook 65, RR Lindwall 4/52) and **8/340 dec** (DCS Compton 103*,
L Hutton 76, WJ Edrich 46, ERH Toshack 4/76)
AUSTRALIA 487 (KR Miller 141*, AR Morris 122, AL Hassett 78, IW Johnson 52)
and **1/215** (AR Morris 124*, DG Bradman 56*)
CAPTAINS WR Hammond [ENG] DG Bradman [AUST]
RESULT draw

148 5th Test Sydney Cricket Ground, February 28, March 1 (no play), 3, 4, 5
ENGLAND 280 (L Hutton 122 retired ill, WJ Edrich 60, RR Lindwall 7/63) and **186**
(DCS Compton 76, CL McCool 5/44)
AUSTRALIA 253 (SG Barnes 71, AR Morris 57, DVP Wright 7/105) and **5/214**
(DG Bradman 63, AL Hassett 47)
CAPTAINS NWD Yardley [ENG] DG Bradman [AUST]
RESULT Australia won by five wickets

1948

*The Invincibles. That's the name given to Bradman's Australian
team that embarked on the '48 tour of England. Australia had four*

big victory margins in five Tests, and it was only at Old Trafford that Australia was unable to force victory. In fact, this was the eighth successive time England-Australia Tests at Old Trafford were either drawn or abandoned.

This was Bradman's farewell tour. It started at Trent Bridge with his 28th Test century (138), he scored another—his last in Tests (173 not out)—at Headingley, and then, needing four runs for a Test average of 100, he was out second ball in his last Test, at The Oval . . . bowled by an Eric Hollies googly.

Hollies, who played 13 Tests dating back to 1934–35, was playing his only Test against Australia. He took five wickets, but only one that most people remember.

In the First Test, Australia gained a lead of 344 on the first innings, thanks to Bradman and also Hassett, whose 137 was his highest score against England.

Compton's highest score against Australia (184) came in the First Test.

At Trent Bridge Jim Laker, who was to take a place in history with 19 wickets against Australia in one Test in 1956, was playing his first Ashes Test. In three Tests, he took only nine wickets at an average of 52 and wasn't able to establish himself in the England side for an Ashes series for another eight years.

Victorian left-armer Bill Johnston was playing his first Test against England in the Trent Bridge match. He took nine wickets, and finished the rubber with 27.

In his sole Test appearance, Alec Coxon took the new ball for England at Lord's, dismissing opener Barnes for a duck in the first innings.

Bradman missed a century in the Second Test, but his second innings 89 made it 14 successive Ashes Tests in which he'd scored at least a half-century (not including the Fifth Test in 1938, in which he did not bat).

Alec Bedser, who Bradman considered—in some conditions—to be the most difficult bowler he batted against, claimed Bradman's wicket in each innings of the first two Tests. He'd also dismissed Bradman in the second innings of the final Test of the previous rubber, making it five times in five innings.

97

With Australia leading the series 2–0, England's selectors dropped Hutton for the Third Test, at Old Trafford. He returned for the final two Tests, passing 50 three times.

Included in the Third Test side for England were two new batsmen—opener George Emmett, who played only one Test, and Jack Crapp, who played seven before becoming a respected umpire.

Compton, England's best batsman for the series, scored another century (145 not out) at Old Trafford after retiring hurt at four— hit while attempting to hook Lindwall.

The duck and the century were good allies during the series. Compton followed his Old Trafford century with a second innings duck, just as Bradman did in the First Test. And in the Second Test, Barnes failed to score in the first innings before hitting 141 in the second.

Barnes was a tough character. He was hit under his ribs while fielding in close in the Third Test, but batted briefly before retiring hurt. He spent the next 10 days in hospital.

Australia's seven-wicket win in the Fourth Test ranks as one of the most famous of all time. Set 404 to win on a spinning pitch, Australia finished at 3/404—the first time a Test team had scored 400 in the fourth innings to win.

Fittingly, Bradman played a major role in the Fourth Test victory with his last Test century. He scored 173 not out, and with Morris (182) put on 301 for the second wicket.

Bradman's century was his fourth in six innings at Headingley. Of his 29 Test centuries, 19 were against England. He finished with 5,028 runs at 89.78 against England, with eight double-centuries and two triple-centuries.

Victorian left-hander Neil Harvey came into the Australian side for the Leeds Test. At 19 years and 121 days, he'd already become the youngest Australian to score a Test century (against India), and now, still 19, he scored a century in his first Test against England. He was the first Australian left-hander to score a century in his maiden Ashes Test.

England's selectors continued to blood new players, with two more on debut in the Fifth Test, at The Oval. Opening bat John Dewes played the first of his five matches and all-rounder Allan Watkins, in the first of his seven Tests, became the first Glamorgan player to represent England.

England's first innings total of 52, with Hutton scoring 30 of them, remains their lowest in Tests in England. Lindwall took six wickets—four of them bowled.

Morris's 196 at The Oval was his third century of the rubber, taking his five-Test aggregate to 696 runs at 87.

1948 AUSTRALIA WON SERIES 4–0

149 1st Test Trent Bridge, Nottingham, June 10, 11, 12, 14, 15
ENGLAND 165 (JC Laker 63, WA Johnston 5/36) and **441** (DCS Compton 184, L Hutton 74, TG Evans 50, J Hardstaff, jr 43, KR Miller 4/125, WA Johnston 4/147)
AUSTRALIA 509 (DG Bradman 138, AL Hassett 137, SG Barnes 62, RR Lindwall 42, JC Laker 4/138) and **2/98** (SG Barnes 64*)
CAPTAINS NWD Yardley [ENG] DG Bradman [AUST]
RESULT Australia won by eight wickets

150 2nd Test Lord's, June 24, 25, 26, 28, 29
AUSTRALIA 350 (AR Morris 105, D Tallon 53, AL Hassett 47, AV Bedser 4/100) and **7/460 dec** (SG Barnes 141, DG Bradman 89, KR Miller 74, AR Morris 62)
ENGLAND 215 (DCS Compton 53, NWD Yardley 44, RR Lindwall 5/70) and **186** (ERH Toshack 5/40)
CAPTAINS DG Bradman [AUST] NWD Yardley [ENG]
RESULT Australia won by 409 runs

151 3rd Test Old Trafford, Manchester, July 8, 9, 10, 12 (no play), 13
ENGLAND 363 (DCS Compton 145*, RR Lindwall 4/99) and **3/174 dec** (C Washbrook 85*, WJ Edrich 53)
AUSTRALIA 221 (AR Morris 51, AV Bedser 4/81) and **1/92** (AR Morris 54*)
CAPTAINS NWD Yardley [ENG] DG Bradman [AUST]
RESULT draw

152 4th Test Headingley, Leeds, July 22, 23, 24, 26, 27
ENGLAND 496 (C Washbrook 143, WJ Edrich 111, L Hutton 81, AV Bedser 79) and **8/365 dec** (DCS Compton 66, C Washbrook 65, L Hutton 57, WJ Edrich 54, TG Evans 47*, WA Johnston 4/95)
AUSTRALIA 458 (RN Harvey 112, SJE Loxton 93, RR Lindwall 77, KR Miller 58) and **3/404** (AR Morris 182, DG Bradman 173*)
CAPTAINS NWD Yardley [ENG] DG Bradman [AUST]
RESULT Australia won by seven wickets

153 5th Test The Oval, August 14, 16, 17, 18
ENGLAND 52 (RR Lindwall 6/20) and **188** (L Hutton 64, WA Johnston 4/40)
AUSTRALIA 389 (AR Morris 196, SG Barnes 61, WE Hollies 5/131)
CAPTAINS NWD Yardley [ENG] DG Bradman [AUST]
RESULT Australia won by an innings and 149 runs

1950–51

Australia without Bradman. After 20 years of trying to counter Australia's batting genius, England were now taking on a team without him. But with Morris, Harvey, Miller, Lindwall and new captain Hassett, this was still a formidable Australian side, which won the first four Tests before England struck in the Fifth.

Off-spinner Jack Iverson came into the Australian side for his debut in the First Test, at the Gabba. He made an immediate impression, spinning Australia to victory with four wickets in the second innings. With his mixture of off and top-spin he took 21 wickets in the series, including a best of 6/27 in the Third Test, in Sydney. This five-Test rubber represented Iverson's entire Test career.

Barnes, who was prone to upset officials with his sometime flippant behaviour, was by now out of the Australian side—his career over after just 13 Tests at an imposing average of 63.05. Of those who have played as many Tests for Australia, only Bradman has a superior average.

Jack Moroney, of NSW, had taken over from Barnes to partner Morris, and scored twin centuries in the Fourth Test against South Africa the previous season. In his first and only Test against England, however, he made a pair.

On a 'sticky' Brisbane wicket, England—with Freddie Brown now the skipper—declared at 7/68 in the first innings, trailing by 160. The move paid dividends with Australia then crashing to 3/0 before declaring at 7/32. Twenty wickets fell after lunch on the third day, with Australia eventually winning a remarkable match by 70 runs.

Brian Close, the youngest player capped by England when he played against New Zealand in 1949, played in the Second Test, in Melbourne, aged 19 years 301 days—still the youngest England player in Tests against Australia. He scored 0 and 1.

Neither side reached 200 in the Second Test, with England set 179 runs to win in three days. Australia won by 28 runs.

Fast bowler John Warr, a surprise selection in the England touring party, was included for the Sydney and Adelaide matches. In his only Tests, he took just one wicket ... 1/281, the most expensive wicket-taker in Test cricket.

The first century of the rubber came in the Third Test when Miller scored 145 not out in Australia's 426. He also took four first innings wickets, giving Australia an innings victory.

Twenty-year-old Jimmy Burke made his debut for Australia in Adelaide, scoring a century in the second innings. It was the first of three hundreds in a 24-Test career.

Morris, who'd struggled in the first three Tests with just 45 runs including two ducks, struck form with his career-best 206 in the Fourth Test.

Hutton became the first England batsman since the turn of the century to twice carry his bat through an innings. He made 156 out of England's first innings 272 in Adelaide.

Brown didn't bat in England's second innings of the Fourth Test, having been involved in a car accident during the match. Compton, who scored three ducks and averaged only seven in the rubber, assumed the England captaincy on the final day.

England's eight-wicket victory in the Fifth Test represented their first win over Australia in more than two decades, dating back to the record innings and 579-run margin at The Oval in 1938. Since that defeat, Australia had gone 25 Tests (against New Zealand, England, India and South Africa) without defeat, including 20 wins.

England's final Test victory was set up by Reg Simpson's unbeaten 156—his only Test hundred against Australia, on his 31st birthday, and also Bedser, whose five wickets in each innings gave him 30 for the series.

Fittingly, Hutton was at the crease when the winning runs were scored in the Fifth Test. Although he scored only one century, he averaged 88.83 for the rubber.

1950–51 AUSTRALIA WON SERIES 4–1

154 1st Test Woolloongabba, Brisbane, December 1, 2 (no play), 4, 5
AUSTRALIA 228 (RN Harvey 74, RR Lindwall 41, AV Bedser 4/45) and **7/32 dec** (TE Bailey 4/22)
ENGLAND 7/68 dec (WA Johnston 5/35) and **122** (L Hutton 62*, JB Iverson 4/43)
CAPTAINS AL Hassett [AUST] FR Brown [ENG]
RESULT Australia won by 70 runs

155 2nd Test Melbourne Cricket Ground, December 22, 23, 26, 27
AUSTRALIA 194 (AL Hassett 52, RN Harvey 42, TE Bailey 4/40, AV Bedser 4/37)
and **181** (KA Archer 46, FR Brown 4/26)
ENGLAND 197 (FR Brown 62, TG Evans 49, JB Iverson 4/37) and **150**
(L Hutton 40, WA Johnston 4/26)
CAPTAINS AL Hassett [AUST] FR Brown [ENG]
RESULT Australia won by 28 runs

156 3rd Test Sydney Cricket Ground, January 5, 6, 8, 9
ENGLAND 290 (FR Brown 79, L Hutton 62, RT Simpson 49, KR Miller 4/37) and
123 (JB Iverson 6/27)
AUSTRALIA 426 (KR Miller 145*, IW Johnson 77, AL Hassett 70, KA Archer 48,
AV Bedser 4/107, FR Brown 4/153)
CAPTAINS FR Brown [ENG] AL Hassett [ENG]
RESULT Australia won by an innings and 13 runs

157 4th Test Adelaide Oval, February 2, 3, 5, 6, 7, 8
AUSTRALIA 371 (AR Morris 206, KR Miller 44, AL Hassett 43, RN Harvey 43,
DVP Wright 4/99) and **8/403 dec** (JW Burke 101*, KR Miller 99, RN Harvey 68)
ENGLAND 272 (L Hutton 156*) and **228** (RT Simpson 61, L Hutton 45,
DS Sheppard 41, WA Johnston 4/73)
CAPTAINS AL Hassett [AUST] FR Brown [ENG]
RESULT Australia won by 274 runs

158 5th Test Melbourne Cricket Ground, February 23, 24 (no play), 26, 27, 28
AUSTRALIA 217 (AL Hassett 92, AR Morris 50, AV Bedser 5/46, FR Brown 5/49)
and **197** (GB Hole 63, RN Harvey 52, AL Hassett 48, AV Bedser 5/59)
ENGLAND 320 (RT Simpson 156*, L Hutton 79, KR Miller 4/76) and **2/95**
(L Hutton 60*)
CAPTAINS AL Hassett [AUST] FR Brown [ENG]
RESULT England won by eight wickets

1953

*After almost 20 years of domination by Australia, England regained
the Ashes in this home series. The first four matches were drawn,
and then England were spun to an eight-wicket win in the final
Test, at The Oval. The England captain by now was Hutton, and
the Ashes triumph came despite his rival Hassett winning the toss
in each of the five Tests.*

In a First Test noted for batting collapses, Australia lost their last
seven wickets for 12 runs in the first innings and their first five
in the space of 40 runs in the second. England had collapses of
3/0 and then 3/16 in the first innings.

Six Australians failed to score in their first innings at Trent Bridge. The only three to reach double figures all passed 50 (Morris 67, Hassett 115 and Miller 55). Hassett and Miller also scored centuries in the Second Test.

Alan Davidson, later to become one of the truly great all-rounders of the game, made his Test debut at Trent Bridge. He played in all five Tests for moderate success—his most notable performance 76 with the bat in the Second Test.

Bedser was the star for England at Trent Bridge. He took 7/55 and 7/44—the match figures of 14/99 remaining a record for a Test at Nottingham. He took another eight wickets in the Second Test—becoming the first England bowler to take 200 Test wickets—and he passed Grimmett's world record of 216 wickets in the Fourth Test.

England's victory hopes in the First Test were dashed by rain, which wiped out the fourth day and the first two sessions of the fifth.

Freddie Brown, skipper in the previous rubber in 1950–51, was by now England's Chairman of Selectors, and came out of retirement for the Second Test—his first in two years. He took four second innings wickets and scored 22 and 28.

England's Willie Watson came into the side for the Second Test, and in his first match against Australia, scored 109 in the second innings. Set 343 to win, England were 4/73 before Watson and Trevor Bailey (71) put on 163 for the fifth-wicket to save the match.

Hutton's only century of the series came in the Lord's Test. He scored 145—his fifth hundred against Australia—in what many rate as his finest innings. As captain, Hutton led England 23 times and did not lose a rubber.

The weather again dominated the match at Old Trafford, with Australia lucky to avoid defeat, collapsing to 8/35 in the second innings—just 77 ahead—when time ran out. Rain had reduced the match by more than half.

Yorkshire wrist-spinner Johnny Wardle claimed 4/7 off five overs in Australia's second innings collapse at Old Trafford. His 28-match and 102-wicket career would end prematurely, with newspaper articles he wrote that were critical of Yorkshire resulting in him being dropped from both the Yorkshire team and the MCC squad for the tour to Australia in 1958–59.

Australia, 99 in front in the first innings at Headingley, made a bold bid for victory. After being held up for 262 minutes by Bailey's second innings 38, Australia needed 177 runs in just under two hours for victory, and finished at 4/147.

Bedser finished the series with 39 wickets, beating Maurice Tate's 1924–25 record by one.

England's Fifth Test win ended Australia's claim on the Ashes, which had lasted three days short of 19 years.

1953 ENGLAND WON SERIES 1–0

159 1st Test Trent Bridge, Nottingham, June 11, 12, 13, 15 (no play), 16
AUSTRALIA 249 (AL Hassett 115, AR Morris 67, KR Miller 55, AV Bedser 7/55) and **123** (AR Morris 60, AV Bedser 7/44)
ENGLAND 144 (L Hutton 43, RR Lindwall 5/57) and **1/120** (L Hutton 60*)
CAPTAINS AL Hassett [AUST] L Hutton [ENG]
RESULT draw

160 2nd Test Lord's, June 25, 26, 27, 29, 30
AUSTRALIA 346 (AL Hassett 104, AK Davidson 76, RN Harvey 59, AV Bedser 5/105, JH Wardle 4/77) and **368** (KR Miller 109, AR Morris 89, RR Lindwall 50, GB Hole 47, FR Brown 4/82)
ENGLAND 372 (L Hutton 145, TW Graveney 78, DCS Compton 57, RR Lindwall 5/66) and **7/282** (W Watson 109, TE Bailey 71)
CAPTAINS AL Hassett [AUST] L Hutton [ENG]
RESULT draw

161 3rd Test Old Trafford, Manchester, July 9, 10, 11, 13 (no play), 14
AUSTRALIA 318 (RN Harvey 122, GB Hole 66, JH de Courcy 41, AV Bedser 5/115) and **8/35** (JH Wardle 4/7)
ENGLAND 276 (L Hutton 66, DCS Compton 45, TG Evans 44*)
CAPTAINS AL Hassett [AUST] L Hutton [ENG]
RESULT draw

162 4th Test Headingley, Leeds, July 23, 24, 25, 27, 28
ENGLAND 167 (TW Graveney 55, RR Lindwall 5/54) and **275** (WJ Edrich 64, DCS Compton 61, JC Laker 48, KR Miller 4/63)
AUSTRALIA 266 (RN Harvey 71, GB Hole 53, AV Bedser 6/95) and **4/147**
CAPTAINS L Hutton [ENG] AL Hassett [AUST]
RESULT draw

163 5th Test The Oval, August 15, 17, 18, 19
AUSTRALIA 275 (RR Lindwall 62, AL Hassett 53, FS Trueman 4/86) and **162** (RG Archer 49, GAR Lock 5/45, JC Laker 4/75)
ENGLAND 306 (L Hutton 82, TE Bailey 64, RR Lindwall 4/70) and **2/132** (WJ Edrich 55*)
CAPTAINS AL Hassett [AUST] L Hutton [ENG]
RESULT England won by eight wickets

1954–55

England, with the Ashes safely in its grasp, took to Australia two secret weapons—the speed twins Frank Tyson and Brian Statham. Between them, they took 46 wickets in the series, ensuring England held on to the Ashes with a 3–1 margin.

MCC, Michael Colin Cowdrey—later to captain England—played the first of his 114 Tests in the opening match, at the Gabba. He reached 40 in each of his first two Tests before his first Test century (102) in the Third, in Melbourne.

For the first time in Australia, the First Test pitch was completely covered, and as a result, England captain Len Hutton made one of cricket's biggest blunders. He misread the pitch and sent Australia in to bat. The result: 8/601 dec.

Morris scored 153 and Harvey 162 in the First Test, but they were Australia's only centuries of the series.

Australia's captain for all but the Second Test of this series was off-spinner Ian Johnson, who was later to become secretary of the Melbourne Cricket Club.

The Tyson onslaught began in the Second Test, in Sydney, assisted in some way by his rival Lindwall. When batting, the 24-year-old Northamptonshire fast bowler was struck by a Lindwall bouncer and knocked unconscious. He responded with a six-wicket second innings as Australia, needing 223 to win, was bowled out for 184. He took 10 wickets in the match.

Tyson also bowled England to victory in the Third Test, taking 7/27 as Australia lost its last 7 wickets for 34.

Peter May, who would be captain of England on the next tour to Australia four years on, scored the first of his three Ashes centuries in the Second Test. In 21 Tests against Australia, May scored 1,566 runs at 46.03. He went on to become president of the MCC and England's Chairman of Selectors.

In the Third Test, in Melbourne, Colin Cowdrey—on the first of his six tours to Australia—became the 50th Englishman to score a century against Australia. He scored 102 out of a total of 191.

Len Maddocks first played for Australia in the Third Test, at his home ground, Melbourne. Although he took seven catches in the last three Tests, his greatest impact came with the bat, with scores of 47, 69 and 32 against the extreme pace of the England attack.

England wrapped up the series with its victory in Adelaide, and for the second Test running, 'Nelson' struck ... Australia all out in their second innings for 111.

Play in the final Test didn't start until well into the fourth day because of rain. When it did, England's Tom Graveney scored his only century against Australia, becoming the 100th player to score a century in Ashes contests. Graveney later played Sheffield Shield cricket for Queensland.

In a match of century milestones, Lindwall claimed his 100th wicket in Ashes Tests when he bowled Bailey in the Fifth Test, in Sydney.

Queenslander Peter Burge, at 22, made his first appearance in the final Test. He scored only 17 and 18 not out, but went on to play 42 Tests and become recognised as one of the most powerful batsmen in world cricket.

The Fifth Test was the last against Australia for Hutton, who'd accumulated 2,428 runs in Ashes Tests at a fine average of 54.46.

1954–55 ENGLAND WON SERIES 3–1

164 1st Test Woolloongabba, Brisbane, November 26, 27, 29, 30, December 1
AUSTRALIA 8/601 dec (RN Harvey 162, AR Morris 153, RR Lindwall 64*, GB Hole 57, KR Miller 49)
ENGLAND 190 (TE Bailey 88, MC Cowdrey 40) and **257** (WJ Edrich 88, PBH May 44)
CAPTAINS IW Johnson [AUST] L Hutton [ENG]
RESULT Australia won by an innings and 154 runs

165 2nd Test Sydney Cricket Ground, December 17, 18, 20, 21, 22
ENGLAND 154 and **296** (PBH May 104, MC Cowdrey 54)
AUSTRALIA 228 (RG Archer 49, JW Burke 44, TE Bailey 4/59, FH Tyson 4/45) and **184** (RN Harvey 92*, FH Tyson 6/85)
CAPTAINS L Hutton [ENG] AR Morris [AUST]
RESULT England won by 38 runs

166 3rd Test Melbourne Cricket Ground, December 31, January 1, 3, 4, 5
ENGLAND 191 (MC Cowdrey 102, RG Archer 4/33) and **279** (PBH May 91, L Hutton 42, WA Johnston 5/85)
AUSTRALIA 231 (LV Maddocks 47, JB Statham 5/60) and **111** (FH Tyson 7/27)
CAPTAINS L Hutton [ENG] IW Johnson [AUST]
RESULT England won by 128 runs

167 4th Test Adelaide Oval, January 28, 29, 31, February 1, 2
AUSTRALIA 323 (LV Maddocks 69, CC McDonald 48, KR Miller 44,
IW Johnson 41) and **111**
ENGLAND 341 (L Hutton 80, MC Cowdrey 79, DCS Compton 44, Benaud 4/120)
and **5/97**
CAPTAINS IW Johnson [AUST] L Hutton [ENG]
RESULT England won by five wickets

168 5th Test Sydney Cricket Ground, February 25 (no play), 26 (no play),
28 (no play), March 1, 2, 3
ENGLAND 7/371 dec (TW Graveney 111, DCS Compton 84, PBH May 79,
TE Bailey 72)
AUSTRALIA 221 (CC McDonald 72, JH Wardle 5/79) and **6/118**
CAPTAINS L Hutton [ENG] IW Johnson [AUST]
RESULT draw

1956

*Peter May assumed the England captaincy for this series—and the
responsibility for holding on to the Ashes so preciously won by his
predecessor, Len Hutton. However, after Australia won the Second
Test, England found themselves needing to come from behind to
win the series. They need not have worried. The remarkable Laker
and Lock took 38 of the 40 Australian wickets to fall in the Third
and Fourth Tests and then another 10 in the final Test to ensure
the Ashes stayed in England.*

Worcestershire opening batsman Peter Richardson played the
first of his 34 Tests at Trent Bridge, with immediate success. He
scored 81 in the first innings and 73 in the second before his
maiden Test century (104) in the Fourth Test, at Old Trafford.

Australia suffered a major blow early in the First Test with
Davidson's serious ankle injury while bowling. He took no further
part in the match and missed the next three Tests.

NSW fast bowler Pat Crawford made a forgettable debut in the
Second Test, breaking down in his fifth over and failing to score.
It was his only Test against England.

At Lord's, the Australian keeper Gil Langley created a long-
standing world record with nine dismissals—eight catches and
one stumping.

The garrulous Yorkshireman 'Fiery' Fred Trueman, in his second Test against Australia, took five wickets in the second innings at Lord's, but after taking only two wickets in the Third Test played no further part in the series.

Miller, at 36 and on his final tour of England, bowled Australia to victory at Lord's with the only 10-wicket haul of his career— 5/72 and 5/80.

Australia ended an eight-year drought in England with their victory in the Second Test, at Lord's.

Just as Freddie Brown had done in 1953, selector Cyril Washbrook came out of retirement for the Third Test. Although 41, it was almost a fairytale comeback, with Washbrook scoring 98 and sharing a vital fourth-wicket partnership of 187 with May (101).

Sussex batsman Alan Oakman played only two Tests—the Third and Fourth Tests of the series. He scored only 4 and 10, but fielding in close on the leg-side to Laker, took seven catches.

The Third Test at Headingley provided Australia with their first nightmares of the spin terrors, Laker and Lock. The former took 11 wickets and the latter seven in giving England its first win over Australia at Leeds.

It was the Fourth Test, at Old Trafford, however, that will always be known simply as 'Laker's Match'. Thirty-four-year-old Surrey off-spinner Jim Laker was handed the ball at the Stretford End and promptly took 9/37 in Australia's first innings ... the other Australian (Burke) falling to Lock. In the second innings, he took all 10 wickets for the amazing match analysis of 68/27/90/19.

Laker's second innings performance at Old Trafford was the first time a bowler has claimed all 10 wickets in a Test innings. His seven wickets in the final Test, at The Oval, gave him an Ashes record 46 in the series.

In Australia's first innings of 84, only the openers McDonald and Burke reached double figures, before all 10 wickets fell for 36.

Two players, Mackay and Harvey, scored a pair in the Fourth Test—the latter getting both ducks on the same day.

Remarkably, Lock bowled more overs than Laker in 'Laker's Match'—69 to 68.

England's victory in the Fourth Test broke a sequence of draws at Old Trafford dating back over half a century, to 1905.

Before Laker created havoc with the ball, England's batsmen scored heavily, with Richardson's maiden Test century, and also the first Ashes century for the Rt Rev David Sheppard, who became the first ordained minister to play Test cricket.

England's selectors recalled another player in the Fifth Test—this time Denis Compton, after having his right kneecap removed, for his final Test. He top-scored with 94. The other two recalled batsmen, Washbrook and Sheppard, had also been successful in their return matches ... Washbrook with 98 in the Third Test and Sheppard with 113 in the Fourth.

Australia's batting woes from Old Trafford continued at The Oval. In the first innings, Australia was 5/47 before making 202, and in the second, they finished at 5/27 when time ran out (more than 12 hours had been lost due to rain).

1956 ENGLAND WON SERIES 2–1

169 1st Test Trent Bridge, Nottingham, June 7, 8 (no play), 9, 11, 12
ENGLAND 8/217 dec (PE Richardson 81, PBH May 73, KR Miller 4/69) and **3/188 dec** (MC Cowdrey 81, PE Richardson 73)
AUSTRALIA 148 (RN Harvey 64, JC Laker 4/58) and **3/120** (JW Burke 58*)
CAPTAINS PBH May [ENG] IW Johnson [AUST]
RESULT draw

170 2nd Test Lord's, June 21, 22, 23, 25, 26
AUSTRALIA 285 (CC McDonald 78, JW Burke 65) and **257** (R Benaud 97, FS Trueman 5/90, TE Bailey 4/64)
ENGLAND 171 (PBH May 63, KR Miller 5/72) and **186** (PBH May 53, KR Miller 5/80, RG Archer 4/71)
CAPTAINS IW Johnson [AUST] PBH May [ENG]
RESULT Australia won by 185 runs

171 3rd Test Headingley, Leeds, July 12, 13, 14 (no play), 16, 17
ENGLAND 325 (PBH May 101, C Washbrook 98, TG Evans 40)
AUSTRALIA 143 (JW Burke 41, KR Miller 41, JC Laker 5/58, GAR Lock 4/41) and **140** (RN Harvey 69, JC Laker 6/55)
CAPTAINS PBH May [ENG] IW Johnson [AUST]
RESULT England won by an innings and 42 runs

172 4th Test Old Trafford, Manchester, July 26, 27, 28, 30, 31
ENGLAND 459 (Rev DS Sheppard 113, PE Richardson 104, MC Cowdrey 80, TG Evans 47, PBH May 43, IW Johnson 4/151)
AUSTRALIA 84 (JC Laker 9/37) and **205** (CC McDonald 89, JC Laker 10/53)
CAPTAINS PBH May [ENG] IW Johnson [AUST]
RESULT England won by an innings and 170 runs

173 5th Test The Oval, August 23, 24, 25, 27 (no play), 28
ENGLAND 247 (DCS Compton 94, PBH May 83*, RG Archer 5/53, KR Miller 4/91)
and **3/182 dec** (Rev DS Sheppard 62)
AUSTRALIA 202 (KR Miller 61, JC Laker 4/80) and **5/27**
CAPTAINS PBH May [ENG] IW Johnson [AUST]
RESULT draw

1958–59

In later years, television was to change the face of Australian cricket, with the acrimonious World Series Cricket split of 1977. The start of that can probably be traced back to this series—the first to be televised. The occasion may have been momentous, but not the cricket, with Trevor 'Barnacle' Bailey batting for almost six hours— 357 minutes—in reaching what was the slowest half-century the game had seen. Still, overall the Australian viewers would have been satisfied. Ironically, Australia was captained in this first televised series by Richie Benaud—for so long the face of Australian cricket—and his team regained the Ashes with a 4–0 victory.

Ian Craig had captained Australia the previous season on the tour of South Africa, but his Test career was ended through a bout of hepatitis. Benaud, his 28-year-old NSW team-mate, was chosen to take over, ahead of the more fancied Harvey. It turned out to be a bold move, with Benaud leading Australia in 27 Tests for only four defeats.

Norm O'Neill made his debut for Australia in the First Test, starting a 42-match career with 34 and 71 not out.

Bailey wasn't the only slow scorer in Brisbane. For Australia, Burke scored only 28 not out in 250 minutes on the final day— comparing unfavourably to Bailey's 68 in 458 minutes.

On the fast, bouncy pitches, Laker wasn't the danger to Australia he had been in England in 1956. He took 15 wickets in the rubber, and missed the Fourth Test. Lock took only five wickets.

Victoria's left-arm paceman Ian Meckiff first confronted England in this series, attracting attention with his controversial action. Opening the bowling with Davidson, Meckiff took 14 wickets in the first two Tests, including his career-best 6/38 in the Second, in Melbourne. He would be no-balled for throwing against South Africa five years later.

West Australian all-rounder Keith Slater was chosen for his only Test in the Third Test, in Sydney. Like Meckiff, some suspected his bowling action, along with a third Australian bowler in this rubber, Gordon Rorke, who made his debut in the Fourth Test.

England made a disastrous start to the Second Test, losing three wickets in five balls to Davidson to crash to 3/7 before May scored the first century by an England captain in Australia for more than 50 years.

Lancashire fast bowler Brian Statham, on one of four tours to Australia, took his career-best figures of 7/57 in Australia's first innings of the Second Test.

Davidson and Meckiff each took nine wickets in the Second Test—Davidson's 6/64 in the first innings his best against England.

Roy Swetman took over from Evans, who had a fractured finger, as England's keeper in both the Third and Fifth Tests—the only Tests of his career. Evans played in the Fourth Test but injured his finger again and passed the gloves to Graveney.

Benaud led from the front with his leg-spin during the series, taking seven wickets in the First Test, and nine in both the Third and Fourth. He finished the series with 31 of his 248 career Test wickets.

Benaud's efforts in the Third Test gave Australia a chance of victory, but needing 150 to win in just under two hours, the Australians settled for a draw.

Australia's 10-wicket win in Adelaide was set up by opener McDonald who, after almost being bowled first ball, went on to make his highest Test score (170), becoming the 50th Australian to score an Ashes century. McDonald's other hundred against England came in the Fifth Test (133).

The Fourth Test victory took the score to 3–0, and meant Australia had regained the Ashes.

Gloucestershire all-rounder John Mortimore, who arrived as a reinforcement for the touring party due to injuries, made his debut in the Fifth Test, in Melbourne. It was one of only two Tests he played against Australia.

The Fifth Test marked the end of the 61-Test career of Bailey, who finished with a pair. The bowler both times was Lindwall, who had, ironically, been 'given' his 100th Ashes wicket by Bailey on the previous Australian tour.

In Melbourne, Lindwall, at 37 nearing the end of his career, played his last Test against England. He took four wickets, and became Australia's leading Test wicket-taker by passing Grimmett's mark of 216.

1958–59 AUSTRALIA WON SERIES 4–0

174 1st Test Woolloongabba, Brisbane, December 5, 6, 8, 9, 10
ENGLAND 134 and **198** (TE Bailey 68, Benaud 4/66)
AUSTRALIA 186 (CC McDonald 42, PJ Loader 4/56) and **2/147** (NC O'Neill 71*)
CAPTAINS PBH May [ENG] R Benaud [AUST]
RESULT Australia won by eight wickets

175 2nd Test Melbourne Cricket Ground, December 31, January 1, 2, 3, 5
ENGLAND 259 (PBH May 113, TE Bailey 48, MC Cowdrey 44, AK Davidson 6/64) and **87** (I Meckiff 6/38)
AUSTRALIA 308 (RN Harvey 167, CC McDonald 47, JB Statham 7/57) and **2/42**
CAPTAINS PBH May [ENG] R Benaud [AUST]
RESULT Australia won by eight wickets

176 3rd Test Sydney Cricket Ground, January 9, 10, 12, 13, 14, 15
ENGLAND 219 (PBH May 42, R Swetman 41, R Benaud 5/83) and **7/287 dec** (MC Cowdrey 100*, PBH May 92, R Benaud 4/94)
AUSTRALIA 357 (NC O'Neill 77, AK Davidson 71, KD Mackay 57, LE Favell 54, CC McDonald 40, JC Laker 5/107, GAR Lock 4/130) and **2/54**
CAPTAINS PBH May [ENG] R Benaud [AUST]
RESULT draw

177 4th Test Adelaide Oval, January 30, 31, February 2, 3, 4, 5
AUSTRALIA 476 (CC McDonald 170, JW Burke 66, NC O'Neill 56, R Benaud 46, AK Davidson 43, RN Harvey 41, FS Trueman 4/90) and **0/36**
ENGLAND 240 (MC Cowdrey 84, TW Graveney 41, R Benaud 5/91) and **270** (PBH May 59, TW Graveney 53*, PE Richardson 43, W Watson 40, R Benaud 4/82)
CAPTAINS R Benaud [AUST] PBH May [ENG]
RESULT Australia won by 10 wickets

178 5th Test Melbourne Cricket Ground, February 13, 14, 16, 17, 18
ENGLAND 205 (PE Richardson 68, JB Mortimore 44*, R Benaud 4/43) and **214** (TW Graveney 54, MC Cowdrey 46)
AUSTRALIA 351 (CC McDonald 133, ATW Grout 74, R Benaud 64, FS Trueman 4/92, JC Laker 4/93) and **1/69** (CC McDonald 51*)
CAPTAINS PBH May [ENG] R Benaud [AUST]
RESULT Australia won by nine wickets

1946/47–1958/59
Questions 1–10

1 Richie Benaud took over as Australian captain for the 1958–59 series. Who did he replace as skipper?

2 Which opener scored 156 not out in the Adelaide Test of 1950–51—becoming the first England batsman to twice carry his bat through a completed Test innings?

3 Denis Compton filled in as England captain during the Fourth Test of 1950–51, and yet he averaged only seven for the series . . . true or false?

4 One of Australia's new players in the 1946–47 series was a leg-spinning all-rounder, who narrowly missed a century in his maiden Test before scoring 104 in his second. Who was that player?

5 Walter Hammond's career ended after the Fourth Test of the 1946–47 series. Who replaced him as England captain for the Fifth Test and was also in charge throughout the 1948 series?

6 The Australian wicketkeeper Gil Langley created a world record at Lord's in 1956. He made:
a) eight dismissals in England's first innings
b) nine dismissals for the match
c) 143 as a nightwatchman

7 Which Australian captain of this era went on to become secretary of the Melbourne Cricket Club?

8 Which England batsman became the first ordained minister to play Test cricket, scoring his first Ashes century in 'Laker's Match' in 1956?

9 Who was the wrist-spinner who took 102 wickets in 28 Tests, but was dropped from the 1958–59 touring team because of his newspaper articles critical of county Yorkshire?

10 Two Australian batsmen each scored 234 in the Second Test of 1946–47 in Sydney. Who were they?

Questions 11–20

11 Who was the extrovert England wicketkeeper, who played 91 Tests in the 1940s and 50s?

12 The great Australian all-rounder Keith Miller took 10 wickets in a match only once in his 55-Test career ... true or false?

13 Which England batsman took almost six hours in reaching a half-century in the First Test of 1958–59?

14 In the 1956 series, Surrey off-spinner Jim Laker took:
a) 39 wickets
b) 42 wickets
c) 46 wickets

15 What was the series scoreline in 1958–59 when Richie Benaud's Australian team regained the Ashes?

16 Who was the Australian left-hander who scored three centuries in his first four Tests of the 1946–47 series?

17 Who bowled Don Bradman for a duck in his final Test innings, at The Oval?

18 Which Australian finished with a 40-Test career batting average of only 11.37, yet averaged 102 on the 1953 Ashes tour?

19 Who captained England in the 1950–51 series?

20 Which Victorian all-rounder hit five sixes in his innings of 93 at Headingley in 1948, and went on to become a State politician?

Questions 21–30

21 The Australian vice-captain in the 1946–47 series had earlier been the AIF captain in the Victory Tests in England. What was his name?

22 Peter May's 113 in Melbourne in 1958–59 was the first century by an England captain in Australia since before the turn of the century ... true or false?

23 Two players from opposite sides scored a century in each innings of the Adelaide Test of 1946–47 ... the first time this had occurred in Test cricket. Name one of them.

24 Jim Laker took 19 wickets at Old Trafford in 1956. Who was the one batsman he failed to dismiss in Australia's first innings?

25 Who's the Victorian left-arm paceman who took 27 wickets in his first Ashes series in 1948?

26 Which Australian batsman averaged 63.05, with three Test hundreds, but played only 13 Tests ... eventually taking the Australian Cricket Board of Control to court when he wasn't again chosen for the Test team?

27 Who was the Middlesex batsman who scored the first of his five centuries in his maiden Ashes Test in 1938, and featured in advertisements as the original 'Brylcream Boy'?

28 Which England bowler—highly regarded by Don Bradman— claimed the great Australian's wicket five times in five innings at the end of the 1946–47 series and the start of 1948?

29 Which Australian batsman averaged the 'devil's number'— 87—on the 1948 tour?
a) Don Bradman   b) Arthur Morris   c) Lindsay Hassett

30 Who's the England player who became the 100th century- maker in Ashes contests, and went on to play Sheffield Shield cricket for Queensland?

Questions 31–40

31 In the 1950s, two England selectors came out of retirement to face Australia ... one in 1953 and the other in 1956. Name one of them.

32 By the time Don Bradman retired at the end of the 1948 tour, he'd scored 19 Ashes centuries, eight double-centuries and how many triple-centuries?

33 Who was the England batsman who made his Test debut just before World War II, and was regarded as the Middlesex twin of Denis Compton?

34 Who was the Victorian left-hander who scored a century as a teenager against India, and then a century in his maiden Ashes Test—still at the age of 19?

35 Who captained Australia for just one Test match against England in the mid-1950s?

36 England regained the Ashes in 1953 after a 19-year reign by Australia. Was the series scoreline:
a) 3–0
b) 2–1
c) 1–0

37 Which Englishman holds the Ashes record of taking 97 minutes to score his first run, in the Fourth Test in Adelaide in 1946–47?

38 Which Ashes series was televised for the first time?

39 Which Australian fast bowler passed Clarrie Grimmett as Australia's record wicket-taker in the final Test of 1958–59?

40 Despite the break of eight years due to World War II, the captains in the first post-war Test were the same as those of immediate pre-War. Who were they?

Questions 41-50

41 The great Australian all-rounder Keith Miller scored 1,511 runs and took 87 wickets in 29 Ashes Tests in the 1940s and '50s. Was Miller playing for Victoria or NSW when he was first chosen for Australia?

42 Which Yorkshireman captained England, and yet played only two Ashes Tests—scoring 0 and 1 in his first match against Australia as a 19-year-old?

43 Who was the Australian leg-spinner who took 31 wickets in the 1958-59 series?

44 Who were the England speed twins who took 46 wickets between them in the 1954-55 series?

45 Who's the England batsman who scored his first Ashes century in Sydney in 1954-55, and went on to become president of the MCC and England's Chairman of Selectors?

46 One of the most amazing declarations came from Australian captain Lindsay Hassett in the First Test, in Brisbane, in 1950-51. Did Hassett declare at:
a) 1/573 b) 0/0 c) 7/32

47 Only three Australians who'd played in the last Ashes Test before World War II also played in the first Ashes Test after the War. Name two of them.

48 In Australia's last Test victory under Don Bradman, the Australian captain scored 173 not out and figured in a triple-century partnership with which other batsman?

49 Which England bowler has the record analysis of 14/99 for a Trent Bridge Test, achieved in the 1953 series when he broke Clarrie Grimmett's then world record of 216 wickets?

50 Who's the Yorkshire fast bowler who took 79 Ashes wickets and went on to become a well-known public speaker and commentator?

ANSWERS *1946/47–1958/59*

1–10

1 Ian Craig
2 Len Hutton
3 True
4 Colin McCool
5 Norman Yardley
6 b) Nine dismissals for the match (eight catches, one stumping)
7 Ian Johnson
8 Rev David Sheppard
9 Johnny Wardle
10 Don Bradman and Sid Barnes

11–20

11 Godfrey Evans
12 True (Lord's, 1956)
13 Trevor Bailey
14 c) 46 wickets
15 4–0
16 Arthur Morris
17 Eric Hollies
18 Bill Johnston
19 Freddie Brown
20 Sam Loxton

21–30

21 Lindsay Hassett
22 False (Archie MacLaren scored a century in 1901–02)
23 The two were Arthur Morris (Australia) and Denis Compton (England)
24 Jim Burke
25 Bill Johnston
26 Sid Barnes
27 Denis Compton
28 Alec Bedser
29 b) Arthur Morris
30 Tom Graveney

31–40

31 The two were Freddie Brown (1953) and Cyril Washbrook (1956)
32 Two
33 Bill Edrich
34 Neil Harvey
35 Arthur Morris
36 c) 1–0
37 Godfrey Evans
38 1958–59
39 Ray Lindwall
40 Don Bradman and Walter Hammond

41–50

41 Victoria
42 Brian Close
43 Richie Benaud
44 Frank Tyson and Brian Statham
45 Peter May
46 c) 7/32 (Australia won the match)
47 The three were Bradman, Barnes and Hassett
48 Arthur Morris (Headingley, 1948)
49 Alec Bedser
50 Fred Trueman

Chapter Five

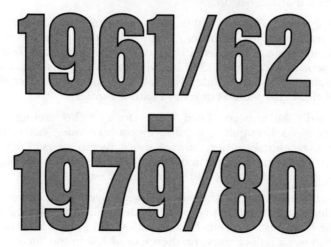

1961/62
-
1979/80

1961

This rubber came just months after the famous series between Australia and the West Indies, featuring the Tied Test at the Gabba. Under Benaud's captaincy, Australian cricket was on a high ... the Ashes won back in 1958–59, and now on English soil, the success continued with a 2–1 victory.

Ashes cricket returned to Edgbaston for the first time in more than 50 years for the First Test. In the only previous Tests at Birmingham, the 1902 match had ended in a draw and England had won comfortably in 1909.

In the First Test, Neil Harvey—on his fourth and final tour of England—scored his 20th Test century, which was the first by an Australian at Edgbaston.

At Edgbaston, Raman Subba Row was making his first Test appearance against Australia ... his 112 making him the twelfth England batsman to score a hundred in his first Ashes Test. He also scored a century (137) in the Fifth Test—his last against Australia—to top the England averages for the rubber. Incredibly, 98 of those 137 runs were scored with a runner.

England's Milan-born 'Lord Ted' Dexter, who among other things was a fine golfer, a pilot, motor-bike rider, broadcaster, model, racehorse owner, and of more recent years, England's somewhat eccentric Chairman of Selectors, achieved his highest score against Australia (180) in the First Test.

Six years after first playing for Victoria, pigeon-fancier and left-handed batsman Bill Lawry made his debut for Australia, opening in the First Test, at Trent Bridge, with Colin McDonald. His first innings was a half-century; he then scored 130 in the Second Test at Lord's and 102 in the Fourth Test at Old Trafford for an average of over 50.

Lawry's famous association with Bob Simpson at the top of the Australian order began in the Fourth Test, when they had the first of their century stands (113) in the second innings. Simpson had come into the Australian side in South Africa in 1957–58.

Harvey captained Australia for the only time in his 79-Test career when a shoulder injury forced Benaud to miss the Second Test at Lord's. His record: one Test, one win. England's defeat was its first in 19 matches.

The first of the great West Australian fast bowlers, Graham McKenzie, made his Test debut at Lord's—two days before his 20th birthday. He took the first of his 96 Ashes wickets in the first innings, and five in the second.

Statham joined the 200-club when he claimed the first Australian wicket of the Lord's Test—that of McDonald.

Queensland wicketkeeper Wally Grout took eight catches in the Second Test, including five in the second innings. With the seventh catch, he reached his hundredth Test dismissal. The batsman was his rival keeper, John 'JT' Murray, who made his debut in the First Test and then took seven catches in the Fourth Test to equal Evans' Ashes record for England.

Murray ended up with 18 dismissals for the series. Grout set an Ashes record of 21 dismissals for the five Tests.

Derbyshire seamer Les Jackson had a Test career spanning 12 years ... for the sum total of two Tests. The first was against New Zealand in 1949, and the second when he was recalled at the age of 40 for the Third Test of this series, at Headingley. He took four wickets for the match.

Trueman took 11 wickets at Headingley, including an amazing second innings spell of 5/0 in dismissing Australia for only 120. It was his best Test against Australia.

NSW batsman Brian Booth, who also played hockey for Australia at the 1956 Olympics, made his debut in the Fourth Test, at Old Trafford, scoring 46.

Simpson, whose leg-spinners had brought him just two wickets in the first three Tests, had a first innings spell of 4/2 to clean up the England tail at Old Trafford. Australia's other leggie, Benaud, took six wickets in the second innings, including a spell of 5/12 to give Australia victory—England losing their last nine wickets for 51 runs.

The Fifth Test, at The Oval, marked the end of Peter May's 66-Test career. He'd taken over the England captaincy from Cowdrey after the Second Test, and led England in a total of 41 Tests.

Australia's Fifth Test centuries, by Burge (181) and O'Neill (117), were their first against England.

1961 AUSTRALIA WON SERIES 2-1

179 1st Test Edgbaston, Birmingham, June 8, 9, 10, 12, 13
ENGLAND 195 (R Subba Row 59, KD Mackay 4/57) and **4/401** (ER Dexter 180,
R Subba Row 112, KF Barrington 48*)
AUSTRALIA 9/516 dec (RN Harvey 114, NC O'Neill 82, RB Simpson 76,
KD Mackay 64, WM Lawry 57)
CAPTAINS MC Cowdrey [ENG] R Benaud [AUST]
RESULT draw

180 2nd Test Lord's, June 22, 23, 24, 26
ENGLAND 206 (R Subba Row 48, AK Davidson 5/42) and **202**
(KF Barrington 66, G Pullar 42, GD McKenzie 5/37)
AUSTRALIA 340 (WM Lawry 130, KD Mackay 54, PJP Burge 46,
FS Trueman 4/118) and **5/71**
CAPTAINS MC Cowdrey [ENG] RN Harvey [AUST]
RESULT Australia won by five wickets

181 3rd Test Headingley, Leeds, July 6, 7, 8
AUSTRALIA 237 (RN Harvey 73, CC McDonald 54, FS Trueman 5/58) and **120**
(RN Harvey 53, FS Trueman 6/30)
ENGLAND 299 (MC Cowdrey 93, G Pullar 53, AK Davidson 5/63) and **2/62**
CAPTAINS R Benaud [AUST] PBH May [ENG]
RESULT England won by eight wickets

182 4th Test Old Trafford, Manchester, July 27, 28, 29, 31, August 1
AUSTRALIA 190 (WM Lawry 74, BC Booth 46, JB Statham 5/53) and **432**
(WM Lawry 102, AK Davidson 77*, NC O'Neill 67, RB Simpson 51, DA Allen 4/58)
ENGLAND 367 (PBH May 95, KF Barrington 78, G Pullar 63, DA Allen 42,
RB Simpson 4/23) and **201** (ER Dexter 76, R Subba Row 49, R Benaud 6/70)
CAPTAINS R Benaud [AUST] PBH May [ENG]
RESULT Australia won by 54 runs

183 5th Test The Oval, August 17, 18, 19, 21, 22
ENGLAND 256 (PBH May 71, KF Barrington 53, AK Davidson 4/83) and **8/370**
(R Subba Row 137, KF Barrington 83, DA Allen 42*, JT Murray 40,
KD Mackay 5/121)
AUSTRALIA 494 (PJP Burge 181, NC O'Neill 117, BC Booth 71,
RB Simpson 40, DA Allen 4/133)
CAPTAINS PBH May [ENG] R Benaud [AUST]
RESULT draw

1962-63

*By now, Dexter had taken over as captain of England, and he took
with him a team looking to regain the Ashes for the first time since*

1956. But it was a big ask, with England's record winless on Australian soil since the Fourth Test, in Adelaide, in February, 1955.

Bowlers had to work hard to remove batsmen in the First Test, at the Gabba, with 14 scores of 50 or more in the match, yet only Booth reached 100. Booth's only other century against England came in the Second Test.

England finally broke through for a long-awaited win in Australia, in the Second Test, in Melbourne—their first in eight matches.

Lawry, who started his career as a free-scoring batsman, finished with a reputation as a dour, defensive opener—the foundation being laid in the second innings of the Second Test when he batted for more than four-and-a-half hours in scoring 57.

England had all but won the Second Test when opener (Rev David) Sheppard, on 113, was run out going for the winning run. It was the second and last of his Ashes Test hundreds.

England's keeper for the first two Tests was Alan 'AC' Smith. John 'JT' Murray kept in the Third Test, in Sydney, but only briefly . . . as he sustained a shoulder injury early in Australia's first innings. Peter Parfitt took the gloves for the remainder of the match.

Victorian pace bowler Colin Guest made his one and only Test appearance in the Third Test, in Sydney. He failed to take a wicket.

Fred Titmus, the England off-spinner whose first-class career spanned five decades, played 19 of his 53 Tests against Australia. His best performance came in the Third Test when he took 7/79.

Like Titmus, Simpson had his career-best return with the ball in the Third Test, with 5/57 in England's first innings. Still looking for his maiden Test century, he also scored 91 in Australia's eight-wicket victory that levelled the series.

Statham took six wickets in the Fourth Test, in Adelaide, taking his career total beyond Alec Bedser's then world record of 236.

Harvey, by now 34, scored the last of his 21 Test hundreds (154) in the Adelaide Test. He retired after the Fifth Test, in Sydney.

Ken Barrington's Fourth Test hundred was posted in style—he did so with a six. He also scored a century in the Fifth Test, and 94 in the second innings.

Davidson's 44-Test career came to an end after the drawn final Test, taking his 186th wicket (and 84th against England) with his final ball.

This was the first time a five-Test Ashes series in Australia had ended with an even scoreline (1-all).

1962–63 SERIES DRAWN 1–ALL

184 1st Test Woolloongabba, Brisbane, November 30, December 1, 3, 4, 5
AUSTRALIA 404 (BC Booth 112, KD Mackay 86*, R Benaud 51,
RB Simpson 50) and **4/362 dec** (WM Lawry 98, RB Simpson 71, RN Harvey 57,
NC O'Neill 56, PJP Burge 47*)
ENGLAND 389 (PH Parfitt 80, KF Barrington 78, ER Dexter 70, R Benaud 6/115)
and **6/278** (ER Dexter 99, G Pullar 56, Rev DS Sheppard 53)
CAPTAINS R Benaud [AUST] ER Dexter [ENG]
RESULT draw

185 2nd Test Melbourne Cricket Ground, December 29, 31, January 1, 2, 3
AUSTRALIA 316 (WM Lawry 52, KD Mackay 49, AK Davidson 40,
FJ Titmus 4/43) and **248** (BC Booth 103, WM Lawry 57, FS Trueman 5/62)
ENGLAND 331 (MC Cowdrey 113, ER Dexter 93, TW Graveney 41, AK Davidson
6/75) and **3/237** (Rev DS Sheppard 113, MC Cowdrey 58*, ER Dexter 52)
CAPTAINS R Benaud [AUST] ER Dexter [ENG]
RESULT England won by seven wickets

186 3rd Test Sydney Cricket Ground, January 11, 12, 14, 15
ENGLAND 279 (MC Cowdrey 85, G Pullar 53, RB Simpson 5/57,
AK Davidson 4/54) and **104** (AK Davidson 5/25)
AUSTRALIA 319 (RB Simpson 91, BK Shepherd 71*, RN Harvey 64,
FJ Titmus 7/79) and **2/67**
CAPTAINS ER Dexter [ENG] R Benaud [AUST]
RESULT Australia won by eight wickets

187 4th Test Adelaide Oval, January 25, 26, 28, 29, 30
AUSTRALIA 393 (RN Harvey 154, NC O'Neill 100, AK Davidson 46) and **293**
(BC Booth 77, RB Simpson 71, R Benaud 48, FS Trueman 4/60)
ENGLAND 331 (KF Barrington 63, ER Dexter 61, FJ Titmus 59*,
GD McKenzie 5/89) and **4/223** (KF Barrington 132*)
CAPTAINS R Benaud [AUST] ER Dexter [ENG]
RESULT draw

188 5th Test Sydney Cricket Ground, February 15, 16, 18, 19, 20
ENGLAND 321 (KF Barrington 101, ER Dexter 47) and **8/268 dec**
(KF Barrington 94, Rev DS Sheppard 68, MC Cowdrey 53)
AUSTRALIA 349 (PJP Burge 103, NC O'Neill 73, R Benaud 57, FJ Titmus 5/103)
and **4/152** (PJP Burge 52*, WM Lawry 45*)
CAPTAINS ER Dexter [ENG] R Benaud [AUST]
RESULT draw

1964

By now, the Benaud era had ended for Australia, and the new man in charge, Bob Simpson, led his side to England. With Harvey and Davidson having also retired, England must have fancied their chances of regaining the Ashes. But rain badly affected the series. Four matches were drawn and Australia's victory at Headingley was sufficient to win the series.

Almost 15 hours' play was lost from the First Test, at Trent Bridge, with the entire third day washed out. And play in the Second Test didn't get underway until the third day.

Geoffrey Boycott, the complex and controversial Yorkshire batsman with a single-minded approach to run-scoring, made his debut in the First Test at the age of 23. He scored the first 48 of his 2,945 Test runs against Australia in the first innings, but didn't bat in the second due to a fractured finger, injured while fielding. The injury forced Boycott to miss the Second Test.

Boycott's first opening partner in Test cricket was off-spinner Titmus, who jumped up the order from number eight when John Edrich withdrew through injury just before the start of play. He scored 16, and in the second innings shared an opening stand of 90 with Dexter, with Boycott unable to bat.

Titmus was given a let-off in the first innings by Grout, who decided not to break the wicket after a run-out collision between Titmus and the Australian bowler, Neil Hawke.

Although Simpson was the new Australian captain, he didn't open the batting with Lawry until the Third Test. Instead, Lawry's Victorian partner Ian Redpath faced the new ball, with Simpson at six.

England's wicketkeeper in this series was Jim Parks, who'd made his Test debut against Pakistan 10 years earlier as a specialist batsman. It wasn't until five years later, in 1959, that he had become a full-time keeper.

Edrich, the cousin of Bill Edrich, celebrated his 27th birthday by returning to the England side for the Second Test, at Lord's, and scoring a century (120) in his first match against Australia.

Victorian all-rounder Bob Cowper, who would later join the elite 300-club of Ashes Test batsmen, made his debut in the Third Test, at Headingley. He scored 2 in his only appearance of the rubber.

At Headingley, South Australian Neil Hawke, who'd made his debut in the Fifth Test, in Sydney, in 1962–63, took his first five-wicket haul in Ashes Tests. He also took 6/47 in the Fifth Test, at The Oval.

Australia recovered from 7/178 to 389 all out in their first innings at Headingley—thanks to Burge who, after struggling against the off-spin of Titmus, relished the new-ball and scored 160.

The Fourth Test, at Old Trafford, was a nightmare for bowlers and a dream-come-true for the batsmen. It's the only time in Test history both teams have scored more than 600 in the first innings. For both sides, four bowlers sent down more than 40 overs, with Australia's Tom Veivers bowling an Ashes record 95.1 overs for a return of 3/155.

McKenzie had his best figures in Ashes Tests of 7/153 at Old Trafford, but sent down 60 overs for that return.

The beneficiaries in the Old Trafford Bowling Massacre were, of course, the batsmen. Four scored centuries (Simpson 311, Barrington 256, Dexter 174 and Lawry 106), and Booth missed becoming a fifth by just two runs.

Simpson's triple-century ended a long wait. He'd played 29 Tests and 51 innings without reaching a maiden Test hundred, and in his 30th Test, he batted for more than twelve-and-a-half hours— 762 minutes—for his 311, which remains the highest score at Old Trafford.

The story of Barrington's Fourth Test career-high 256 was also remarkable. It was his 10th Test hundred, and yet, his first in England.

England tried two new bowlers for the Fourth Test, Tom Cartwright and Fred Rumsey. Both played only five Tests— perhaps scared away by the introductory pitch. Cartwright bowled 77 overs and Rumsey 35.5, taking two wickets each.

However, the most significant of all milestones at The Oval was produced by a bowler. Trueman, at 33 and in the twilight of his career, became the first player to reach 300 Test wickets. He finished his 67-match career with 307.

1964 AUSTRALIA WON SERIES 1–NIL

189 1st Test Trent Bridge, Nottingham, June 4, 5, 6 (no play), 8, 9
ENGLAND 8/216 dec (G Boycott 48) and **9/193 dec** (ER Dexter 68, GD McKenzie 5/53)
AUSTRALIA 168 (RB Simpson 50) and **2/40**
CAPTAINS ER Dexter [ENG] RB Simpson [AUST]
RESULT draw

190 2nd Test Lord's, June 18 (no play), 19 (no play), 20, 22, 23
AUSTRALIA 176 (TR Veivers 54, FS Trueman 5/48) and **4/168** (PJP Burge 59)
ENGLAND 246 (JH Edrich 120, GE Corling 4/60)
CAPTAINS RB Simpson [AUST] ER Dexter [ENG]
RESULT draw

191 3rd Test Headingley, Leeds, July 2, 3, 4, 6
ENGLAND 268 (JM Parks 68, ER Dexter 66, NJN Hawke 5/75, GD McKenzie 4/74) and **229** (KF Barrington 85)
AUSTRALIA 389 (PJP Burge 160, WM Lawry 78, FJ Titmus 4/69) and **3/111** (IR Redpath 58*)
CAPTAINS ER Dexter [ENG] RB Simpson [AUST]
RESULT Australia won by seven wickets

192 4th Test Old Trafford, Manchester, July 23, 24, 25, 27, 28
AUSTRALIA 8/656 dec (RB Simpson 311, WM Lawry 106, BC Booth 98, NC O'Neill 47) and **0/4**
ENGLAND 611 (KF Barrington 256, ER Dexter 174, JM Parks 60, G Boycott 58, GD McKenzie 7/153)
CAPTAINS RB Simpson [AUST] ER Dexter [ENG]
RESULT draw

193 5th Test The Oval, August 13, 14, 15, 17, 18 (no play)
ENGLAND 182 (KF Barrington 47, NJN Hawke 6/47) and **4/381** (G Boycott 113, MC Cowdrey 93*, FJ Titmus 56, KF Barrington 54*)
AUSTRALIA 379 (WM Lawry 94, BC Booth 74, TR Veivers 67*, IR Redpath 45, FS Trueman 4/87)
CAPTAINS ER Dexter [ENG] RB Simpson [AUST]
RESULT draw

1965–66

By now, it was 10 years and five rubbers since England had held the Ashes. On this trip, the captain was 32-year-old Mike Smith, whose previous appearance in an Ashes Test was more than four years back when he scored a first innings duck. England led the series 1-nil after their big victory in the Third Test, but hopes of regaining the Ashes were snuffed out by Simpson and Lawry in the following match.

This series belonged to Lawry, who scored three centuries in seven innings, with 592 runs at an average of 84.5. The first of those centuries came in the First Test, at the Gabba, with two half-centuries in the Second Test and two more hundreds in the Fourth and Fifth Tests.

The boy from Dungog in NSW, Doug Walters, made his debut in the First Test, scoring a century (155) at the age of 19 ... just as Harvey and Jackson had done before him. Three weeks later, and by now 20, he scored another century (115) in his second Test. This equalled Ponsford's feat in scoring centuries in his first two Tests.

In contrast to Walters, Australia's other debut player in the First Test, Queensland paceman Peter Allan, lasted only one Test. He took two wickets, was selected again for the Fourth Test, but withdrew through injury.

Simpson missed the Gabba Test because of a fractured wrist and the Third Test, in Sydney, due to chickenpox. In his absence, Brian Booth led the Australian side.

In the Second Test, in Melbourne, both Australian openers scored half-centuries in each innings without getting to 100: Simpson (59 and 67) and Lawry (88 and 78).

In the Second Test, Cowper, still looking for his first century against England, joined Hill, Macartney, Chipperfield and Miller in being dismissed for 99.

The powerful Queenslander Peter Burge scored 120 in the Second Test. It was his fourth and final Test century—all of them against England.

Just as Hobbs had enjoyed a love affair with the MCG pitch, Cowdrey was beginning one of his own. In the Second Test, he scored his third Test century in Melbourne, and his fourth against Australia overall.

In the Third Test, in Sydney, England had an opening partnership of 234 in almost even-time. Boycott scored 84, and left-hander Bob Barber made 185—his only Test century.

Caught Grout, bowled Hawke. That became the story of England's only innings in the Third Test. Cowdrey, Smith, Brown and Parks were all dismissed that way. Grout took five catches in the innings—Hawke a career-best 7/105.

Edrich, who scored 109 in Melbourne, made it two hundreds in two innings with 103 in Sydney.

Off-spinner Titmus had a fabulous series with the bat. He had scores of 60, 56 not out, 14, 33, 53 and 42 not out ... the tailender finishing with 258 runs at 64.5, and during his innings of 14 in the Third Test, he passed the 1000-run mark to compliment his 100 Test wickets.

Victorian Keith Stackpole, who went on to make his name as an opening batsman, made his debut in the Fourth Test, scoring 43 at number eight and taking the wickets of Cowdrey and then Smith with his leg-spinners.

Simpson (225) and Lawry (119) posted a 244-run opening stand in the Fifth Test, in Adelaide—an Ashes record which stood until 1989. It remains Australia's best start in a Test in Australia.

While Hobbs and Cowdrey may have loved Melbourne, Ken Barrington had an intimate relationship with the Adelaide Oval. In the Fourth Test—his last in Adelaide—he scored 60 and 102, making it 10 consecutive first-class scores of at least 50 in Adelaide for an aggregate of 748 runs at 93.5.

Barrington scored his fifth century against Australia in the final Test in Melbourne ... reaching the three-figure mark with a six—just as he had against the Australians in Adelaide in 1962–63. He's the only man to bring up a century with a six twice in Ashes Tests.

The Welsh left-arm paceman Jeff Jones took 15 wickets in four of the five Tests, including 6/118 in Adelaide, becoming the first Glamorgan player to take five or more wickets in a Test innings.

Cowper's first Test century against England came in a big way in the Fifth Test in Melbourne. Dropped for the Fourth Test, his Fifth Test innings had a certain 'I'll show 'em' flavour. He batted for more than 12 hours and scored 307—Australia's only triple-century in Australia, and Cowper's only century in nine Tests against England.

A member of the Australian side for the final two Tests was 22-year-old South Australian Ian Chappell, who'd made his Test debut against Pakistan the previous summer. These were his first

Tests against England, and he went on to become possibly Australia's greatest captain.

The series ended with the retirement of Australia's Wally Grout, who'd made 187 dismissals in 51 Tests. Sadly, by the time England next played in Australia, Grout was dead, after suffering a heart attack at the age of 41.

1965–66 SERIES DRAWN 1–ALL

194 1st Test Woolloongabba, Brisbane, December 10, 11 (no play), 13, 14, 15
AUSTRALIA 6/443 dec (WM Lawry 166, KD Walters 155, TR Veivers 56*)
ENGLAND 280 (FJ Titmus 60, KF Barrington 53, JM Parks 52, G Boycott 45, PI Philpott 5/90) and **3/186** (G Boycott 63*)
CAPTAINS BC Booth [AUST] MJK Smith [ENG]
RESULT draw

195 2nd Test Melbourne Cricket Ground, December 30, 31, January 1, 3, 4
AUSTRALIA 358 (RM Cowper 99, WM Lawry 88, RB Simpson 59, BR Knight 4/84) and **426** (PJP Burge 120, KD Walters 115, WM Lawry 78, RB Simpson 67)
ENGLAND 558 (JH Edrich 109, MC Cowdrey 104, JM Parks 71, KF Barrington 63, FJ Titmus 56*, G Boycott 51, RW Barber 48, MJK Smith 41, GD McKenzie 5/134) and **0/5**
CAPTAINS RB Simpson [AUST] MJK Smith [ENG]
RESULT draw

196 3rd Test Sydney Cricket Ground, January 7, 8, 10, 11
ENGLAND 488 (RW Barber 185, JH Edrich 103, G Boycott 84, DA Allen 50*, NJN Hawke 7/105)
AUSTRALIA 221 (RM Cowper 60, G Thomas 51, DJ Brown 5/63) and **174** (FJ Titmus 4/40, DA Allen 4/47)
CAPTAINS MJK Smith [ENG] BC Booth [AUST]
RESULT England won by an innings and 93 runs

197 4th Test Adelaide Oval, January 28, 29, 31, February 1
ENGLAND 241 (KF Barrington 60, JM Parks 49, GD McKenzie 6/48) and **266** (KF Barrington 102, FJ Titmus 53, NJN Hawke 5/54)
AUSTRALIA 516 (RB Simpson 225, WM Lawry 119, G Thomas 52, KR Stackpole 43, IJ Jones 6/118)
CAPTAINS MJK Smith [ENG] RB Simpson [AUST]
RESULT Australia won by an innings and nine runs

198 5th Test Melbourne Cricket Ground, February 11, 12, 14, 15 (no play), 16
ENGLAND 9/485 dec (KF Barrington 115, JM Parks 89, JH Edrich 85, MC Cowdrey 79, FJ Titmus 42*, KD Walters 4/53) and **3/69**
AUSTRALIA 8/543 dec (RM Cowper 307, WM Lawry 108, KD Walters 60)
CAPTAINS MJK Smith [ENG] RB Simpson [AUST]
RESULT draw

1968

This series brought together two new captains, Bill Lawry and Colin Cowdrey, for an Ashes rubber, and also a group of new players who were destined to play a big part in the shape of cricket in the 1970s. They included the South African-born Basil D'Oliveira, who, the same year, became the centre of an international incident when the England tour of South Africa was cancelled because the South African authorities refused him entry to his homeland because of the colour of his skin. England's hopes of regaining the Ashes received a setback with Australia's win in the opening Test, at Old Trafford, and despite England's big victory at The Oval, the series was drawn

Doug Walters, who was to tour England four times without scoring a Test hundred, came close to doing so in his maiden Test on England soil. He scored 81 in the first innings and 86 in the second.

John Snow, the Sussex vicar's son who started county cricket as a batsman, first played against Australia in the First Test, at Old Trafford. He took 17 wickets for the series, but his best was yet to come—playing a key role in England regaining the Ashes in 1970–71.

Off-spinner Pat Pocock can feel harshly treated in playing just one Ashes Test. After taking punishment from Lawry in the first innings at Old Trafford, he took six wickets in the second ... only to be dropped for the Second Test.

Like Pocock, D'Oliveira starred in the second innings at Old Trafford—this time with the bat. He top-scored with 87 not out (he was the only England batsman to pass 50 in the match), but like Pocock, was dropped for the Lord's Test.

The Second Test was the 200th Ashes contest, and to mark the occasion, the former Australian Prime Minister, Sir Robert Menzies, presented the captains with a gold sovereign for the toss. Cowdrey won the toss, but the rain-affected match was drawn.

England ended their high turnover of wicketkeepers since the retirement of Godfrey Evans, with Kent's effervescent Alan Knott taking the gloves in this rubber for the first time against Australia. He would make 105 dismissals in his 34 Ashes Tests.

Australia's first innings total of 78 at Lord's was their lowest in England for more than 50 years—the damage caused by Warwickshire paceman Dave Brown with his Ashes-best of 5/42.

At Lord's, Cowdrey created a world record when he took the third of his first innings catches, giving him a Test total of 111.

Both captains were injured in the Third Test, at Edgbaston ... Cowdrey sustaining a leg injury while batting, while a fractured finger forced Lawry to retire hurt in Australia's first innings.

At Edgbaston, the records continued for Cowdrey. Now 35, he became the first cricketer to play 100 Tests. He celebrated by scoring another century (104) with assistance from his runner (Boycott), and during that innings he passed 7000 Test runs.

The injuries from the Edgbaston match prevented both captains from playing in the Fourth Test, at Headingley. Their replacements, and leading their countries in Tests for the only time, were Tom Graveney and the Australian wicketkeeper Barry Jarman.

Three players made their debuts at Headingley: West Australian batsman John Inverarity, and Keith Fletcher and Roger Prideaux for England. Fletcher, or 'The Gnome' as he was called, went on to become England's cricket manager of the 1990s, while opening batsman Prideaux played only one Ashes Test. He top-scored with 64 in the first innings, but missed the Fifth Test through injury.

D'Oliveria returned to the England side for the Fifth Test, and his 158 was his highest score in 13 matches against Australia.

NSW-born South Australian off-spinner Ashley Mallett played his maiden Test at The Oval—less than 12 months after his first-class debut. He took the first of his five wickets in the game with his fifth ball in Test cricket, and scored 43 not out, which remained his best score in Ashes Tests.

But it was the England left-arm spinner Derek Underwood who was the star bowler of the final Test. He spun England to a dramatic victory with 7/50—his best return in 29 Tests against Australia.

England's win at The Oval was achieved with just five minutes to spare, with Australia losing 5/15 in the last 31 minutes.

1968 SERIES DRAWN 1–ALL

199 1st Test Old Trafford, Manchester, June 6, 7, 8, 10, 11
AUSTRALIA 357 (AP Sheahan 88, WM Lawry 81, KD Walters 81, IM Chappell 73, JA Snow 4/97) and **220** (KD Walters 86, BN Jarman 41, PI Pocock 6/79)
ENGLAND 165 (JH Edrich 49, RM Cowper 4/48) and **253** (BL D'Oliveira 87*, RW Barber 46)
CAPTAINS WM Lawry [AUST] MC Cowdrey [ENG]
RESULT Australia won by 159 runs

200 2nd Test Lord's, June 20, 21, 22, 24, 25
ENGLAND 7/351 dec (C Milburn 83, KF Barrington 75, G Boycott 49, MC Cowdrey 45)
AUSTRALIA 78 (DJ Brown 5/42) and **4/127** (IR Redpath 53)
CAPTAINS MC Cowdrey [ENG] WM Lawry [AUST]
RESULT draw

201 3rd Test Edgbaston, Birmingham, July 11 (no play), 12, 13, 15, 16
ENGLAND 409 (MC Cowdrey 104, TW Graveney 96, JH Edrich 88, EW Freeman 4/78) and **3/142** (JH Edrich 64*)
AUSTRALIA 222 (IM Chappell 71, RM Cowper 57, KD Walters 46) and **1/68**
CAPTAINS MC Cowdrey [ENG] WM Lawry [AUST]
RESULT draw

202 4th Test Headingley, Leeds, July 25, 26, 27, 29, 30
AUSTRALIA 315 (IR Redpath 92, IM Chappell 65, KD Walters 42, DL Underwood 4/41) and **312** (IM Chappell 81, KD Walters 56, IR Redpath 48, R Illingworth 6/87)
ENGLAND 302 (RM Prideaux 64, JH Edrich 62, KF Barrington 49, DL Underwood 45*, AN Connolly 5/72) and **4/230** (JH Edrich 65, KF Barrington 46*, TW Graveney 41)
CAPTAINS BN Jarman [AUST] TW Graveney [ENG]
RESULT draw

203 5th Test The Oval, August 22, 23, 24, 26, 27
ENGLAND 494 (JH Edrich 164, BL D'Oliveira 158, TW Graveney 63) and **181** (AN Connolly 4/65)
AUSTRALIA 324 (WM Lawry 135, IR Redpath 67, AA Mallett 43*) and **125** (RJ Inverarity 56, DL Underwood 7/50)
CAPTAINS MC Cowdrey [ENG] WM Lawry [AUST]
RESULT England won by 226 runs

1970–71

The longest rubber in Test history ushered in the dawning of a new era in Australian cricket. Three youngsters who were to establish themselves as record-breaking champions all first tasted Test cricket during this series, which went to a Seventh Test (although the Third Test was abandoned without a ball being bowled). The names of the newcomers: Rod Marsh, Greg Chappell and Dennis Lillee. But for all the promise of these future stars, the rubber belonged to England, who won the Fourth Test and the Seventh to recapture the Ashes.

England's captain for the series was 38-year-old Yorkshireman Ray Illingworth, whose fine performances in the 1968 home series included his Ashes-best bowling of 6/87 in the Fourth Test, at Headingley. Former captain Cowdrey was still in the England side, and became the world run-scoring record-holder during the First Test, in Brisbane.

Marsh, the 23-year-old West Australian dubbed 'Iron Gloves', was the first of the young trio to play Test cricket. He was chosen for the First Test, along with two other first-gamers, leg-spinner Terry Jenner and the Victorian fast bowler with the wrong-foot delivery style, Alan 'Froggy' Thomson.

In Brisbane, Stackpole opened the batting for the first time against England, and scored his career-high 207. He helped Australia to 3/418 before the last seven wickets fell for 15 runs.

By now, John Snow was at his peak, with his pace causing discomfort for the Australians. During the series he took 31 wickets, with six of them in the first innings in Brisbane.

Snow's new-ball partner was Leicestershire paceman Ken Shuttleworth, on debut in the First Test, where he took five wickets in the second innings.

The Second Test was the first to be staged in Perth, with Greg Chappell making a memorable debut. Batting at number seven, he became the sixth Australian to score a century (108) in his first Test innings. It was the start of an 87-Test career reaping more than 7000 runs, with 24 centuries.

During the Perth Test, Lawry passed 5000 Test runs and his Victorian team-mate Redpath scored 171—his highest score in 66 Tests.

Kent opener Brian Luckhurst, who'd played his maiden Test aged 31 in Brisbane, was a revelation on tour. After 74 in the First Test, he scored 131 in Perth, then 109 in the Fifth Test—finishing with an average of 56.87 in five Tests. During his first century, he injured a thumb, and during the second he fractured a finger.

John Hampshire, who later played for Tasmania and then became a Test umpire, was England's 12th man in Perth. Of the three Australian second innings wickets to fall, Hampshire took two catches.

Along with the celebrated Australians to debut during the series was an Englishman who was to reach great heights. Twenty-one-year-old fast bowler Robert George Dylan (after the American folk singer) Willis, who joined the touring party as a late replacement for Alan Ward, came into the side for the Fourth Test, in Sydney. Twelve years later, he was to return to Australia as the England captain.

England's Fifth Test win was set up by Boycott's batting (77 and 142 not out), and then completed by Snow's finest performance in 20 Ashes Tests. He took 7/40 to dismiss Australia for 116.

Through the Fourth Test second innings debacle, Lawry carried his bat for Australia with 60 not out—the first Australian to do so in Sydney.

The Fourth Test marked a sad Test farewell for the great Australian fast bowler Graham McKenzie, who'd taken 246 Test wickets—two short of Benaud's Australian record—but was never picked again. His career ended while batting—retiring hurt after being struck in the face by a short ball from Snow.

The Fifth Test, in Melbourne, was a late addition to the fixture, replacing a match against Victoria to make up for the rained-out Third Test. It finished just three days before the start of the Sixth Test, in Adelaide.

Ian Chappell, now batting at number three, led the way for Australia in the Fifth Test, scoring a century with the second 50 in almost even-time.

Marsh reached 92 in Australia's first innings of the Fifth Test before Lawry made one of his most memorable decisions. He declared with Australia 9/493, robbing Marsh of the chance to become the first Australian wicketkeeper to score a Test hundred.

Queensland fast bowler Ross Duncan was chosen for the Sydney match—the only Test of his career. He failed to take a wicket.

Lillee, the 21-year-old West Australian tearaway, first appeared in the Sixth Test, in Adelaide. He took the first of his 23 five-wicket hauls in the first innings—his first victim, John Edrich.

Lillee's new-ball partner in his maiden Test was Thomson—but it was Alan and not Jeff, with whom he formed a famous partnership in later years.

Stackpole continued his good form in Adelaide with scores of 87 and 136, but this was to be the final Test for his partner Lawry, who was dropped from the side and replaced as skipper by Ian Chappell.

In the final Test in Sydney, Illingworth led an England walk-off on the second day, triggered by the crowd's reaction to Snow after the England paceman had struck Australian tailender Jenner on the head with a bouncer.

The Australian selectors tried two new players in the Seventh Test. Queensland fast bowler Tony Dell took five wickets, but played only two Tests, and 35-year-old Victorian opener Ken Eastwood came in for Lawry in his only Test. He scored 5 and 0 and took the wicket of Fletcher in his brief moment of fame.

England's win in the Seventh Test came after being sent in by Ian Chappell, and the victory was enough for the tourists to regain the Ashes.

1970–71 ENGLAND WON SERIES 2–0

204 1st Test Woolloongabba, Brisbane, November 27, 28, 29, December 1, 2
AUSTRALIA 433 (KR Stackpole 207, KD Walters 112, IM Chappell 59, JA Snow 6/114) and **214** (WM Lawry 84, K Shuttleworth 5/47)
ENGLAND 464 (JH Edrich 79, BW Luckhurst 74, APE Knott 73, BL D'Oliveira 57) and **1/39**
CAPTAINS WM Lawry [AUST] R Illingworth [ENG]
RESULT draw

205 2nd Test WACA Ground, Perth, December 11, 12, 13, 15, 16
ENGLAND 397 (BW Luckhurst 131, G Boycott 70, JH Edrich 47, MC Cowdrey 40, GD McKenzie 4/66) and **6/287 dec** (JH Edrich 115*, G Boycott 50)
AUSTRALIA 440 (IR Redpath 171, GS Chappell 108, IM Chappell 50, RW Marsh 44, JA Snow 4/143) and **3/100**
CAPTAINS R Illingworth [ENG] WM Lawry [AUST]
RESULT draw

* The 3rd Test, scheduled for Melbourne, was abandoned without a ball being bowled.

206 4th Test Sydney Cricket Ground, January 9, 10, 11, 13, 14
ENGLAND 332 (G Boycott 77, JH Edrich 55, JW Gleeson 4/83, AA Mallett 4/40) and **5/319 dec** (G Boycott 142*, BL D'Oliveira 56*, R Illingworth 53)
AUSTRALIA 236 (IR Redpath 64, KD Walters 55, DL Underwood 4/66) and **116**

(WM Lawry 60*, JA Snow 7/40)
CAPTAINS R Illingworth [ENG] WM Lawry [AUST]
RESULT England won by 299 runs

207 5th Test Melbourne Cricket Ground, January 21, 22, 23, 25, 26
AUSTRALIA 9/493 dec (IM Chappell 111, RW Marsh 92*, IR Redpath 72, WM Lawry 56, KD Walters 55) and **4/169 dec** (WM Lawry 42)
ENGLAND 392 (BL D'Oliveira 117, BW Luckhurst 109, R Illingworth 41) and **0/161** (G Boycott 76*, JH Edrich 74*)
CAPTAINS WM Lawry [AUST] R Illingworth [ENG]
RESULT draw

208 6th Test Adelaide Oval, January 29, 30, February 1, 2, 3
ENGLAND 470 (JH Edrich 130, KWR Fletcher 80, G Boycott 58, JH Hampshire 55, BL D'Oliveira 47, DK Lillee 5/84) and **4/233 dec** (G Boycott 119, R Illingworth 48*, JH Edrich 40)
AUSTRALIA 235 (KR Stackpole 87, P Lever 4/49) and **3/328** (KR Stackpole 136, IM Chappell 104)
CAPTAINS R Illingworth [ENG] WM Lawry [AUST]
RESULT draw

209 7th Test Sydney Cricket Ground, February 12, 13, 14, 16, 17
ENGLAND 184 (R Illingworth 42) and **302** (BW Luckhurst 59, JH Edrich 57, BL D'Oliveira 47)
AUSTRALIA 264 (GS Chappell 65, IR Redpath 59, KD Walters 42) and **160** (KR Stackpole 67)
CAPTAINS R Illingworth [ENG] IM Chappell [AUST]
RESULT England won by 62 runs

1972

To the tune of Here Come The Aussies, *the Australians left for England with Ian Chappell now firmly ensconced as captain for his first full Ashes series. He was fast developing a reputation as a winner—aggressive, adventurous and inspirational. He was up against the hardened pro, 40-year-old Ray Illingworth, who'd led England to regaining the Ashes in Australia 18 months earlier. It had the makings of an enthralling series.*

South African-born Sussex all-rounder Tony Greig was chosen for his England debut in the First Test, at Old Trafford, starting a controversial career which included the England captaincy and a key role in the establishment of World Series Cricket. He had a fine match, top-scoring in each innings with half-centuries, and taking five wickets.

Greig had become known to Australian crowds the previous summer when playing for the Rest of the World team. During that series, he'd struck Graeme Watson with a short ball. Watson required 40 pints of blood, but fought back to win a place in the touring party.

Greig's first Test wicket was Ian Chappell for a duck. The pair were later to become colleagues in the television commentary box.

Opening batsman Bruce Francis also made his debut in the First Test. He played in the first three Tests without success and wasn't selected again. Francis later played a key role in organising a rebel tour to South Africa by an Australian team in the mid-1980s.

Marsh had another near-miss in his bid to score a Test century, when he made 91 at Old Trafford.

Lillee, who was to be a key player in the series, took six second innings wickets in the First Test, including three in four balls. He also took three in four balls in the Fifth Test, at The Oval, finishing the rubber with 31 victims.

England's 89-run win at Old Trafford was the first time the home side had won the opening Ashes Test in England for 42 years.

Australia introduced two new players for the Second Test, at Lord's—batsman Ross Edwards and his West Australian team-mate, the right-arm swing bowler Bob Massie. This was to be remembered as 'Massie's Match', after the debutant returned the remarkable figures of 16/137.

Massie took eight wickets in the first innings and eight in the second. Lillee took the other two wickets in each innings. Only England's Jim Laker and Sydney Barnes have taken more wickets in a Test match, but no-one has taken as many wickets on debut. Massie's maiden Test haul represented more than half of his Test career total of 31 wickets in six Tests.

Australia's win at Old Trafford ended an 11-match streak without victory against England—their longest on record.

No England batsman scored a century in the series. Opening batsman Brian Luckhurst went closest with 96 in the Third Test, at Trent Bridge.

Stackpole, who'd scored three half-centuries in the first two Tests, scored one of his three Ashes hundreds (114) in the match at Trent Bridge. He ended up with 485 runs for the rubber at 53.8. In all Tests against England, Stackpole averaged over 50—well up on his 43-Test career average of 37.42.

Marsh took five catches in England's second innings at Old Trafford and the same in the first innings at Trent Bridge. In the first innings of the Fourth Test at Headingley, he made two of his career-total 12 stumpings—one each off the bowling of Mallett and Inverarity.

NSW all-rounder David Colley started his Test career in the First Test of the series—and ended it with the Third. He took only six wickets, but scored a half-century in his final Test.

In his second Test, Edwards scored 170 not out in the second innings at Trent Bridge when asked to open with Stackpole. It was the first of his two Ashes centuries. He also opened in the Fourth Test and scored a 'pair'.

England's nine-wicket win in the Fourth Test ensured the Ashes stayed with the home team. The match was played on a controversial grassless pitch, suffering an attack of 'Fusarium Oxysporum' after recent flooding. Underwood took 10 wickets.

Lancashire opener Barry Wood made his debut for England in the Fifth Test, at The Oval, scoring 90 in the second innings. It turned out to be his highest score in four Tests against Australia.

England's chances in the Fifth Test were weakened by injuries to three bowlers—Snow, D'Oliveira and Illingworth. When Illingworth left the field with an ankle injury late on the fifth day, Edrich captained England for the remainder of this six-day Test.

Australia's win at the Oval, to square the series, was set up by the Chappell brothers. Ian scored 118 and Greg 113—the first time brothers had scored centuries in the same innings of a Test.

The Australian team for the final Test contained six West Australians, three South Australians and two Victorians—and, for the first time in England, no player from NSW.

1972 SERIES DRAWN 2–ALL

210 1st Test Old Trafford, Manchester, June 8, 9, 10, 12, 13
ENGLAND 249 (AW Greig 57, JH Edrich 49) and **234** (AW Greig 62, G Boycott 47, DK Lillee 6/66)
AUSTRALIA 142 (KR Stackpole 53, JA Snow 4/41, GG Arnold 4/62) and **252**

(RW Marsh 91, KR Stackpole 67, JA Snow 4/87, AW Greig 4/53)
CAPTAINS R Illingworth [ENG] IM Chappell [AUST]
RESULT England won by 89 runs

211 2nd Test Lord's, June 22, 23, 24, 26
ENGLAND 272 (AW Greig 54, APE Knott 43, RAL Massie 8/84) and **116**
(RAL Massie 8/53)
AUSTRALIA 308 (GS Chappell 131, IM Chappell 56, RW Marsh 50, JA Snow 5/57)
and **2/81** (KR Stackpole 57*)
CAPTAINS R Illingworth [ENG] IM Chappell [AUST]
RESULT Australia won by eight wickets

212 3rd Test Trent Bridge, Nottingham, July 13, 14, 15, 17, 18
AUSTRALIA 315 (KR Stackpole 114, DJ Colley 54, RW Marsh 41, JA Snow 5/92)
and **4/324 dec** (R Edwards 170*, GS Chappell 72, IM Chappell 50)
ENGLAND 189 (DK Lillee 4/35, RAL Massie 4/43) and **4/290** (BW Luckhurst 96,
BL D'Oliveira 50*, PH Parfitt 46)
CAPTAINS IM Chappell [AUST] R Illingworth [ENG]
RESULT draw

213 4th Test Headingley, Leeds, July 27, 28, 29
AUSTRALIA 146 (KR Stackpole 52, DL Underwood 4/37) and **136**
(AP Sheahan 41*, DL Underwood 6/45)
ENGLAND 263 (R Illingworth 57, JA Snow 48, JH Edrich 45, AA Mallett 5/114)
and **1/21**
CAPTAINS IM Chappell [AUST] R Illingworth [ENG]
RESULT England won by nine wickets

214 5th Test The Oval, August 10, 11, 12, 14, 15, 16
ENGLAND 284 (APE Knott 92, PH Parfitt 51, JH Hampshire 42, DK Lillee 5/58)
and **356** (B Wood 90, APE Knott 63, BL D'Oliveira 43, DK Lillee 5/123)
AUSTRALIA 399 (IM Chappell 118, GS Chappell 113, R Edwards 79,
DL Underwood 4/90) and **5/242** (KR Stackpole 79, AP Sheahan 44*,
RW Marsh 43*)
CAPTAINS R Illingworth [ENG] IM Chappell [AUST]
RESULT Australia won by five wickets

1974–75

*Lillee and Thomson. Those names are synonymous with Australian
cricket in the 1970s, and they were at the peak of their powers
during this six-Test rubber. Lillee took 24 wickets and Thomson,
who missed the final Test through injury, took 33. England's shell-
shocked batsmen failed to reach an innings total of 300 until the*

final Test when the Lillee-Thomson partnership was broken. The Ashes returned to Australia.

In the period from the previous Test against England (at The Oval in 1972), Lillee had suffered a severe back injury, with stress fractures in his spine. This was his comeback series after a courageous battle to regain fitness.

Thomson first played for Australia against Pakistan two seasons earlier, but it wasn't until this series that he was recognised as a world-class bowler. In the First Test, he took nine wickets—six in the second innings.

Australia brought a new opening batsman into the team for the First Test—West Australian left-hander Wally Edwards (no relation to Ross who batted at number five). Wally Edwards scored 4 and 5 in the First Test and two ducks in the next four innings saw his Test career over after three matches.

England, on this tour, were led by the Scotsman Mike Denness, whose struggle against Lillee and Thomson was such that he dropped himself from the team for the Fourth Test, in Sydney. It meant that Edrich was the England captain when Australia regained the Ashes.

The only England batsman to counter the Australian quicks in Brisbane was Tony Greig, whose first innings 110 was England's first century at the 'Gabba since Maurice Leyland 38 years earlier.

Alan Knott claimed from Godfrey Evans the world record for catches by a wicketkeeper when he dismissed Ross Edwards in Brisbane—Knott's 174th Test catch.

By now, Tasmanian-born Max 'Tangles' Walker was in the Australian side—having taken 26 wickets in Australia's 1973 series win in the Caribbean. His medium-pace provided the ideal foil for Lillee and Thomson, with 15 wickets in the first five Tests before he struck in the last. Thomson missed the match and Lillee bowled only six overs before suffering a bruised foot, leaving Walker to take a career-best 8/143 in England's only innings.

England called for a reinforcement a few days before the start of the Second Test, in Perth. Amiss and Edrich had hand injuries from the First Test, and Colin Cowdrey—by now just a fortnight shy of his 42nd birthday—arrived to boost the England party, four days before playing in the Second Test. In nine innings in the series, he failed to reach 50 and averaged only 18.3.

141

The Perth Test is remembered for the feat of Doug Walters, who scored a century between tea and stumps on the second day—his century coming up off the last ball of the day with a six over square-leg off Bob Willis.

The Perth Test also represented the return to Test cricket of 42-year-old off-spinner Fred Titmus, who first played for England back in 1955. This was his first Test since losing four toes in a boating accident during the Caribbean tour of 1968.

Greg Chappell, one of the finest of all slips fieldsmen, took seven catches in the Second Test. In the Fourth Test, in Sydney, he scored 144—the biggest of his nine hundreds against England.

Ian Chappell was never afraid to gamble. In Perth, he won the toss and asked England to bat, and did the same in the Third Test, in Melbourne—the first time a captain had done that in successive Australia-England Tests.

England's injury woes against the Australian pacemen continued with David Lloyd retiring hurt for a time during the Second Test after being hit in the groin by Thomson. Edrich, in his match as England's stand-in captain, sustained two fractured ribs after being hit by Lillee off the first ball he faced in the second innings.

Rick McCosker, in the first of his 25 appearances for Australia, made his debut in the Fourth Test, in Sydney, scoring 80 in the first innings. Three years later McCosker was to emerge a hero in the Centenary Test in Melbourne.

Australia's Fourth Test victory to regain the Ashes was completed when Mallett took his 100th Test wicket.

Denness returned to the England side for the Fifth Test and celebrated with a dramatic form reversal. He scored a half-century, which was a prelude to his score of 188 in the final Test ... the highest score by an England captain in Australia.

The Fifth Test was exceptional for Allan Knott, who scored his first century against Australia (106 not out) and also made his 200th Test dismissal.

The series came to an end for Thomson on the rest day of the Fifth Test when he injured his shoulder while playing tennis ... his 33 wickets in the series effectively coming in four-and-a-half Tests.

Lancashire paceman Peter Lever triggered Australia's downfall in the final Test, with a spell of 4/5 leading to Australia's first innings 152 all out. He finished with 6/38—his best return in Test cricket.

The Sixth Test brought to an end the record 114-Test career of Cowdrey ... 43 of those matches against Australia with 2,433 runs in Ashes Tests.

1974–75 AUSTRALIA WON SERIES 4–1

215 1st Test Woolloongabba, Brisbane, November 29, 30, December 1, 3, 4
AUSTRALIA 309 (IM Chappell 90, GS Chappell 58, MHN Walker 41*,
RGD Willis 4/56) and **5/288 dec** (GS Chappell 71, KD Walters 62*, R Edwards 53,
RW Marsh 46*)
ENGLAND 265 (AW Greig 110, JH Edrich 48, MHN Walker 4/73) and **166**
(JR Thomson 6/46)
CAPTAINS IM Chappell [AUST] MH Denness [ENG]
RESULT Australia won by 166 runs

216 2nd Test WACA Ground, Perth, December 13, 14, 15, 17
ENGLAND 208 (APE Knott 51, D Lloyd 49) and **293** (FJ Titmus 61, CM Old 43,
MC Cowdrey 41, JR Thomson 5/93)
AUSTRALIA 481 (R Edwards 115, KD Walters 103, GS Chappell 62,
IR Redpath 41, RW Marsh 41) and **1/23**
CAPTAINS MH Denness [ENG] IM Chappell [AUST]
RESULT Australia won by nine wickets

217 3rd Test Melbourne Cricket Ground, December 26, 27, 28, 30, 31
ENGLAND 242 (APE Knott 52, JH Edrich 49, JR Thomson 4/72) and **244**
(DL Amiss 90, AW Greig 60, D Lloyd 44, JR Thomson 4/71, AA Mallett 4/60)
AUSTRALIA 241 (IR Redpath 55, RW Marsh 44, RGD Willis 5/61) and **8/238**
(GS Chappell 61, RW Marsh 40, AW Greig 4/56)
CAPTAINS MH Denness [ENG] IM Chappell [AUST]
RESULT draw

218 4th Test Sydney Cricket Ground, January 4, 5, 6, 8, 9
AUSTRALIA 405 (GS Chappell 84, RB McCosker 80, IM Chappell 53, GG Arnold
5/86, AW Greig 4/104) and **4/289 dec** (GS Chappell 144, IR Redpath 105)
ENGLAND 295 (APE Knott 82, JH Edrich 50, JR Thomson 4/74) and **228**
(AW Greig 54, AA Mallett 4/21)
CAPTAINS IM Chappell [AUST] JH Edrich [ENG]
RESULT Australia won by 171 runs

219 5th Test Adelaide Oval, January 25 (no play), 26, 27, 29, 30
AUSTRALIA 304 (TJ Jenner 74, KD Walters 55, MHN Walker 41,
DL Underwood 7/113) and **5/272 dec** (KD Walters 71*, RW Marsh 55,
IR Redpath 52, IM Chappell 41, DL Underwood 4/102)
ENGLAND 172 (MH Denness 51, KWR Fletcher 40, DK Lillee 4/49) and **241**
(APE Knott 106*, KWR Fletcher 63, DK Lillee 4/69)
CAPTAINS IM Chappell [AUST] MH Denness [ENG]
RESULT Australia won by 163 runs

220 6th Test Melbourne Cricket Ground, February 8, 9, 10, 12, 13
AUSTRALIA 152 (IM Chappell 65, P Lever 6/38) and **373** (GS Chappell 102,
IR Redpath 83, RB McCosker 76, IM Chappell 50, AW Greig 4/88)
ENGLAND 529 (MH Denness 188, KWR Fletcher 146, AW Greig 89,
JH Edrich 70, MHN Walker 8/143)
CAPTAINS IM Chappell [AUST] MH Denness [ENG]
RESULT England won by an innings and four runs

1975

*Ever since World War II, Ashes contests had gone at least five
Tests—twice to six and once even seven. This time, though, it was
back to four matches, and 12 months earlier than would have been
reasonably anticipated. The series came hard on the heels of the
inaugural World Cup, won by the West Indies. Ian Chappell and
Mike Denness were still in charge of the respective teams, and
Denness had a big job to regain the ground lost so comprehensively
in Australia a few months earlier.*

Twenty-one-year-old Essex batsman Graham Gooch made his
England debut in the First Test, at Edgbaston. He made a pair
and was dropped for the Second Test.

Lillee and Walker took five wickets each to wreck England's first
innings at Edgbaston—thanks to a pitch left rain-affected after a
storm struck at the start of the England innings.

Australia's First Test victory was their first in five Tests at
Edgbaston dating back to the start of the century.

David Steele, grey-haired, bespectacled and looking a decade older
than his 33 years, made his debut in the Second Test, at Lord's. After
getting lost in the Lord's pavilion, Steele found his way quickly in
Test cricket, scoring 50 in the first innings and passing 30 in each
of his six innings to top England's averages at 60.83.

Denness continued his struggle against Australia, failing in the
First Test. He was then replaced as captain by Greig—a South
African replacing a Scotsman as England captain. Greig was to
lead England in four Tests against Australia without a victory.

Edrich, by now 38 and the mainstay of England's batting, scored the biggest of his seven Ashes hundreds (175) in the Lord's Test.

Lillee, not renowned for his batting prowess, came to Australia's rescue at Lord's, scoring his highest Test score of 73 not out.

Ross Edwards joined the '99-club' at Lord's, falling short of what would have been a third Test hundred.

Phillippe Henri Edmonds, the Rhodesian-raised son of an English father and Belgian mother, made his England debut in the Third Test, at Headingley. The Middlesex left-arm spinner made a sensational start to his international career, taking 5/17 in his first 12 overs.

Australia had long been searching for 'the new Alan Davidson', and when Gary Gilmour arrived on the scene, he seemed to be just the man. He took nine wickets at Headingley—six of them in the first innings. But he was to play only 15 Tests.

The Headingley Test was set up for an enthralling finish. Australia, set 445 to win, were to resume at 3/220, with McCosker on 95 and looking for his first Test century. However, overnight the pitch was vandalised with knives and oil—the work of a group campaigning for the release of an imprisoned criminal. The match was abandoned as a draw.

McCosker's maiden century came in the Fourth Test, at The Oval—his 127 the highest of his four Test centuries. McCosker shared a second-wicket partnership of 277 with Ian Chappell, whose 192 was his highest score against England. They helped Australia to what appeared to be a match-winning first innings lead of 341. But then came the England fightback.

England's second innings at The Oval of 538 (after 191 in the first innings) was due largely to Kent all-rounder Bob Woolmer, who'd made his debut in the Second Test before being dropped for the Third.

The 538 total at The Oval was England's highest in the second innings in a Test against Australia.

The final Test was played over six days—the last six-day Test in England, and the longest at 32 hours 17 minutes.

1975 AUSTRALIA WON SERIES 1–0

221 1st Test Edgbaston, Birmingham, July 10, 11, 12, 14
AUSTRALIA 359 (RW Marsh 61, RB McCosker 59, R Edwards 56, IM Chappell 52, JR Thomson 49)

ENGLAND 101 (DK Lillee 5/15, MHN Walker 5/48) and **173** (KWR Fletcher 51, JR Thomson 5/38)
CAPTAINS IM Chappell [AUST] MH Denness [ENG]
RESULT Australia won by an innings and 85 runs

222 2nd Test Lord's, July 31, August 1, 2, 4, 5
ENGLAND 315 (AW Greig 96, APE Knott 69, DS Steele 50, DK Lillee 4/84) and **7/436 dec** (JH Edrich 175, B Wood 52, DS Steele 45, AW Greig 41)
AUSTRALIA 268 (R Edwards 99, DK Lillee 73*, JA Snow 4/66) and **3/329** (IM Chappell 86, RB McCosker 79, GS Chappell 73*, R Edwards 52*)
CAPTAINS AW Greig [ENG] IM Chappell [AUST]
RESULT draw

223 3rd Test Headingley, Leeds, August 14, 15, 16, 18, 19 (no play)
ENGLAND 288 (DS Steele 73, JH Edrich 62, AW Greig 51, GJ Gilmour 6/85) and **291** (DS Steele 92, AW Greig 49)
AUSTRALIA 135 (PH Edmonds 5/28) and **3/220** (RB McCosker 95*, IM Chappell 62)
CAPTAINS AW Greig [ENG] IM Chappell [AUST]
RESULT draw

224 4th Test The Oval, August 28, 29, 30, September 1, 2, 3
AUSTRALIA 9/532 dec (IM Chappell 192, RB McCosker 127, KD Walters 65, R Edwards 44) and **2/40**
ENGLAND 191 (JR Thomson 4/50, MHN Walker 4/63) and **538** (RA Woolmer 149, JH Edrich 96, GRJ Roope 77, DS Steele 66, APE Knott 64, DK Lillee 4/91, KD Walters 4/34)
CAPTAINS IM Chappell [AUST] AW Greig [ENG]
RESULT draw

Centenary Test, 1977

The Centenary Test was staged to celebrate the 100th anniversary of the First Test between the teams led by Dave Gregory and James Lillywhite on the same ground back in 1877. In that time, 224 matches had been contested by the two countries in one of sport's most enduring rivalries. The architect of the Centenary Test was 72-year-old former Victorian and Australian medium pacer Hans Ebeling, who had played a lone Test, on the England tour of 1934. The result, as it was 100 years earlier . . . Australia by 45 runs.

By now, Ian Chappell had retired from Test cricket (although he resumed for World Series Cricket the following season and then returned briefly to the Test arena). Greg Chappell was leading Australia for the first time against England.

Remarkably, neither team reached 140 in the first innings, but both scored over 400 in the second.

Australia's openers were the NSW pair of Ian Davis, in his first Test against England, and McCosker, who suffered a broken jaw in the first innings when he missed a hook off Willis. He had the jaw wired and batted at number 10 in Australia's second innings, scoring 25 and sharing a vital 54-run partnership with Marsh.

Leg-spinner Kerry O'Keeffe, after a first innings duck at number nine, opened Australia's second innings with Davis, scoring 14 in a 33-run stand.

Twenty-one-year-old South Australian left-hander David Hookes was the only newcomer to Test cricket for this match. He'd been in sensational form during the summer with four successive centuries to force his way into the team. His second innings of 56 included five successive boundaries off Greig.

Mike Brearley, the scholarly Middlesex captain, was making his first appearance against Australia, opening with Woolmer. Brearley was soon to become one of England's most successful captains.

Marsh, who broke Wally Grout's Australian record of 187 Test dismissals during England's first innings, then produced his long-awaited maiden century in Ashes Tests. He scored 110 not out, becoming the first Australian keeper to score a hundred against England.

Derek Randall, the eccentric fielding whiz from Nottinghamshire, was making his first appearance against Australia in this match— his second innings 174 the highest of his three hundreds against Australia, and giving England a chance of victory.

England, set 463 for victory, were within 100 of the target with five wickets in hand, but O'Keeffe and Lillee then dismissed the tail . . . England losing 5/48.

Lillee, who took the final wicket (Underwood), finished with 11 for the match (6/26 and 5/139). It was one of four occasions he took 10 or more wickets in a match against England.

The Ashes weren't at stake in this one-off Test.

CENTENARY TEST, 1976–77

225 Melbourne Cricket Ground, March 12, 13, 14, 16, 17
AUSTRALIA 138 (GS Chappell 40) and **9/419 dec** (RW Marsh 110*, IC Davis 68, KD Walters 66, DW Hookes 56, CM Old 4/104)
ENGLAND 95 (DK Lillee 6/26, MHN Walker 4/54) and **417** (DW Randall 174, DL Amiss 64, JM Brearley 43, APE Knott 42, AW Greig 41, DK Lillee 5/139)
CAPTAINS GS Chappell [AUST] AW Greig [ENG]
RESULT Australia won by 45 runs

1977

This series was staged in the shadow of the most dramatic shake-up in cricket history. Kerry Packer's World Series Cricket was set to split the game wide open, involving most of the world's leading players. Most of the Australian tourists were about to defect, while Tony Greig's close involvement cost him the England captaincy— replaced by Mike Brearley. Played amid such acrimony, claim and counter-claim, the cricket was of secondary interest, and England regained the Ashes.

Three players made their Australian debuts for the First Test, at Lord's. Richie Robinson, the reserve wicketkeeper, played as an opening batsman; West Australian Craig Serjeant scored 81 batting at number four; and NSW fast bowler Len Pascoe (or Len Durtanovich as he was christened by his Yugoslav parents) took five wickets as the new-ball partner for his old Bankstown mate Thomson. Lillee missed the series through injury.

Woolmer scored three centuries in his 10 Ashes Tests—two of them in the first two Tests of this rubber (120 at Lord's and 137 at Old Trafford).

Willis had by now become the spearhead of the England attack. He took seven wickets in the first innings at Lord's and 27 for the series.

Brearley's first Test win over Australia came at Old Trafford in the second match of the rubber. He led his country in 18 England-Australia Tests for 11 wins.

The Third Test, at Trent Bridge, marked the debut of 21-year-old Somerset all-rounder Ian Botham who, over the years, was to become a match-winner for England and a villain for Australia. He took five wickets in Australia's first innings—the first of his 383 Test wickets, the Australian skipper Greg Chappell. He also took five wickets in the first innings of the Fourth Test, but was out injured for the Fifth.

Geoff Boycott hadn't played against Australia since 'Massie's Match' at Lord's in 1972. Eventually, he decided to return to Test cricket and was selected for the Third Test, scoring 107 and 80 not out, becoming the first England player to bat on each day of a five-day Test.

Boycott also scored 191 in the Fourth Test, at Headingley—the highest of his seven Ashes hundreds, and his 100th first-class century.

At Trent Bridge, Knott scored the biggest of his five Test centuries—his 135 the highest score by a wicketkeeper in England-Australia Tests. During that innings, he became the first wicketkeeper to reach 4000 Test runs.

England's innings victory at Headingley made it 3–nil, and under Brearley, England had regained the Ashes.

Kim Hughes, the bright batting star from Perth who was to become a key personality in Australian cricket over the next decade, made his debut in the Fifth Test, at The Oval. It was Australia's final Test before the advent of World Series Cricket. Ironically, Hughes became—perhaps more than any other player—caught in the rebels' crossfire over the next few seasons.

Another West Australian made his debut in the Fifth Test. Pace bowler Mick Malone took 5/63 in the first innings, and scored 46. Yet, due to his decision to sign with WSC, this turned out to be his only Test.

1977 ENGLAND WON SERIES 3–0

226 1st Test Lord's, June 16, 17, 18, 20, 21
ENGLAND 216 (RA Woolmer 79, DW Randall 53, JR Thomson 4/41) and **305** (RA Woolmer 120, AW Greig 91, JM Brearley 49, JR Thomson 4/86)
AUSTRALIA 296 (CS Serjeant 81, GS Chappell 66, KD Walters 53, RGD Willis 7/78) and **6/114** (DW Hookes 50)
CAPTAINS JM Brearley [ENG] GS Chappell [AUST]
RESULT draw

227 2nd Test Old Trafford, Manchester, July 7, 8, 9, 11, 12
AUSTRALIA 297 (KD Walters 88, GS Chappell 44) and **218** (GS Chappell 112, DL Underwood 6/66)
ENGLAND 437 (RA Woolmer 137, DW Randall 79, AW Greig 76) and **1/82** (JM Brearley 44)
CAPTAINS GS Chappell [AUST] JM Brearley [ENG]
RESULT England won by nine wickets

228 3rd Test Trent Bridge, Nottingham, July 28, 29, 30, August 1, 2
AUSTRALIA 243 (RB McCosker 51, KJ O'Keeffe 48*, IT Botham 5/74) and **309** (RB McCosker 107, DW Hookes 42, RGD Willis 5/88)
ENGLAND 364 (APE Knott 135, G Boycott 107, LS Pascoe 4/80) and **3/189** (JM Brearley 81, G Boycott 80*)
CAPTAINS GS Chappell [AUST] JM Brearley [ENG]
RESULT England won by seven wickets

229 4th Test Headingley, Leeds, August 11, 12, 13, 15
ENGLAND 436 (G Boycott 191, APE Knott 57, AW Greig 43, JR Thomson 4/113), LS Pascoe 4/91)
AUSTRALIA 103 (IT Botham 5/21, M Hendrick 4/41) and **248** RW Marsh 63, M Hendrick 4/54)
CAPTAINS JM Brearley [ENG] GS Chappell [AUST]
RESULT England won by an innings and 85 runs

230 5th Test The Oval, August 25 (no play), 26, 27, 29, 30
ENGLAND 214 (MF Malone 5/63), JR Thomson 4/87) and **2/57**
AUSTRALIA 385 (DW Hookes 85, MHN Walker 78*, RW Marsh 57, MF Malone 46, RGD Willis 5/102)
CAPTAINS JM Brearley [ENG] GS Chappell [AUST]
RESULT draw

1978–79

Without Greg Chappell and the established stars, Australia went into this six-Test rubber with a new-look team ill-prepared for an Ashes battle . . . especially against an England side headed by Brearley, whose leadership success was based on planning and pragmatism rather than by weight of runs. As a batsman, Brearley was a flop, failing to reach double figures in six of his 10 innings. But as a skipper he was a success, with England winning the series 5–1.

Graham Yallop, a 26-year-old Victorian left-hander, assumed the Australian captaincy for the First Test in his first encounter with

England, leading by example with a century in the second innings. He scored another in the Sixth Test—121 out of Australia's total of 198, and the only batsman to pass 20.

Both sides had new wicketkeepers in the First Test . . . Marsh and Knott had both gone to WSC, and their replacements were Queenslander John Maclean and Derbyshire veteran Bob Taylor. Both took five catches in the first innings.

South Australian fast bowler Rodney Hogg made the first of his 38 Test appearances in the opening match at the Gabba. His first innings 6/74 was to remain his best figures and his maiden score of 36 was his highest against England. Hogg shouldered the Australian attack and took 41 wickets for the series—breaking Arthur Mailey's record against England—and he took five wickets in each innings of the Second and Third Tests.

Australia's second innings in Brisbane featured not only Yallop's century, but also one by Hughes (129) . . . the first of three he was to score in 22 Tests against England.

David Gower, the elegant left-hander from Leicestershire, first played against Australia in the First Test, and in Perth he scored his first Ashes hundred (102).

During the series, Australia used four opening batsmen—Graeme Wood, Gary Cosier, Rick Darling and Andrew Hilditch. In each of the Tests, one of the openers was run out . . . Darling and Wood twice, Cosier and Hilditch once. The running between wickets of Wood and Darling was particularly nerve-wracking and they became known as the 'Kamikaze Kids'.

Senior Australian umpire Tom Brooks, under fire during the Perth Test, announced his retirement on the final day.

Allan Border, the chunky left-hander from Sydney, made his debut as a 23-year-old in the Third Test, in Melbourne, scoring 29 and the first of only three ducks in Tests against England. Australia welcomed Border with their only victory of the series.

The first of Border's record 156 catches was Gooch and the first of his 39 wickets was Brearley.

Border's fighting qualities became evident in his second match, when he scored 60 not out and 45 not out as wickets fell around him in Australia's 93-run defeat.

Australia's win in the Third Test ended a magical start for England under Brearley's leadership. It was his first loss in 16 Tests. England, though, won the Fourth Test, in Sydney, to retain the Ashes . . . the first time it had done so in Australia since 1954–55.

Maclean's international career started in the First Test and ended in the Fourth, when he left the field during England's first innings due to heat exhaustion. Yallop kept in his absence, catching Botham. Maclean was dropped for the Fifth Test, replaced by West Australian Kevin Wright.

The Fourth Test was one Boycott would rather forget. It gave him the only first-ball duck (lbw Hogg) of his long career.

Darling, whose 91 in the Fourth Test turned out to be his highest score in 14 Test matches, was carried from the Adelaide Oval on a stretcher during the Fifth Test. He'd been struck under the heart by a ball from Willis, and received life-saving treatment by England's John Emburey and umpire Max O'Connell.

England keeper Bob Taylor joined Darling as a player destined to narrowly miss an Ashes hundred. He scored 97 in the Fifth Test—his highest against Australia.

The series ended with England's 9-wicket win in the Sixth Test in Sydney. England, requiring another four runs for victory, lost a wicket and new batsman Randall was greeted by a rubber snake— courtesy of Rodney Hogg.

The final scoreline was 5–1. It was the first time England had won five Tests in a series in Australia.

1978–79 ENGLAND WON SERIES 5–1

231 1st Test Woolloongabba, Brisbane, December 1, 2, 3, 5, 6
AUSTRALIA 116 (RGD Willis 4/44) and **339** (KJ Hughes 129, GN Yallop 102)
ENGLAND 286 (DW Randall 75, IT Botham 49, DI Gower 44, RM Hogg 6/74, AG Hurst 4/93) and **3/170** (DW Randall 74, DI Gower 48*)
CAPTAINS GN Yallop [AUST] JM Brearley [ENG]
RESULT England won by seven wickets

232 2nd Test WACA Ground, Perth, December 15, 16, 17, 19, 20
ENGLAND 309 (DI Gower 102, G Boycott 77, G Miller 40, RM Hogg 5/65) and **208** (DW Randall 45, GA Gooch 43, RM Hogg 5/57)
AUSTRALIA 190 (PM Toohey 81*, RGD Willis 5/44) and **161** (GM Wood 64, GJ Cosier 47, JK Lever 4/28)
CAPTAINS JM Brearley [ENG] GN Yallop [AUST]
RESULT England won by 166 runs

233 3rd Test Melbourne Cricket Ground, December 29, 30, January 1, 2, 3
AUSTRALIA 258 (GM Wood 100, GN Yallop 41) and **167** (KJ Hughes 48)

ENGLAND 143 (RM Hogg 5/30) and **179** (DI Gower 49, GA Gooch 40, RM Hogg 5/36)
CAPTAINS GN Yallop [AUST] JM Brearley [ENG]
RESULT Australia won by 103 runs

234 4th Test Sydney Cricket Ground, January 6, 7, 8, 10, 11
ENGLAND 152 (IT Botham 59, AG Hurst 5/28) and **346** (DW Randall 150, JM Brearley 53, JD Higgs 5/148, RM Hogg 4/67)
AUSTRALIA 294 (WM Darling 91, AR Border 60*, KJ Hughes 48, GN Yallop 44) and **111** (AR Border 45*, JE Emburey 4/46)
CAPTAINS JM Brearley [ENG] GN Yallop [AUST]
RESULT England won by 93 runs

235 5th Test Adelaide Oval, January 27, 28, 29, 31, February 1
ENGLAND 169 (IT Botham 74, RM Hogg 4/26) and **360** (RW Taylor 97, G Miller 64, G Boycott 49, JE Emburey 42, AG Hurst 4/97)
AUSTRALIA 164 (IT Botham 4/42) and **160** (KJ Hughes 46)
CAPTAINS JM Brearley [ENG] GN Yallop [AUST]
RESULT England won by 205 runs

236 6th Test Sydney Cricket Ground, February 10, 11, 12, 14
AUSTRALIA 198 (GN Yallop 121, IT Botham 4/57) and **143** (B Yardley 61*, G Miller 5/44, JE Emburey 4/52)
ENGLAND 308 (GA Gooch 74, DI Gower 65, JM Brearley 46, JD Higgs 4/69) and **1/35**
CAPTAINS GN Yallop [AUST] JM Brearley [ENG]
RESULT England won by nine wickets

1979–80

The truce between cricket's establishment and Kerry Packer brought the World Series Cricket 'rebels' back to the fold. Australia played two Test rivals over the summer, the West Indies and England . . . both over three Tests, meaning the Ashes weren't up for grabs. Lucky for England, because with Greg Chappell regaining the Australian captaincy, Australia dominated the series, winning 3–0. The Ashes, though, stayed in England.

The First England-Australia Test in Perth became known as 'The Aluminium Bat Affair'. Lillee used an aluminium bat before being ordered to change it for a traditional appliance.

The man who was bowling to Lillee during 'The Aluminium Bat Affair' was Botham, who took 11 wickets in the match, and in the Third Test, in Melbourne, scored his first century against Australia (119 not out). There were to be many more heroic performances in 1981.

In the second innings of the Perth Test, Lillee was caught Willey bowled Dilley.

In the First Test, Border reach 1000 Test runs—just under 12 months after his debut. That was the quickest of all Australians in the 103 years of Test cricket to that stage. His second innings century (115) was his first against England.

Australia's woeful record of run-outs by opening batsmen in Tests against England extended to eight successive Tests. After one run-out in each of the six Tests of 1978–79, Victorian Julien Wiener, who made his debut in Perth, was run out in both the First and Second Tests. They were to be his only Tests against England in a six-match career.

This was a series of missed hundreds:
- Boycott finished unbeaten on 99 in the First Test, becoming the first England batsman to carry his bat through a completed innings without reaching a century. He was also the first player to finish 99 not out in a Test.
- Hughes scored 99 in Perth.
- Gower scored 3 and 98 not out in the Second Test, in Sydney—exactly the same scores as Greg Chappell in the same match.
- Gooch was out for 99 in the Third Test—run out going for the run that would have completed his maiden Test century.

Former captain Ian Chappell returned to the Australian side to face England for the first time since 1975. He played in the final two Tests to complete a 30-Test career against England.

Both Ian and Greg Chappell reached 2000 runs against England—Ian in the Second Test and Greg in the Third.

Bowling milestones in the series included:
- Thomson's 150th Test wicket (First Test, Miller).
- Underwood's 100th wicket against Australia (Second Test, Ian Chappell).
- Lillee's 100th wicket against England (First Test, Brearley) and 200th Test wicket (Third Test, Lever).

Lillee took 6/60 and 5/78 in Australia's Third Test win.

1979–80 AUSTRALIA WON SERIES 3–0

237 1st Test WACA Ground, Perth, December 14, 15, 16, 18, 19
AUSTRALIA 244 (KJ Hughes 99, RW Marsh 42, IT Botham 6/78) and **337** (AR Border 115, JM Wiener 58, GS Chappell 43, IT Botham 5/98)
ENGLAND 228 (JM Brearley 64, DK Lillee 4/73) and **215** (G Boycott 99*, G Dymock 6/34)
CAPTAINS GS Chappell [AUST] JM Brearley [ENG]
RESULT Australia won by 138 runs

238 2nd Test Sydney Cricket Ground, January 4, 5, 6, 8
ENGLAND 123 (DK Lillee 4/40, G Dymock 4/42) and **237** (DI Gower 98*, DL Underwood 43)
AUSTRALIA 145 (IM Chappell 42, IT Botham 4/29) and **4/219** (GS Chappell 98*, KJ Hughes 47, RB McCosker 41)
CAPTAINS JM Brearley [ENG] GS Chappell [AUST]
RESULT Australia won by six wickets

239 3rd Test Melbourne Cricket Ground, February 1, 2, 3, 5, 6
ENGLAND 306 (GA Gooch 99, JM Brearley 60*, G Boycott 44, DK Lillee 6/60) and **273** (IT Botham 119*, GA Gooch 51, DK Lillee 5/78, LS Pascoe 4/80)
AUSTRALIA 477 (GS Chappell 114, IM Chappell 75, BM Laird 74, AR Border 63, JK Lever 4/111) and **2/103** (GS Chappell 40*)
CAPTAINS JM Brearley [ENG] GS Chappell [ENG]
RESULT Australia won by eight wickets

Centenary Test, 1980

After the huge success of the 1977 Centenary Test in Melbourne, celebrating 100 years of Test cricket, another was held at Lord's in 1980—this time marking the centenary of the first Test match played in England. The Ashes were not at stake, and with rain interruptions, the match failed to live up to the drama of the Melbourne match three years earlier.

Botham led England for the first time against Australia, but failed to score and took only one wicket.

The West Australians Wood (112) and Hughes (117) scored Australia's centuries, with Hughes batting on all five days of the match.

Boycott, who'd also batted on each day of a five-day Test three years earlier, scored an unconquered century (128 not out) in the second innings, passing 7000 Test runs along the way.

Pascoe, whose Test career had been cut short by World Series Cricket, took five wickets in the first innings—his best return in six matches against England.

Umpires for the Centenary Test were Harold 'Dickie' Bird and David Constant . . . the latter of whom was threatened by angry members in front of Lord's Long Room after a pitch inspection.

CENTENARY TEST, 1980

240 Lord's, August 28, 29, 30, September 1, 2
AUSTRALIA 5/385 dec (KJ Hughes 117, GM Wood 112, AR Border 56*, GS Chappell 47) and **4/189 dec** (KJ Hughes 84, GS Chappell 59)
ENGLAND 205 (G Boycott 62, DI Gower 45, LS Pascoe 5/59, DK Lillee 4/43) and **3/244** (G Boycott 128*, MW Gatting 51*)
CAPTAINS GS Chappell [AUST] IT Botham [ENG]
RESULT draw

1961–1980
Questions 1–10

1 Who replaced John Maclean as Australia's wicketkeeper for the final two Tests of 1978–79?

2 Bob Simpson's maiden Test century, in his 30th Test, was 311 in England in 1964. At which venue?

3 Which England batsman had 10 consecutive scores of at least 50 in Adelaide, scoring 748 runs at 93.5?

4 Both captains were injured for the Fourth Test, at Edgbaston, in 1968, enabling two players to lead their countries in Tests for the only time in their careers. Who were they?

5 England lost the wicket of David Sheppard with only one run needed to win the Second Test of 1962–63. Was Sheppard:
a) Bowled
b) Run Out
c) Dismissed Hit Wicket

6 Which Victorian batsman scored two centuries on his maiden Ashes tour of 1961, averaging over 50?

7 Rod Marsh, Greg Chappell and Dennis Lillee all made their Test debuts in the 1970–71 series. Marsh and Chappell were two of three Australian first-gamers in the First Test in Brisbane . . . true or false?

8 England lost the services of three bowlers during The Oval Test of 1972. One was John Snow. Name one of the others.

9 Who opened the batting for Australia with Rick McCosker in the First Test, at Lord's, in 1977?

10 Which Australian batsman made his debut in the 1965–66 series, emulating the feat of Bill Ponsford with centuries in his first two Tests?

Questions 11–20

11 Australia's captain Bob Simpson missed the Brisbane Test of 1965–66 due to a fractured wrist, and the Sydney Test due to chickenpox. Who led Australia in his absence?

12 Only once in Ashes history has there been a 'Seventh Test'. Where and when was the Seventh Test?

13 Who was England's captain when Australia regained the Ashes in the Fourth Test of 1974–75?

14 Who was Bob Woolmer's opening partner for England in the 1977 Centenary Test?

15 What was the rhyming dismissal from the Perth Test in 1979–80?

16 Neil Harvey retired at the end of the 1962–63 series, having scored 21 Test centuries. How many of those centuries were against England?
a) six
b) 10
c) 11

17 Who was the Australian who finished his career averaging better than 50 against England, and yet started in Tests as a leg-spinner batting at number eight?

18 Which England captain of this era was also a pilot, a model, a racehorse owner, motor-bike rider, broadcaster and a fine golfer?

19 Lillee's first new-ball partner in Test cricket was Thomson . . . true or false?

20 Who's the 1956 Australian Olympian who scored two Ashes centuries, both in the 1962–63 series?

Questions 21–30

21 Which 42-year-old, who first played Test cricket in 1955, returned to the England side in the Perth match of 1974–75 for the first time in more than six years?

22 Which England batsman was dismissed for 99 in the Melbourne Test of 1979–80—run out going for his maiden Test century?

23 Australia's captain Richie Benaud missed the 1961 Lord's Test because of a shoulder injury. Who led Australia in his absence?

24 Australian bowler Tom Veivers took 3/155 in England's only innings at Old Trafford in 1964. Did he bowl:
   a) 47.3 overs
   b) 61.1 overs
   c) 95.1 overs

25 Which England bowler broke Alec Bedser's world record of 236 wickets in the Adelaide Test of 1962–63?

26 Who was the Australian batsman who, after being dropped for the Fourth Test of 1965–66, scored 307 when reinstated for the Fifth?

27 John Edrich, who scored a century in his maiden Ashes Test in 1964, is the son of Bill Edrich . . . true or false?

28 Who's the batsman who was chosen in the Australian side as Bill Lawry's replacement after Lawry was sacked as Australian skipper for the final Test of 1970–71?

29 Which Australian took 6/74 on debut in 1978–79, and an Ashes record 41 wickets for the series?

30 Who was the Kent opening batsman who scored the first Test century in Perth, and finished with a Test average of 56 on the 1970–71 tour?

Questions 31-40

31 Fast bowler Bob Willis made his first Australian tour in 1970–71, joining the touring party as a late replacement for which injured team-mate?

32 At which ground did Bob Massie take 16/137 on debut in 1972?

33 Which England batsman scored his 10th Test century, but his first in England, at Old Trafford in 1964 with 256?

34 What scoring feat do Hill, Macartney, Chipperfield, Miller, Bob Cowper in 1965–66 and Ross Edwards in 1975, all have in common?

35 Who was the Northamptonshire batsman who made his Test debut at Lord's in 1975, and, after becoming lost in the Lord's Pavilion, topped England's averages for the series?

36 Ian Chappell captained Australia in the 1977 Centenary Test . . . true or false?

37 Tony Greig captained England in four Ashes Tests for:
a) Four wins
b) Two wins
c) No wins

38 Which Australian fast bowler made his Test debut at Lord's in 1961, taking the first of his 96 Ashes wickets?

39 Who were the two captains for the 1972 series?

40 Which Australian bowler took his 84th and final Ashes wicket with the last ball he bowled in Tests, in Sydney in 1962–63?

Questions 41–50

41 The off-spinner Fred Titmus was Geoff Boycott's first opening partner in Test cricket . . . true or false?

42 Who's the Queensland batsman of the 1950s and 1960s who scored four Test centuries . . . all against England?

43 Which England bowler became the first player to reach 300 Test wickets?

44 Peter May captained England in the 1956 and 1958–59 series, and regained the captaincy for the last three Tests of 1961. Who led England in the first two Tests of that series?

45 Which son of a Sussex vicar started his county career as a batsman, and made his Ashes debut in 1968?

46 What was controversial about Bill Lawry's declaration with Australia 9/493 in the Fifth Test of 1970–71?

47 Which future Australian captain made his debut in the last Ashes Test before World Series Cricket?
a) Graham Yallop
b) Kim Hughes
c) Allan Border

48 Which West Australian batsman made his debut in 'Massie's Match', and scored 170 not out as an opener at Trent Bridge?

49 Who was the Australian opening batsman who played only two Ashes Tests, and was run out in both of them, during the 1979–80 series?

50 Which Australian batsman was 95 not out when play was abandoned at Headingley in 1975 after the pitch was vandalised?

ANSWERS *1961–1979/80*

1–10

1 Kevin Wright
2 Old Trafford
3 Ken Barrington
4 Barry Jarman (Australia) and Tom Graveney (England)
5 b) Run Out
6 Bill Lawry
7 False (Marsh played in the First Test, but Chappell's debut came in the Second Test, in Perth)
8 The other two were Basil D'Oliveira and Ray Illingworth
9 Richie Robinson (the reserve wicketkeeper)
10 Doug Walters

11–20

11 Brian Booth
12 Sydney, 1970–71
13 John Edrich (Mike Denness had stood down for the match due to poor form)
14 Mike Brearley
15 Lillee was caught Willey bowled Dilley
16 a) Six
17 Keith Stackpole
18 Ted Dexter
19 True (Alan 'Froggy' Thomson—not Jeff)
20 Brian Booth

21–30

21 Fred Titmus
22 Graham Gooch
23 Neil Harvey
24 c) 95.1 overs
25 Brian Statham
26 Bob Cowper
27 False (they were cousins)
28 Ken Eastwood
29 Rodney Hogg
30 Brian Luckhurst

31–40

31 Alan Ward
32 Lord's
33 Ken Barrington
34 They were all dismissed for 99 in a Test against England
35 David Steele
36 False (Greg Chappell was the captain)
37 c) No wins
38 Graham McKenzie
39 Ian Chappell and Ray Illingworth
40 Alan Davidson

41–50

41 True (he was elevated from number eight when John Edrich withdrew through injury just before the start of play)
42 Peter Burge
43 Fred Trueman
44 Colin Cowdrey
45 John Snow
46 Rod Marsh was 92 not out, and was denied the chance of becoming the first Australian wicketkeeper to score a Test hundred
47 b) Kim Hughes
48 Ross Edwards
49 Julien Wiener
50 Rick McCosker

Photo Quiz

Answers to photo quiz p. 215

9 **Third Test, Edgbaston, 1989.** a) **Who is the batsman?** b) **Who is the bowler?** c) **Who is the catcher?**

10 a) **What was the news?** b) **Where was the match?** c) **Which year?**

11 What did these Ashes players share in common in the 1968 series?

12 WG Grace. Legend has it that one Australian bowler once sent a delivery straight through his beard. Who was that bowler?

13 Second Test, Lord's, 1953. a) Who is the batsman? b) Who is the wicketkeeper? c) Who is the fieldsman?

14 This man played only one Test, but left his name firmly in the history of England–Australia Tests. Who is he and why?

15 This youngster went on to captain Australia. Who is he?

16 Third Test, Adelaide, 1982. a) Who is the batsman? b) Who is the bowler? c) Who is the catcher? d) Who is the wicketkeeper?

17 a) Who is the Australian fieldsman taking the first of his 31 catches in Tests against England? b) Who is the bowler?

Chapter Six

1981
-
1993

1981

The nightmare series. That's how Australians recall this six-match rubber, turned so dramatically by Ian Botham. After two Tests, with Botham struggling for form as England captain, Australia led 1–0, and seemed on course to regain the Ashes. But when Brearley took over for the Third Test, Botham cut loose, leading England to remarkable fightback victories at Headingley and Edgbaston. With a third win at Old Trafford, the home side clinched the series 3–1.

After more than a century of cricket in England, the First Test was the first time a Test was played without a scheduled rest day—and with play on a Sunday.

With Greg Chappell not touring, Hughes led the Australians—the first time he'd been captain in a Test against England.

Australia introduced two new players for the First Test, at Trent Bridge. Trevor Chappell, the younger brother of Ian and Greg, played in the first three Tests to start and finish his Test career. His selection meant that, for the first time, three brothers had represented Australia in Test matches. More successful was West Australian swing bowler Terry Alderman, who took the new ball with Lillee. His first wicket in the First Test was Boycott ... he took another eight for the match and, in total, a record 42 for the series.

Marsh took three catches off Alderman at Trent Bridge—the first of them (Woolmer) giving him a world record 244 Test catches, and 100 against England. He claimed the world record for overall dismissals in the Third Test (from Alan Knott). In the final Test, Marsh passed 3000 Test runs.

Australia's First Test win was their first at Trent Bridge since Bradman's final tour, in 1948. Defeat for England was the fourth, in 11 matches under Botham. Another draw in the Second Test, at Lord's, brought to an end his winless stint at captaincy.

Geoff Lawson, the young paceman from Wagga Wagga, was playing his first Ashes series, failing to take a wicket in the First Test, but then 7/81—his best against England—in the first innings of the Second. He missed the last three Tests through injury.

At Lord's, Boycott, by now 40, was making his 100th Test appearance.

England's 18-run win in the Third Test, at Headingley, came after Australia led by 227 on the first innings. Botham took six first innings wickets before top-scoring with 50. Then, with England 5/105 in their second innings—still 122 behind—he blasted 149 not out to give England a chance. He became the first England player to score a century and take five wickets in an innings in the same match against Australia.

With Botham having set up the Headingley comeback, Willis completed it. Australia, needing 130 to win, lost 9/55, with Willis taking his career-best 8/43.

England's situation was so bleak at Headingley that, on the morning of the fourth day, with England 1/6 in their second innings—still 221 runs in arrears—the bookmakers offered odds of 500/1 about an England win. Lillee and Marsh both placed bets in the unlikely event of their opponents getting up. They caused an outcry when news of their profits became known.

During the series, Brearley became England's most successful captain against Australia—his victory at Headingley was his ninth, passing the record of WG Grace.

Australia's torture continued in the Fourth Test, at Edgbaston, when, needing 151 to win, the last six wickets fell for only 16 runs—Botham taking 5/1—to give England a 29-run victory.

Queensland batsman Martin Kent, who'd already played for 'Australia' in World Series Cricket, made his official Test debut at Edgbaston. In the last three Tests, he had scores of 46, 52 and 54, but they were the only Tests of his career, which was cut short soon afterwards by a back injury.

Young NSW pace bowler Mike Whitney won a fairytale call-up from England league cricket to bolster Australia's attack for the final two Tests. He took five wickets and scored three ducks in four innings. Whitney went on to play 12 Tests, but was never selected for a full Ashes tour.

Lancashire's Paul Allott made his debut for England in the Fifth Test—memorable not for his bowling, but his batting, as he scored his maiden first-class half-century (at number 10).

At Old Trafford, Willis took his 100th wicket against Australia (Dyson) and Lillee took his 150th against England (Willis), while

Knott became the first England keeper to make 100 dismissals against Australia (Kent).

In the final Test, Willis became England's highest wicket-taker against Australia, taking the record from Wilfred Rhodes.

Botham scored two centuries in the series—his hundred (149 not out) in the Third Test coming off 87 balls, and his hundred (118) in the Fifth Test coming off 86 deliveries. He hit six sixes at Old Trafford ... the most for an England batsman in one innings against Australia. He also took 34 wickets, with 10 at The Oval taking his career total to 200—all in less than five years.

England used three wicketkeepers during the rubber—Paul Downton, Bob Taylor and Alan Knott.

Dirk Wellham, who went on to become the only player to captain three Sheffield Shield sides, made his debut at The Oval, scoring a century (103) ... just as he'd scored a century in his maiden first-class match.

Border, who was to eventually lead Australia in regaining the Ashes in England, scored unbeaten centuries in each of the final two Tests.

The reign of England captain Mike Brearley in Ashes Tests ended with the drawn final Test. Under Brearley, England were never beaten at home, and of 18 matches under his leadership, England won 11 and lost 4.

1981 ENGLAND WON SERIES 3–1

241 1st Test Trent Bridge, Nottingham, June 18, 19, 20, 21
ENGLAND 185 (MW Gatting 52, TM Alderman 4/68) and **125** (DK Lillee 5/46, TM Alderman 5/62)
AUSTRALIA 179 (AR Border 63) and **6/132** (GR Dilley 4/24)
CAPTAINS IT Botham [ENG] KJ Hughes [AUST]
RESULT Australia won by four wickets

242 2nd Test Lord's, July 2, 3, 4, 6, 7
ENGLAND 311 (P Willey 82, MW Gatting 59, GA Gooch 44, GF Lawson 7/81) and **8/265 dec** (DI Gower 89, G Boycott 60)
AUSTRALIA 345 (AR Border 64, RW Marsh 47, GM Wood 44, KJ Hughes 42, DK Lillee 40*) and **4/90** (GM Wood 62*)
CAPTAINS IT Botham [ENG] KJ Hughes [AUST]
RESULT draw

243 3rd Test Headingley, Leeds, July 16, 17, 18, 20, 21
AUSTRALIA 9/401 dec (J Dyson 102, KJ Hughes 89, GN Yallop 58, IT Botham 6/95) and **111** (RGD Willis 8/43)

ENGLAND 174 (IT Botham 50, DK Lillee 4/49) and **356** (IT Botham 149*, GR Dilley 56, G Boycott 46, TM Alderman 6/135)
CAPTAINS KJ Hughes [AUST] JM Brearley [ENG]
RESULT England won by 18 runs

244 4th Test Edgbaston, Birmingham, July 30, 31, August 1, 2
ENGLAND 189 (JM Brearley 48, TM Alderman 5/42) and **219** (RJ Bright 5/68)
AUSTRALIA 258 (KJ Hughes 47, MF Kent 46, JE Emburey 4/43) and **121** (AR Border 40, IT Botham 5/11)
CAPTAINS JM Brearley [ENG] KJ Hughes [AUST]
RESULT England won by 29 runs

245 5th Test Old Trafford, Manchester, August 13, 14, 15, 16, 17
ENGLAND 231 (CJ Tavare 69, PJW Allott 52*, DK Lillee 4/55, TM Alderman 4/88) and **404** (IT Botham 118, CJ Tavare 78, APE Knott 59, JE Emburey 57, TM Alderman 5/109)
AUSTRALIA 130 (MF Kent 52, RGD Willis 4/63) and **402** (AR Border 123*, GN Yallop 114, RW Marsh 47, KJ Hughes 43)
CAPTAINS JM Brearley [ENG] KJ Hughes [AUST]
RESULT England won by 103 runs

246 6th Test The Oval, August 27, 28, 29, 31, September 1
AUSTRALIA 352 (AR Border 106*, GM Wood 66, MF Kent 54, IT Botham 6/125, RGD Willis 4/91) and **9/344 dec** (DM Wellham 103, AR Border 84, RW Marsh 52, M Hendrick 4/82, IT Botham 4/128)
ENGLAND 314 (G Boycott 137, MW Gatting 53, DK Lillee 7/89) and **7/261** (MW Gatting 56, APE Knott 70*, JM Brearley 51, DK Lillee 4/70)
CAPTAINS KJ Hughes [AUST] JM Brearley [ENG]
RESULT draw

1982–83

With the Mike Brearley era over, England headed to Australia for a five-Test rubber under Bob Willis. The Australians still had the ageing stars Lillee and Marsh, while Greg Chappell—after missing the 1981 tour—was back as captain ahead of Hughes. Wins in Brisbane and Adelaide, followed by defeat in Melbourne, enabled Australia to regain the Ashes.

Australia suffered a setback on the second day of the opening Test in Perth, with Alderman—the star of the previous tour to England—suffering a dislocated shoulder after tackling an intruding spectator. The incident, which almost ended Alderman's career, led to the Australians leaving the field.

Off-spinner Bruce Yardley, who started out as a medium-pace bowler, claimed his best figures against England (5/107) in the First Test, when he also passed 100 Test wickets. He took 22 wickets for the series, and won the International Cricketer of the Year Award.

Botham began the series quietly, but in the First Test he took his Test runs tally to 3000 and his wicket tally to 250—the first player to achieve such a double.

Kent opener Chris Tavare earned the wrath of the Perth crowd. In total, he scored 98 (89 and 9), with two non-scoring patches amounting to 153 minutes ... he spent an hour and a half on 66, and then took over an hour to get off the mark in the second innings.

Kepler Wessels, born in South Africa and a man who'd later return to captain that country, made his debut for Australia in the Second Test, in Brisbane, scoring a century (162).

Carl Rackemann, a strapping paceman from the Queensland town of Wondai, also made his debut at the Gabba. But Australia's new-ball star was Lawson, who had his best match against England, with 11 wickets.

Marsh took an Ashes record six catches in the second innings in Brisbane and nine for the match, giving him 300 in total. His 28 catches for the rubber was a world record.

Willis failed to respect history when he won the toss in the Third Test. Peter May in 1958–59 and Mike Denness in 1974–75 had won the toss in Adelaide and sent Australia into bat. Willis did the same, and again it backfired ... Australia winning easily.

Lawson was to finish his 46-Test career with a batting average of 15.96 ... but in the Third Test he twice batted in the top half. As a nightwatchman, he went in at number five in the first innings and three in the second.

Chappell's Third Test century (115) was his first in Adelaide, and the last of his nine against England.

The Boxing Day Test in Melbourne provided one of cricket's great finishes. Australia, set 292 to win, were 9/218 before Border (62 not out) and Thomson (21) put on 70 for the last wicket ... four runs short of victory. Tavare missed the final catch, but Miller took it, off Botham's bowling—giving Botham 100 wickets and 1000 runs against Australia.

England's three-run win in Melbourne was their narrowest winning margin in 250 Ashes Tests. Australia had once had a three-run victory, at Old Trafford 80 years earlier.

Nottinghamshire off-spinner Eddie Hemmings—like Yardley, a late bloomer who started as a medium-pacer—first played against Australia in this series. In the Fifth Test, in Sydney, he was sent in as a nightwatchman, and scored 95.

1982–83 AUSTRALIA WON SERIES 2–1

247 1st Test WACA Ground, Perth, November 12, 13, 14, 16, 17
ENGLAND 411 (CJ Tavare 89, DW Randall 78, DI Gower 72, AJ Lamb 46, B Yardley 5/107) and **358** (DW Randall 115, AJ Lamb 56, DR Pringle 47*, GF Lawson 5/108)
AUSTRALIA 9/424 dec (GS Chappell 117, KJ Hughes 62, DW Hookes 56, J Dyson 52, GF Lawson 50, G Miller 4/70) and **2/73**
CAPTAINS RGD Willis [ENG] GS Chappell [AUST]
RESULT draw

248 2nd Test Woolloongabba, Brisbane, November 26, 27, 28, 30, December 1
ENGLAND 219 (AJ Lamb 72, IT Botham 40, GF Lawson 6/47) and **309** (G Fowler 83, G Miller 60, GF Lawson 5/87), JR Thomson 5/73)
AUSTRALIA 341 (KC Wessels 162, GS Chappell 53, B Yardley 53, RGD Willis 5/66) and **3/190** (DW Hookes 66*, KC Wessels 46)
CAPTAINS RGD Willis [ENG] GS Chappell [AUST]
RESULT Australia won by seven wickets

249 3rd Test Adelaide Oval, December 10, 11, 12, 14, 15
AUSTRALIA 438 (GS Chappell 115, KJ Hughes 88, KC Wessels 44, J Dyson 44, IT Botham 4/112) and **2/83**
ENGLAND 216 (AJ Lamb 82, DI Gower 60, GF Lawson 4/56) and **304** (DI Gower 114, IT Botham 58, GF Lawson 5/66)
CAPTAINS GS Chappell [AUST] RGD Willis [ENG]
RESULT Australia won by eight wickets

250 4th Test Melbourne Cricket Ground, December 26, 27, 28, 29, 30
ENGLAND 284 (CJ Tavare 89, AJ Lamb 83, RM Hogg 4/69, B Yardley 4/89) and **294** (G Fowler 65, IT Botham 46, DR Pringle 42, GF Lawson 4/66)
AUSTRALIA 287 (KJ Hughes 66, DW Hookes 53, RW Marsh 53, KC Wessels 47) and **288** (DW Hookes 68, AR Border 62*, KJ Hughes 48, NG Cowans 6/77)
CAPTAINS RGD Willis [ENG] GS Chappell [AUST]
RESULT England won by three runs

251 5th Test Sydney Cricket Ground, January 2, 3, 4, 6, 7
AUSTRALIA 314 (AR Border 89, J Dyson 79, IT Botham 4/75) and **382** (KJ Hughes 137, AR Border 83, KC Wessels 53, RW Marsh 41)
ENGLAND 237 (DI Gower 70, DW Randall 70, JR Thomson 5/50) and **7/314** (EE Hemmings 95, DW Randall 44, B Yardley 4/139)
CAPTAINS GS Chappell [AUST] RGD Willis [ENG]
RESULT draw

1985

With the ghosts of the 1981 tour still lingering, Australia returned to England for this six-Test series. It was the first under the leadership of Border, who ultimately, was to become the first captain since Woodfull in 1934 to regain the Ashes in England. But not this time. It was one-all with two Tests to play before the wheels fell off—England winning both by an innings, and under Gower, regaining the Ashes lost two years earlier.

Young Victorian all-rounder Simon O'Donnell made his Australian debut in the First Test, at Headingley. He played in the first five Tests, but then only one more before being diagnosed as suffering cancer in 1987. He successfully fought the disease but failed to add to his Test match tally.

Australia's vice-captain was Andrew Hilditch, whose roller-coaster career included NSW captaincy at 21 and Australian vice-captaincy at 22 (1978–79) before missing out on both sides at the end of World Series Cricket. By now in South Australia, he scored a century (119) in the First Test, but was then brought undone by the hook shot as the series wore on.

Nottinghamshire opener Tim Robinson became the 15th England batsman to score a century (175) in his first Ashes appearance. He led a remarkably consistent batting line-up to England's highest total against Australia at Headingley (533), with all but Gooch reaching double figures. Robinson also scored 148 in the Fifth Test, at Edgbaston, sharing a triple-century partnership with Gower for the second-wicket.

With Alderman in South Africa, Australia's new-ball attack was led by Lawson and 20-year-old Craig McDermott, who finished the series with 30 wickets, including 6/70 in England's first innings at Lord's and 8/141 in England's only innings at Old Trafford of 9/482 dec. (The other wicket to fall was run out.) He became the youngest Australian to take eight wickets in a Test innings.

Australia's reluctant wicketkeeper in all Tests was former opening batsman Wayne Phillips. Batting at number seven, he joined the '90s club', scoring 91 in the First Test. That remained his highest score against England.

Botham took seven wickets in each of the first two Tests and 31 for the rubber. In the Second Test he passed Willis as England's leading Test wicket-taker.

Australia's victory in the Second Test, at Lord's, was set up by a big first innings lead, with Border scoring 196 ... the highest score by an Australian captain at Lord's.

The Lord's win was completed by veteran leg-spinner Bob 'Dutchy' Holland, who was making his first Ashes appearance, at the age of 38. He took five wickets in the second innings.

Australia's innings of 539 in the Third Test was their highest at Trent Bridge—but was surpassed four years later. Wood's 172 was the highest, and last, of his three hundreds against England.

Australia's other century at Trent Bridge came from stocky Queenslander Greg Ritchie (146). He'd narrowly missed a century at Lord's and this turned out to be his only Test hundred against England.

Gower led from the front for England. His 166 in the Third Test is the highest by an England captain at Trent Bridge. His 215 in the Fifth Test remains England's highest score against Australia at Edgbaston, and his 157 in the final Test took his series aggregate to 732 at 81.3—passing Compton's record aggregate for an Ashes series in England.

New-ball bowler Arnie Sidebottom made his first and last appearance against Australia when he made his Test debut at Trent Bridge. He took just one wicket (Holland). He was the first Yorkshire player to represent England since Boycott's retirement.

Replacing Sidebottom for the Fourth Test was Leicestershire's Jonathon Agnew, who failed to take a wicket in his only Ashes appearance. Agnew is now a BBC commentator.

England's 9/482 dec in the Fourth Test, at Old Trafford, was dominated by Gatting—his 160 was his first century against Australia. His second (100 not out) came in the next match, at Edgbaston.

Australia had a stand-in opener in their second innings at Old Trafford—all-rounder Greg Matthews, in his first match against England, opened with Hilditch.

Thomson turned 35 on the second day of the Fifth Test, at Edgbaston. On the third day, he took the wicket of Gooch—his 100th against England and 200th overall in Tests. It was to be his final Test and last Test wicket.

Botham's record-breaking continued in the Fifth Test when he became England's highest wicket-taker against Australia—passing the mark set by Bob Willis.

Kent paceman Richard Ellison was a match-winner in his first Ashes appearance. At Edgbaston, he took six wickets in the first innings and four in 15 balls in the second to give England its innings victory. He also took seven wickets in the Sixth Test—his tally, a career-total of two Ashes Test was 17 wickets at 10.8.

Of England's 464 in the Sixth Test, at The Oval, 351 were scored in a second-wicket partnership between Gooch (196) and Gower (157). It was the second successive match in which Gower had figured in a triple-century stand, and it was Gooch's first century against Australia after 22 Ashes Tests.

1985 ENGLAND WON SERIES 3–1

252 1st Test Headingley, Leeds, June 13, 14, 15, 17, 18
AUSTRALIA 331 (AMJ Hilditch 119, GM Ritchie 46) and **324** (WB Phillips 91, AMJ Hilditch 80, KC Wessels 64, JE Emburey 5/82), IT Botham 4/107)
ENGLAND 533 (RT Robinson 175, IT Botham 60, PR Downton 54, MW Gatting 53, CJ McDermott 4/134) and **5/123**
CAPTAINS AR Border [AUST] DI Gower [ENG]
RESULT England won by five wickets

253 2nd Test Lord's, June 27, 28, 29, July 1, 2
ENGLAND 290 (DI Gower 86, AJ Lamb 47, CJ McDermott 6/70) and **261** (IT Botham 85, MW Gatting 75*, RG Holland 5/68)
AUSTRALIA 425 (AR Border 196, GM Ritchie 94, SP O'Donnell 48, IT Botham 5/109) and **6/127** (AR Border 41*)
CAPTAINS DI Gower [ENG] AR Border [AUST]
RESULT Australia won by four wickets

254 3rd Test Trent Bridge, Nottingham, July 11, 12, 13, 15, 16
ENGLAND 456 (DI Gower 166, MW Gatting 74, GA Gooch 70, GF Lawson 5/103) and **2/196** (RT Robinson 77*, GA Gooch 48)
AUSTRALIA 539 (GM Wood 172, GM Ritchie 146, AMJ Hilditch 47, SP O'Donnell 46)
CAPTAINS DI Gower [ENG] AR Border [AUST]
RESULT draw

255 4th Test Old Trafford, Manchester, August 1, 2, 3, 5, 6
AUSTRALIA 257 (DC Boon 61, AMJ Hilditch 49, SP O'Donnell 45, IT Botham 4/79, PH Edmonds 4/40) and **5/340** (AR Border 146*, KC Wessels 50, AMJ Hilditch 40, JE Emburey 4/99)
ENGLAND 9/482 dec (MW Gatting 160, GA Gooch 74, AJ Lamb 67, DI Gower 47, CJ McDermott 8/141)
CAPTAINS AR Border [AUST] DI Gower [ENG]
RESULT draw

256 5th Test Edgbaston, Birmingham, August 15, 16, 17, 19, 20
AUSTRALIA 335 (KC Wessels 83, GF Lawson 53, AR Border 45, RM Ellison 6/77)
and **142** (WB Phillips 59, RM Ellison 4/27)
ENGLAND 5/595 dec (DI Gower 215, RT Robinson 148, MW Gatting 100*,
AJ Lamb 46)
CAPTAINS AR Border [AUST] DI Gower [ENG]
RESULT England won by an innings and 118 runs

257 6th Test The Oval, August 29, 30, 31, September 2
ENGLAND 464 (GA Gooch 196, DI Gower 157, GF Lawson 4/101,
CJ McDermott 4/108)
AUSTRALIA 241 (GM Ritchie 64*) and **129** (AR Border 58, RM Ellison 5/46)
CAPTAINS DI Gower [ENG] AR Border [AUST]
RESULT England won by an innings and 94 runs

1986–87

*Over the past decade Australian cricket had been traumatised by
World Series Cricket, and then by the rebel tour to South Africa.
Under Border, the rebuilding programme was taking shape as
Gatting led England on this five-Test series. Success for Australia
wasn't far away, but not yet. England—although without a single
tourist from Yorkshire or Lancashire for the first time—won the
First Test, and then victory in the Fourth Test ensured the retention
of the Ashes, despite Australia's belated win in the final match.*

A new look was beginning to appear about the Australian side.
Giant Perth left-arm paceman Bruce Reid—the tallest man to play
in Ashes Tests—took 20 wickets in his first series against England,
while Victorian Merv Hughes took 10 wickets . . . also in his first
Ashes rubber.

A third member of Australia's First Test attack was another Perth
left-armer on debut, Chris Matthews. He took three wickets but
struggled for control and his Test career lasted only three
matches.

England was widely criticised going into the First Test, with a now-
famous barb: 'England can't bat, can't bowl and can't field'.

The only 'Z' to represent Australia, Tim Zoehrer, was Australia's
wicketkeeper in four Tests—his only matches against England. He

missed the Third Test through injury, when Greg Dyer made his Test debut.

England also had a new keeper—Surrey's Jack Richards who, in the Second Test, in Perth, joined Les Ames and Alan Knott as England keepers to score an Ashes hundred (133).

England introduced 20-year-old all-rounder Philip de Freitas to Ashes cricket for the First Test, in Brisbane. Born in Dominica, de Freitas made quite an impression, scoring 40 and taking five wickets for the match.

However, it was England's senior all-rounder who stole the show in Brisbane. Botham's 138 remains England's highest score at the Gabba, and it included an Ashes record 22 off one over from Hughes.

Geoff Marsh and David Boon combined as openers for the first time in an Ashes Test in Brisbane. Marsh scored 56 and 110 in his maiden appearance against England. Boon also scored a century, in the Third Test, but otherwise struggled and was dropped for Wellham for the final Test.

England's 8/592 dec in Perth was their highest score in Australia for almost 60 years, with opener Chris Broad's 162 the highest by an England player at the WACA. His partner Bill Athey scored 96 in an England opening stand of 223. Broad also scored centuries in Adelaide and Melbourne, joining Hobbs, Sutcliffe and Hammond as the only England batsmen to score three hundreds in a series in Australia.

Border's 125 in Perth was Australia's 200th hundred in an Ashes Test. His seventh century against England (100 not out) came in the Third Test, in Adelaide.

Twenty-one-year-old all-rounder Steve Waugh hit back at his doubters in the Perth Test. Batting at three, he scored 71 and then took 5/69 in England's second innings. He also scored 79 not out in the Third Test, and 73 in the Fifth.

Gatting's first innings 100 in Adelaide was followed by a second innings duck. Likewise Boon, who failed to score after his 103.

James Whitaker made his Test debut in Adelaide, and with Gower and de Freitas, Leicestershire had three players in a Test for the first time.

England's innings victory in the Fourth Test, in Melbourne, came in three days—their first three-day win in Australia for more than

80 years, with Gatting joining Chapman, Hutton and Brearley as the only England captains to retain the Ashes in Australia this century.

Gladstone Small, who'd played Sheffield Shield cricket for South Australia, made his first Ashes appearance in Melbourne, taking seven wickets.

Little-known off-spinner Peter Taylor was chosen for his Test debut in the final match, in Sydney . . . some reckoned it was a mistake by the selectors, with opening batsman Mark Taylor hotly pressing his claims. But 'Peter Who?' turned out to be a match-winner with a match aggregate of eight wickets and 53 runs.

Victorian Dean Jones scored the first and biggest of his three Ashes hundreds (184 not out) in a lone hand in Australia's first innings in Sydney.

Emburey's best performance against Australia came in the Sydney Test when he took seven wickets in Australia's second innings. But when he was bowled by leg-spinner Peter Sleep late on the final day, Australia had won . . . ending a sequence of 14 matches without victory.

Sleep's five-wicket second innings haul was the best of his 14-Test career.

1986–87 ENGLAND WON SERIES 2–1

258 1st Test Woolloongabba, Brisbane, November 14, 15, 16, 18, 19
ENGLAND 456 (IT Botham 138, CWJ Athey 76, MW Gatting 61, DI Gower 51, AJ Lamb 40, PAJ DeFreitas 40) and **3/77**
AUSTRALIA 248 (GR Marsh 56, GRJ Matthews 56*, GM Ritchie 41, GR Dilley 5/68) and **282** (GR Marsh 110, GM Ritchie 45, JE Emburey 5/80)
CAPTAINS MW Gatting [ENG] AR Border [AUST]
RESULT England won by seven wickets

259 2nd Test WACA Ground, Perth, November 28, 29, 30, December 2, 3
ENGLAND 8/592 dec (BC Broad 162, DI Gower 136, CJ Richards 133, CWJ Athey 96, BA Reid 4/115) and **8/199 dec** (MW Gatting 70, DI Gower 48, SR Waugh 5/69)
AUSTRALIA 401 (AR Border 125, SR Waugh 71, GRJ Matthews 45, GR Dilley 4/79) and **4/197** (DM Jones 69, GR Marsh 49)
CAPTAINS MW Gatting [ENG] AR Border [AUST]
RESULT draw

260 3rd Test Adelaide Oval, December 12, 13, 14, 15, 16
AUSTRALIA 5/514 dec (DC Boon 103, DM Jones 93, SR Waugh 79*, GRJ Matthews 73*, AR Border 70, GR Marsh 43) and **3/201 dec** (AR Border 100*, GM Ritchie 46*, GR Marsh 41)

ENGLAND 455 (BC Broad 116, MW Gatting 100, CWJ Athey 55, JE Emburey 49, BA Reid 4/64, PR Sleep 4/132) and **2/39**
CAPTAINS AR Border [AUST] MW Gatting [ENG]
RESULT draw

261 4th Test Melbourne Cricket Ground, December 26, 27, 28
AUSTRALIA 141 (DM Jones 59, GC Small 5/48, IT Botham 5/41) and **194** (GR Marsh 60, SR Waugh 49)
ENGLAND 349 (BC Broad 112, AJ Lamb 43, MW Gatting 40, CJ McDermott 4/83, BA Reid 4/78)
CAPTAINS AR Border [AUST] MW Gatting [ENG]
RESULT England won by an innings and 14 runs

262 5th Test Sydney Cricket Ground, January 10, 11, 12, 14, 15
AUSTRALIA 343 (DM Jones 184*, GC Small 5/75) and **251** (SR Waugh 73, AR Border 49, PL Taylor 42, JE Emburey 7/78)
ENGLAND 275 (DI Gower 72, JE Emburey 69, CJ Richards 46, PL Taylor 6/78) and **264** (MW Gatting 96, PR Sleep 5/72)
CAPTAINS AR Border [AUST] MW Gatting [ENG]
RESULT Australia won by 55 runs

Bicentenary Test, 1988

This Test was staged to celebrate the 200th anniversary of white settlement in Australia, but it failed to live up to the pre-match hype. For three days England was in control, but a rearguard fightback by Australia ensured the match would end in a draw.

Only the not out batsman (Hemmings) failed to reach double figures in a consistent England batting display—highlighted by a century (139) by Broad. It was his fourth hundred in six Tests in Australia, and all were scored at different venues. At the end of it all, he smashed his stumps and was heavily fined by the England tour management.

England had three players new to England-Australia Tests. Martin Moxon opened the batting with Broad, and all-rounder David Capel and wicketkeeper Bruce French were both playing against Australia for the first time.

Australia had two players appearing against England for the first time—batsman Mike Veletta, and Tony Dodemaide, who shared the new-ball with McDermott. It was to be their only Test matches against England.

Dyer was chosen for his second and final Test against England. He took one catch and made two stumpings before being hit on the nose. Veletta took the gloves for the final part of England's innings.

Peter Taylor was the star the previous time England had played at the SCG. He again did well in this match, taking the Australian bowling honours with 4/84.

Trailing by 211 on the first innings, Australia was forced to follow-on on the fourth day. Boon (184 not out) and Marsh (56) then put on 162 for the first wicket to thwart England's hopes of victory. This remains Australia's highest opening partnership against England in Sydney.

BICENTENARY TEST, 1987–88

263 Sydney Cricket Ground, January 29, 30, 31, February 1, 2
ENGLAND 425 (BC Broad 139, BN French 47, RT Robinson 43, MD Moxon 40, PL Taylor 4/84)
AUSTRALIA 214 (DM Jones 56, PR Sleep 41) and **2/328** (DC Boon 184*, GR Marsh 56, AR Border 48*)
CAPTAINS MW Gatting [ENG] AR Border [AUST]
RESULT draw

1989

Australia had waited a long time for this series. Border's team arrived in England unheralded, and a close series was anticipated. But the Australians found dry pitches to the liking of their array of young batting talent, and they had Alderman back for the first time since his record-breaking rout of 1981. Gower was back in charge of the England side, but his wasn't a happy lot. Australia steam-rolled through the series, winning 4–0 and regaining the Ashes lost four years earlier. And significantly, it was the first time Australia had regained the Ashes in England since 1934.

Tasmanian paceman Greg Campbell—a surprise choice in the touring party—made his debut in the First Test, at Headingley.

He took the wicket of Derek Pringle, then played no further part in the series. It was to be his only Ashes Test.

Alderman picked up from where he left off eight years earlier, with five wickets in each innings at Headingley. He took at least five wickets in an innings in each Test except the Third, at Edgbaston, and finished with 41 wickets—becoming the first bowler to twice take more than 40 wickets in a series.

Australia's 7/601 dec was a record for all Tests at Headingley, with the NSW pair of Mark Taylor (136) and Steve Waugh (177 not out) both scoring their first centuries against England. It was Taylor's maiden Test against England, while Waugh continued his good form with 152 not out in the Second Test, at Lord's.

Waugh finally gained an average—393—when he was out for 43 in the Third Test, at Edgbaston.

Australia's First Test win was their first at Headingley since 1964 and took the ground's Ashes record to 6 wins apiece.

South African-born Allan Lamb, who migrated to England in 1977, scored his first Ashes hundred (125) in the Headingley match, passing 3,000 Test runs along the way.

Australia's impressive record at Lord's extended to 11 wins, with only five defeats—the last in 1934.

RJ Sims, a name not usually associated with Test cricket, will always remember the Lord's Test. Sims was a member of the MCC groundstaff and found himself substituting in the field for England on the final day, when he accepted a catch from Border . . . the Australian skipper out for 1.

England had made four changes after the First Test, and another four after the Second, when Botham returned to the side after a long absence. He failed to make an impression in three Tests.

The Third Test was the eighth Ashes encounter at Edgbaston. Jones' 157 was Australia's highest score at the ground—passing the only other century, 114 by Harvey in 1961.

Middlesex medium-pacer Angus Fraser made his England debut in the Third Test, taking four wickets.

Drama on the final morning of the Fourth Test, at Old Trafford, with news that Emburey, Robinson and Foster were among players who'd signed to join a rebel tour of South Africa. They were overlooked for the final two Tests.

Former England Test batsman and Tasmanian Shield player John Hampshire made his Test umpiring debut in the match at Old Trafford.

Australia's nine-wicket win to regain the Ashes at Old Trafford— completed by Tasmanian David Boon—was their 100th against England.

England wicketkeeper Jack Russell scored a fighting century in the Fourth Test (128 not out), becoming the first England player to score his maiden first-class century in a Test against Australia.

Mike Atherton, who would assume the England captaincy during the next home Ashes series, made his debut in the Fifth Test, at Trent Bridge, falling for a duck in his first innings.

The Fifth Test was dominated by Australia's openers, Marsh (138) and Taylor (219), who became the first pair to bat throughout a full day in England. They ended up with 329—an Ashes record and a record for all Tests in England. Taylor's double-century was Australia's first against England since Stackpole's 207 in 1970-71. Taylor ended up with a series aggregate of 839 runs—the third highest in Test history behind Bradman and Hammond.

In reply to Australia's 6/602 dec, England made a disastrous start, with Alderman dismissing Moxon (0), Atherton (0) and Curtis (2) to leave England 3/14.

Australia's win at Trent Bridge by an innings and 180 runs was their biggest innings victory in England.

Gower was elevated to open the England second innings at Trent Bridge with Curtis (Moxon dropping down to five).

Two more England players (Alan Igglesden and John Stephenson) made their debuts in the Sixth Test, at The Oval, taking the number of England players used in the series to 29— one short of the 1921 record.

Australia passed 600 twice in the series, 500 once more, and 400 in each first innings of the remaining three Tests.

1989 AUSTRALIA WON SERIES 4-0

264 1st Test Headingley, Leeds, June 8, 9, 10, 12, 13
AUSTRALIA 7/601 dec (SR Waugh 177*, MA Taylor 136, DM Jones 79, MG Hughes 71, AR Border 66) and **3/230 dec** (MA Taylor 60, AR Border 60*, DC Boon 43, DM Jones 40*)

ENGLAND 430 (AJ Lamb 125, KJ Barnett 80, RA Smith 66, TM Alderman 5/107) and **191** (GA Gooch 68, TM Alderman 5/44)
CAPTAINS AR Border [AUST] DI Gower [ENG]
RESULT Australia won by 210 runs

265 2nd Test Lord's, June 22, 23, 24, 26, 27
ENGLAND 286 (RC Russell 64*, GA Gooch 60, DI Gower 57, MG Hughes 4/71) and **359** (DI Gower 106, RA Smith 96, TM Alderman 6/128)
AUSTRALIA 528 (SR Waugh 152*, DC Boon 94, GF Lawson 74, MA Taylor 62, JE Emburey 4/88) and **4/119** (DC Boon 58*)
CAPTAINS DI Gower [ENG] AR Border [AUST]
RESULT Australia won by six wickets

266 3rd Test Edgbaston, Birmingham, July 6, 7, 8, 10, 11
AUSTRALIA 424 (DM Jones 157, MA Taylor 43, SR Waugh 43, GR Marsh 42, TV Hohns 40, ARC Fraser 4/63) and **2/158** (MA Taylor 51, GR Marsh 42)
ENGLAND 242 (IT Botham 46, RC Russell 42, TS Curtis 41)
CAPTAINS AR Border [AUST] DI Gower [ENG]
RESULT draw

267 4th Test Old Trafford, Manchester, July 27, 28, 29, 31, August 1
ENGLAND 260 (RA Smith 143, GF Lawson 6/72) and **264** (RC Russell 128*, JE Emburey 64, TM Alderman 5/66)
AUSTRALIA 447 (SR Waugh 92, MA Taylor 85, AR Border 80, DM Jones 69, GR Marsh 47) and **1/81**
CAPTAINS DI Gower [ENG] AR Border [AUST]
RESULT Australia won by nine wickets

268 5th Test Trent Bridge, Nottingham, August 10, 11, 12, 14
AUSTRALIA 6/602 dec (MA Taylor 219, GR Marsh 138, DC Boon 73, AR Border 65*)
ENGLAND 255 (RA Smith 101, TM Alderman 5/69) and 167 (MA Atherton 47)
CAPTAINS AR Border [AUST] DI Gower [ENG]
RESULT Australia won by an innings and 180 runs

269 6th Test The Oval, August 24, 25, 26, 28, 29
AUSTRALIA 468 (DM Jones 122, AR Border 76, MA Taylor 71, DC Boon 46, IA Healy 44, DR Pringle 4/70) and **4/219 dec** (AR Border 51*, DM Jones 50, MA Taylor 48)
ENGLAND 285 (DI Gower 79, GC Small 59, TM Alderman 5/66) and **5/143** (RA Smith 77*)
CAPTAINS AR Border [AUST] DI Gower [ENG]
RESULT draw

1990–91

Graham Gooch was the man in England's hotseat for this series. With England licking their wounds after the 4–0 drubbing in

1989, Gooch assumed the captaincy—his style simple: leadership through weight of runs. He'd just amassed more than 1,000 runs in six Tests against New Zealand and India, and England needed more of the same here. Gooch didn't let his side down but his team- mates did, letting slip opportunities to take control of matches as Australia's fighting spirit came to the fore. Apart from the '89 stars, Australia had an additional trump card—Bruce Reid, who set the home side on course for a 3–0 win to retain the Ashes.

Reid was making his third comeback after five back operations which culminated in a five centimetre plate being inserted in his lower spine. After five wickets in the First Test, at the Gabba, he took 13/148 in the Second, in Melbourne. It was the first time he'd taken five wickets in a Test innings, and naturally, his first bag of 10 or more wickets.

Gooch missed the opening Test due to surgery on a poisoned finger—injured while fielding off his own bowling against team- mate Robin Smith at practice on the fourth day of the tour. He played in the Second Test, in Melbourne, but made a poor start— lbw to bogeyman Alderman for the seventh time. However, then followed five scores of 50 or more and he was the only England batsman to average better than 50.

Allan Lamb captained England in the First Test in the absence of Gooch. During the match, he passed 4000 Test runs.

Australian opener Mark Taylor also suffered a finger injury, at his home town of Wagga, two weeks before the First Test. He missed a Shield match, but was declared fit for the Gabba Test, scoring 67 not out in guiding Australia to its 10-wicket win. However, he had a poor series, averaging only 23.6.

Border, on his home ground in Brisbane, was appearing in his 200th Test innings. He scored only 9.

Man-of-the-match Alderman came back to haunt England in the second innings at the Gabba, with his career best figures of 6/47 as England crashed to 114—its lowest score in Brisbane. It was the 14th and final time he took five or more wickets in a Test innings.

Queensland Shield player Peter Cantrell had a taste of Test cricket at the Gabba, taking the catches of Stewart and Fraser while fielding as a substitute.

Australia's First Test victory came inside three days—the first time for Australia in an Ashes Test since Headingley in 1938.

In the Second Test, in Melbourne, Border was leading Australia for the 20th consecutive match against England—an Ashes record.

Gower, in his final Test in Melbourne, reached 3000 runs against Australia with his eighth Ashes century (100) ... yet his first at the MCG. In the second innings, he was out for a duck—his first in 119 Test innings.

Wicketkeeper Jack Russell made six dismissals in Australia's first innings in Melbourne—a record for England against Australia. Three catches came off Fraser's bowling—his figures a career-best 6/82.

Boon (94 not out) and Marsh (79 not out) led Australia to their eight-wicket win in Melbourne—both passing 1,000 runs against England along the way.

In the Third Test, in Sydney, 22-year-old Lancastrian Mike Atherton scored the slowest century (105) in Tests between Australia and England—424 minutes. He'd been dropped twice and given not out when replays indicated he had been run out on 94.

Gooch scored his 6000th run in the Sydney Test, while Gower, with a second successive Test century (123), passed 8,000 runs during the match.

Australian fast bowler Carl Rackemann entered the batting record books in the Sydney Test—the longest time for an Australian to get off the mark, 72 minutes, in helping Australia avoid possible defeat.

All-rounder Greg Matthews scored his fourth Test century (128) on his home ground during the Third Test. He finished second to Boon in the batting aggregates (353) and averages (70.6).

Cockney left-arm spinner Phil Tufnell, after failing to take a wicket on debut in the Second Test, took five wickets in Australia's second innings in Sydney, and almost took a hat-trick. He'd had Border caught by Gooch ... next ball he caught and bowled Jones ... and then Steve Waugh was dropped first-ball by Gower at bat-pad.

During the Third Test, Healy was struck above the eye by a Matthews delivery. He left the field for stitches and Taylor took the gloves.

After the Third Test, Gower and team-mate John Morris hired a Tiger Moth and 'buzzed' the Carrara ground on the Gold Coast during play against Queensland as a salute to Robin Smith's return to form. England's tour management fined each player 1000 pounds, of which Gower remarked: "I'm not ecstatic about paying a thousand pounds for 20 minutes in the air. It's more than commercial rates and, in these times of deregulation, it's a scandal."

Mark Waugh was chosen to make his Australian debut in the Fourth Test, in Adelaide—at the expense of older twin Steve, who broke the news to him. After 100 first-class matches, Mark scored 138 in his Test debut.

England replaced regular keeper Russell in the Fourth Test for an extra batsman, with Alec Stewart behind the stumps.

Taylor was run out twice in the Adelaide Test—just as he was against the West Indies at the same ground two seasons earlier.

McDermott, in his comeback match after two years on the outer, took 5/97 in England's first innings in Adelaide. He then completed the series by taking 8/97 in the first innings of the final Test, in Perth, and 11 for the match.

England had to bat through the final day to save the Fourth Test, and a record opening stand for England in Adelaide of 203 between Gooch (117) and Atherton (87) ensured the draw.

England called on two additional players during the tour ... Hugh Morris as a back-up for Gooch, and paceman Phil Newport for Angus Fraser, who missed the Third Test with a hip injury, and then aggravated the injury in the Fourth Test. Newport played in the final Test.

Alderman's three second innings wickets in Perth took him to 100 against England in 17 Tests—equal-fastest with Charles 'Terror' Turner a century earlier.

Australia's series win was their third 3–0 scoreline in an Ashes series, following the 1921 and 1946–47 series.

1990–91 AUSTRALIA WON SERIES 3–0

270 1st Test Woolloongabba, Brisbane, November 23, 24, 25
ENGLAND 194 (DI Gower 61, BA Reid 4/53) and **114** (TM Alderman 6/47)
AUSTRALIA 152 and **0/157** (GR Marsh 72*, MA Taylor 67*)

CAPTAINS AJ Lamb [ENG] AR Border [AUST]
RESULT Australia won by 10 wickets

271 2nd Test Melbourne Cricket Ground, December 26, 27, 28, 29, 30
ENGLAND 352 (DI Gower 100, AJ Stewart 79, W Larkins 64, BA Reid 6/97) and
150 (GA Gooch 58, W Larkins 54, BA Reid 7/51)
AUSTRALIA 306 (AR Border 62, MA Taylor 61, DM Jones 44, ARC Fraser 6/82)
and **2/197** (DC Boon 94*, GR Marsh 79*)
CAPTAINS GA Gooch [ENG] AR Border [AUST]
RESULT Australia won by eight wickets

272 3rd Test Sydney Cricket Ground, January 4, 5, 6, 7, 8
AUSTRALIA 518 (GRJ Matthews 128, DC Boon 97, AR Border 78, DM Jones
60, SR Waugh 48, DE Malcolm 4/128) and **205** (IA Healy 69, PCR Tufnell 5/61)
ENGLAND 8/469 dec (DI Gower 123, MA Atherton 105, AJ Stewart 91, GA Gooch
59) and **4/113** (GA Gooch 54)
CAPTAINS AR Border [AUST] GA Gooch [ENG]
RESULT draw

273 4th Test Adelaide Oval, January 25, 26, 27, 28, 29
AUSTRALIA 386 (ME Waugh 138, GRJ Matthews 65, DC Boon 49,
CJ McDermott 42*, PAJ DeFreitas 4/56) and **6/314** (DC Boon 121, AR Border 83*)
ENGLAND 229 (GA Gooch 87, RA Smith 53, PAJ DeFreitas 45,
CJ McDermott 5/97, BA Reid 4/53) and **5/335** (GA Gooch 117, MA Atherton 87,
AJ Lamb 53)
CAPTAINS AR Border [AUST] GA Gooch [ENG]
RESULT draw

274 5th Test WACA Ground, Perth, February 1, 2, 3, 5
ENGLAND 244 (AJ Lamb 91, RA Smith 58, CJ McDermott 8/97) and **182**
(RA Smith 43, PJ Newport 40*, MG Hughes 4/37)
AUSTRALIA 307 (DC Boon 64, GRJ Matthews 60*, IA Healy 42) and **1/120**
(GR Marsh 63*)
CAPTAINS GA Gooch [ENG] AR Border [AUST]
RESULT Australia won by nine wickets

1993

*So much had been achieved by Australia in England in 1989 that
the '93 tourists had inherited a tough act to follow. Without
Alderman and Lawson, the attack didn't seem as menacing, and
surely England couldn't be in as much disarray as four years
earlier ... But this was to be Border's Ashes swansong and the
Australians planned to farewell him with another demolition of the
old enemy. And that's just the way it turned out. Australia had
retained the Ashes with a 3–0 lead after four Tests, then made it*

4–0 at Edgbaston before England broke through for a long-awaited win in the final match at The Oval. Australia 4–1.

Two players made their debuts for England in the First Test at Old Trafford ... former New Zealander Andy Caddick, who took just one wicket, and Scottish-born off-spinner Peter Such, whose first innings 6/67 was the best Ashes debut by an England bowler since Fred Martin's 12-wicket match in 1890. Such ended up with 16 wickets for the series—England's leading wicket-taker.

Australia also had two players on debut at Old Trafford ... West Australian all-rounder Brendon Julien (also born in New Zealand), and NSW opener Michael Slater, who scored 58 in his first innings and shared a 128-run opening partnership with Taylor (124) ... a record for Wagga Wagga opening batsmen in Test cricket!

Leg-spinner Shane Warne, in his first Ashes match, claimed a wicket with his first ball—bowling Gatting with what became known as a 'Jaffa'. He took 34 wickets for the series and his off-spinning partner Tim May took 21—between them a record 55 wickets for an Australian spin pair in England.

Gooch, who captained England in the first four Tests before resigning, scored his third Ashes century (133) in the second innings at Old Trafford before being given out 'handled ball' ... the first England player to be dismissed in such a way in a Test match.

Healy hadn't scored a first-class hundred going into the series, but at Old Trafford he scored 102 not out, becoming the first Australian since Harry Graham 100 years earlier to score his maiden first-class century in an Ashes Test. He also joined Rod Marsh and Wayne Phillips as the only Australian keepers to score Test hundreds.

Australia's first three batsmen, Taylor (111), Slater (152) and Boon (164 not out) all scored centuries in the first innings of the Second Test, at Lord's, while Mark Waugh then joined the '99-Club'. Atherton joined him in England's second innings.

Slater's maiden Test century came in his second match, and with Taylor, he put on an Ashes all-wicket record at Lords of 260. Australia's 4/632 dec was their second-highest total at Lord's.

Boon's century at Lord's was his first in England after falling seven runs short of a hundred at Old Trafford. His second century in

England (101) came in the Third Test, at Trent Bridge, and his third (107) in the Fourth Test, at Headingley. It was the first time an Australian had scored three centuries in successive Ashes Tests since Bradman in 1938.

Video replays were being used in this series for the first time in Ashes Tests, with Smith the first player given out when he was stumped by Healy at Lord's.

McDermott played only the First Test (without taking a wicket) before falling seriously ill. He had surgery in England before returning home.

Kent fast bowler Martin McCague, who grew up in Australia, made his England debut in the Third Test, taking four wickets. He shared the new-ball with another first-gamer, Mark Ilott.

Graham Thorpe also made his England debut at Trent Bridge, scoring a century (114 not out) in his first match.

Border had waited over six years to score his eighth Ashes century, but it came in a big way in the Fourth Test. His 200 not out was his second Test double-century and highest score against England. He followed Billy Murdoch and Bob Simpson as Australian captains to score a Test double-century in England.

Border and Steve Waugh (157 not out) put on an unbroken partnership of 332 for the fifth-wicket at Headingley—Waugh's century his third against England and all over 150 and unbeaten.

Hughes, who shouldered the Australian pace attack in the absence of McDermott, took his 200th Test wicket at Headingley—the seventh Australia to reach 200 wickets.

Victorian Paul Reiffel, in his first Test against England, took five wickets in the first innings of the Fourth Test, and finished with 19 wickets in the last three matches.

Gooch's resignation after the Fourth Test brought Atherton into the spotlight as England's new captain. He scored 72 in his first innings as skipper. But like Alec Stewart, Allan Lamb, Graham Gooch, Chris Cowdrey, John Emburey, Mike Gatting and David Gower immediately before him, Atherton's first match as England captain ended in defeat.

Mark Waugh's century at Edgbaston (137) was Australia's 10th of the series. He shared an Edgbaston record fifth-wicket partnership of 153 with Steve Waugh.

Australia's Edgbaston win took to 18 the record number of Ashes

Tests without defeat it had played under Border. The sequence was broken with England's victory in the final match, at The Oval.

Gooch scored two half-centuries (56 and 79) in the Sixth Test to overtake Gower as England's leading Test run-scorer (8293).

Warne's 34 wickets was a record for a leg-spinner in an Ashes series in England, surpassing Grimmett's 1930 tally of 29.

Healy finished the rubber with 26 dismissals—a record for a series in England.

The final Test brought to an end the Ashes career of Allan Border, who scored 3548 runs in 47 Tests against England, averaging 56.32 with eight centuries.

1993 AUSTRALIA WON SERIES 4–1

275 1st Test Old Trafford, Manchester, June 3, 4, 5, 6, 7
AUSTRALIA 289 (MA Taylor 124, MJ Slater 58, PM Such 6/67) and **5/432 dec** (IA Healy 102*, DC Boon 93, SR Waugh 78*, ME Waugh 64)
ENGLAND 210 (GA Gooch 65, MG Hughes 4/59, SK Warne 4/51) and **332** (GA Gooch 133, CC Lewis 43, MG Hughes 4/92, SK Warne 4/86)
CAPTAINS AR Border [AUST] GA Gooch [ENG]
RESULT Australia won by 179 runs

276 2nd Test Lord's, June 17, 18, 19, 20, 21
AUSTRALIA 4/632 dec (DC Boon 164*, MJ Slater 152, MA Taylor 111, ME Waugh 99, AR Border 77)
ENGLAND 205 (MA Atherton 80, MG Hughes 4/52, SK Warne 4/57) and **365** (MA Atherton 99, GA Hick 64, AJ Stewart 62, MW Gatting 59, TBA May 4/81, SK Warne 4/102)
CAPTAINS AR Border [AUST] GA Gooch [ENG]
RESULT Australia won by an innings and 62 runs

277 3rd Test Trent Bridge, Nottingham, July 1, 2, 3, 5, 6
ENGLAND 321 (RA Smith 86, N Hussain 71, MG Hughes 5/92) and **6/422 dec** (GA Gooch 120, GP Thorpe 114*, RA Smith 50, N Hussain 47*)
AUSTRALIA 373 (DC Boon 101, ME Waugh 70, MJ Slater 40, MJ McCague 4/121) and **6/202** (BP Julian 56*, SR Waugh 47*)
CAPTAINS GA Gooch [ENG] AR Border [AUST]
RESULT draw

278 4th Test Headingley, Leeds, July 22, 23, 24, 25, 26
AUSTRALIA 4/653 dec (AR Border 200*, SR Waugh 157*, DC Boon 107, MJ Slater 67, ME Waugh 52)
ENGLAND 200 (GA Gooch 59, MA Atherton 55, PR Reiffel 5/65) and **305** (AJ Stewart 78, MA Atherton 63, TBA May 4/65)
CAPTAINS AR Border [AUST] GA Gooch [ENG]
RESULT Australia won by an innings and 148 runs

279 5th Test Edgbaston, Birmingham, August 5, 6, 7, 8, 9
ENGLAND 276 (MA Atherton 72, JE Emburey 55*, AJ Stewart 45, PR Reiffel 6/71) and **251** (GP Thorpe 60, GA Gooch 48, TBA May 5/89, SK Warne 5/82)
AUSTRALIA 408 (ME Waugh 137, IA Healy 80, SR Waugh 59) and **2/120** (ME Waugh 62*)
CAPTAINS MA Atherton [ENG] AR Border [AUST]
RESULT Australia won by eight wickets

280 6th Test The Oval, August 19, 20, 21, 22, 23
ENGLAND 380 (GA Hick 80, AJ Stewart 76, GA Gooch 56, MA Atherton 50) and **313** (GA Gooch 79, MR Ramprakash 64, MA Atherton 42)
AUSTRALIA 303 (IA Healy 83*, MA Taylor 70, AR Border 48, ARC Fraser 5/87) and **229** (ME Waugh 49, PR Reiffel 42, SL Watkin 4/65)
CAPTAINS MA Atherton [ENG] AR Border [AUST]
RESULT England won by 161 runs

1981–1993
Questions 1–10

1 Which England opening batsman had two non-scoring periods totalling 153 minutes during the Perth Test of 1982–83?

2 Which Australian bowler took exactly 50 per cent of his Test wickets in Ashes Tests, and turned 35 during his final Test appearance?

3 With which scoring feat did England opener Chris Broad join the illustrious group of Hobbs, Sutcliffe and Hammond, during the Australian tour of 1986–87?

4 Which batsman scored the winning run for Australia to regain the Ashes at Old Trafford in 1989?

5 Which England bowler almost took a hat-trick in Sydney in 1990–91 ... dismissing Border and Jones, only to have Steve Waugh dropped first ball?

6 When did Ian Botham first captain England against Australia?

7 England's remarkable 18-run win at Headingley in 1981 came after a first innings deficit of:
a) 227 runs
b) 283 runs
c) 356 runs

8 Which Australian fast bowler took 7/81 in England's first innings at Lord's in 1981, only to miss the final three Tests through injury?

9 Which was the first series of the 1980s where Australia regained the Ashes?

10 All-rounder Greg Matthews opened the batting in his first Test against England ... true or false?

Questions 11–20

11 Which bowler played only one Test, in the 1985 series, becoming the first Yorkshire player to be selected for England since the retirement of Geoff Boycott three years earlier?

12 Which leg-spinner took five wickets in England's second innings in Sydney in 1986–87, giving Australia victory?

13 Which English umpire was threatened by members in front of the Lord's Long Room during the 1980 Centenary Test?

14 In 18 matches under Mike Brearley, England:
a) Won 16 and lost none
b) Won 14 and lost two
c) Won 11 and lost four

15 Who was the Australian vice-captain in England on the 1985 tour, scoring 119 in the First Test, at Headingley?

16 Who was the Kent paceman who played only two Ashes Tests in the 1980s, taking 17 wickets at 10.8?

17 Who was David Gower's Tiger Moth flying partner when he 'buzzed' the Carrara ground during England's innings on the 1990–91 tour?

18 Geoff Boycott became the first English player to play 100 Tests ... true or false?

19 Alan Knott, Bob Taylor and which other wicketkeeper all played for England in the 1981 series?

20 Which Australian off-spinner took 22 wickets in the 1982–83 series?

Questions 21–30

21 Which Australian batsman scored his only Test century in his debut match, at The Oval in 1981?

22 Bob Willis took over the England captaincy from Ian Botham after the first two Tests of 1981 . . . true or false?

23 Which Australian tailender batted at number three in the first innings and number five in the second in the Third Test, in Adelaide, in 1982–83?

24 Leg-spinner Bob Holland took 5/68 in the second innings at Lord's in 1985 in his first Ashes Test. How old was Holland?
 a) 38
 b) 39
 c) 40

25 Which England batsman shared a triple-century partnership with David Gower at Edgbaston in 1985?

26 Which two Australian fast bowlers took a combined 30 wickets in their first Ashes series in 1986–87?

27 Mark Taylor's 1989 tour aggregate of 839 was surpassed by only two players in the history of Ashes rubbers. Who were they?

28 Which England batsman was dismissed 'handled ball' in the 1993 series?

29 In which series did Trevor Chappell have his taste of Test cricket?

30 Who captained England during the 1989 series . . . Mike Gatting, David Gower or Ian Botham?

Questions 31–40

31 Which two England players featured in the final catch, off Botham's bowling, to give England a three-run win in Melbourne in 1982–83?

32 Which Australian wicketkeeper of the 1980s joined the '90s club'—narrowly missing an Ashes century?

33 The now-BBC commentator Jonathon Agnew played in just one Ashes Test, in 1985. How many wickets did he take?

34 Ian Botham scored 138 in the Brisbane Test of 1986–87, with one over from Merv Hughes realising an Ashes record:
a) 19 runs
b) 22 runs
c) 29 runs

35 Who are the two Australians whose only Test against England was the Bicentenary Test of 1988?

36 England failed to win a single Test under Ian Botham's captaincy . . . true or false?

37 Which Lancashire seamer made his debut in the Fifth Test of 1981, scoring his maiden first-class half-century at number 10?

38 Who were the two Australian wicketkeepers during the 1986–87 series?

39 Who was regarded as Graham Gooch's lbw bogeyman in the late 1980s and early '90s?

40 Which England batsman had three scores in excess of 150 and totalled 732 runs at 81.3 in the 1985 series?

Questions 41–50

41 Craig McDermott took 8/141 in England's innings of 9/482 dec at Old Trafford in 1985. Who took the other wicket?

42 Who became the third England wicketkeeper to score an Ashes hundred, in Perth in 1986–87?

43 Steve Waugh's first batting average for Tests in England was:
a) 177
b) 243
c) 393

44 Which England bowler took 8/43 to complete England's victory at Headingley in 1981?

45 Apart from the Headingley Test, where was Australia's other nightmare loss in 1981, when they were dismissed for 121 chasing 151 for victory?

46 Which England nightwatchman scored 95 in the Fifth Test, in Sydney, in 1982–83?

47 Greg Chappell captained Australia for the last four Tests of the 1981 tour . . . true or false?

48 Who were the three members of England's 1989 Fourth Test side who had signed for a rebel tour of South Africa, and were subsequently dropped for the final two Tests?

49 Fast bowler Martin McCague made his England debut at Trent Bridge in 1993, sharing the new-ball with which other first-gamer?

50 Which two players were out for 99 at Lord's in 1993?

ANSWERS *1981–1993*

1–10

1 Chris Tavare
2 Jeff Thomson (100 wickets against England, and 200 overall)
3 He scored three Test centuries on tour
4 David Boon
5 Phil Tufnell
6 1980 Centenary Test
7 a) 227 runs
8 Geoff Lawson
9 1982–83
10 True (in the second innings he opened with Andrew Hilditch)

11–20

11 Arnie Sidebottom
12 Peter Sleep
13 David Constant
14 c) Won 11 and lost four
15 Andrew Hilditch
16 Richard Ellison
17 John Morris
18 False (Colin Cowdrey was the first to 100)
19 Paul Downton
20 Bruce Yardley

21–30

21 Dirk Wellham
22 False (Mike Brearley took over from Botham)
23 Geoff Lawson
24 a) 38
25 Tim Robinson
26 Bruce Reid and Merv Hughes
27 Don Bradman and Walter Hammond
28 Graham Gooch
29 1981
30 David Gower

31–40

31 Chris Tavare and Geoff Miller (Tavare spilled the catch, but Miller took it on the rebound)
32 Wayne Phillips
33 None
34 b) 22 runs
35 Mike Veletta and Tony Dodemaide
36 True
37 Paul Allott
38 Tim Zoehrer and Greg Dyer
39 Terry Alderman
40 David Gower

41–50

41 The other wicket (Lamb) was run out
42 Jack Richards
43 c) 393 (with scores of 177*, 152*, 21* and 43)
44 Bob Willis
45 Edgbaston
46 Eddie Hemmings
47 False (Chappell didn't tour England in 1981)
48 John Emburey, Tim Robinson and Neil Foster
49 Mark Ilott
50 Mark Waugh and Mike Atherton

Chapter Seven

Specialist Categories

The Captains

1 The England captains of the 1980s and '90s David Gower, Mike Gatting, John Emburey, Chris Cowdrey, Graham Gooch, Allan Lamb, Alec Stewart and Mike Atherton all had a common factor in their first matches as captain. What was it?

2 Who was the 41-year-old who captained England in one Ashes Test?

3 Allan Border captained Australia in 29 Ashes Tests—more than any other player. Who holds the record for England?

4 Three wicketkeepers have captained Australia in Tests against England. Name two of them.

5 Only one captain has led England to more than 10 Test victories over Australia. Who was that captain?

6 Douglas Jardine's deputy on the 1932–33 Bodyline tour was appointed England captain for the 1934 home series. What was his name?

7 Which Australian captain led Australia to a record eight consecutive Ashes Test victories?

8 Who led England in the First Test of the 1990–91 series, in the absence of the injured Graham Gooch?

9 Of these long-serving Australian captains, which has the greatest winning percentage in Ashes Tests?
a) Monty Noble
b) Don Bradman
c) Allan Border
d) Ian Chappell

10 The respective captains in the 1905 series were born on the same day. Who were they?

11 Only four England captains this century have retained the Ashes in Australia. Name three of them.

12 Three Australians have 100 per cent winning records as captains in Ashes Tests. Name two of them.

13 The first time the two captains have scored centuries in the same Ashes Test was at Lord's in 1930. Who were those players?

14 Which future England captain made his Test debut at Edgbaston in 1975, scored a pair, and was subsequently dropped for the next match?

15 Who are the three Australian captains to have scored 200 or better in a Test innings in England?

Where Were They Born?

1 Which England captain was born in Scotland?

2 Which member of the England team for the 1932–33 Bodyline series was born in Australia?

3 Who were the two New Zealand-born bowlers in the 1993 Ashes series?

4 Which England captain was born in India?

5 The England all-rounder Philip de Freitas was born in . . .

6 Where was the Australian-raised England fast bowler Martin McCague born?

7 Which member of the Australian team for the first Test match was born in Ireland?

8 Which Australian bowler of the early 1970s was born in Hampshire, England?

9 Billy Midwinter, a member of Australia's team for the first Test match, also played for England. In which country was he born?

10 Which England spinner, who finished an Ashes series as his side's leading wicket-taker, was born in Scotland?

11 Who was the exciting young Australian batsman of the late 1920s and early 1930s who was born at Rutherglen in Scotland?

12 Which England captain was born in Italy?

13 In which country was Clarrie Grimmett born?

14 Which England captain was born in Lima, Peru, in 1910?

15 Barnsby 'BB' Cooper was educated in England and played for Australia in the first Test match, yet he was born in neither country. In which country was he born?

The Venues

1 The highest innings total in Ashes Tests is England's 7/903 dec in 1938. At which ground?

2 Where is Australia's most successful home venue—in percentage terms—in Tests against England?

3 How many grounds have been used for Ashes Test matches?

4 The playing pitch at which English venue suffered an attack of 'Fusarium Oxysporum' in 1972, enabling Derek Underwood to take 10 wickets?

5 The first Test match in England was staged at The Oval in 1880. Where was the Centenary Test played 100 years later?

6 At which ground was Brisbane's first Ashes Test in 1928–29?

7 The biggest crowd to attend an Australia-England Test was 350,534, at:
a) Sydney Cricket Ground
b) Melbourne Cricket Ground
c) The Oval
d) Lord's

8 Which English venue hosted Ashes Tests in 1902 and 1909, but not another for more than 50 years?

9 Which ground has hosted the most Australia-England Test matches?

10 At which English ground did Don Bradman score successive Test triple-centuries, in 1930 (334) and 1934 (304)?

11 The first day of which ground's maiden Test match was washed out?

12 Which English venue has hosted only one Ashes Test, on the 1902 tour?

13 At which ground did Walter Hammond finish with a career average in Ashes Tests of 161.6?

14 Which was the third Australian venue to host Test matches?

15 Australia and England both have 100 per cent winning records at certain venues. Which ones?

Other Sports

1 Which Australian fast bowler of the 1930s was a member of South Melbourne's 1933 premiership side in the VFL?

2 Which England captain also played a rugby union international at fly-half against Wales?

3 Which player represented Australia at hockey in the 1956 Olympic Games before playing Test cricket, where he scored two Ashes hundreds?

4 Who was the England player of the 1920s and '30s who scored three Ashes centuries, and also represented England in the 'Victory' soccer international in 1919?

5 The Waugh twins, Steve and Mark, represented NSW at schoolboy level in cricket and which two other sports?

6 Jeff Thomson had taken 33 wickets in the 1974–75 series before being injured playing which other sport on the rest day of the Fifth Test, in Adelaide?

7 Which England captain held the world long-jump record for 21 years?

8 Which Australian fast bowler played first-grade rugby league for Sydney club St George in the 1940s?

9 Australian swing bowler Max Walker played VFL football for which club?

10 Which Australian captain later became involved in the development of golf clubs?

11 Who was the Australian batsman of the 1950s and '60s who was offered a contract to play professional baseball in the United States?

12 Which long-serving Australian batsman was one of the leading figures in the establishment of rugby league in Australia?

13 Johnny 'JWHT' Douglas won an Olympic Games gold medal, in which sport?

14 Which Australian batsman of the 1920s and '30s could also claim excellence at football, baseball, gymnastics, hockey and athletics?

15 Which England opening batsman played two Ashes Tests— both in the 1958–59 series—and was also a soccer international and leading player for Arsenal?

Injuries & Illnesses

1 England captain Graham Gooch missed the First Test of 1990–91 due to surgery on a poisoned finger. In which city was he hospitalised for treatment?

2 Which Australian tailender was struck by a John Snow bouncer in Sydney in 1970–71, triggering a crowd reaction against Snow and an England walk-off?

3 Which England player returned to Test cricket after having had his right kneecap removed?

4 Which England player began his long Test career at Trent Bridge in 1964, but wasn't able to bat in the second innings— or the next Test—due to a fractured finger?

5 Who was the Australian batsman who passed 40 in each of his three Tests, only to have his career then curtailed by a back injury?

6 Who was the Australian batsman who batted after being struck in the ribs while fielding at Old Trafford in 1948— only to then spend 10 days in hospital?

7 Why didn't England captain Freddie Brown bat in the second innings of the Adelaide Test in 1950–51?

8 Which England bowler administered life-saving assistance to Rick Darling after the Australian opener had been struck under the heart by a Bob Willis delivery in Adelaide in 1978–79?

9 Which member of Australia's 1972 touring party required transfusions of 40 pints of blood after being struck in the face by a Tony Greig delivery six months earlier?

10 Which player was called up to reinforce the England party of 1974–75 after Dennis Amiss and John Edrich had suffered hand injuries in the First Test?

11 Who was the England bowler called into the side for the Perth Test of 1990–91 as a replacement for Angus Fraser, who had a hip injury?

12 Why was Australia's wicketkeeper John Maclean forced to leave the field during England's first innings of his final Test, in 1978–79?

13 In the Adelaide Bodyline Test, Australian wicketkeeper Bert Oldfield suffered a fractured skull while hooking. Who kept wicket in England's second innings?

14 Which England captain scored 63 and 36 in a Headingley Test, batting virtually one-handed after injuring his left hand while fielding?

15 Who was the bowler who struck Rick McCosker with a bouncer in the 1977 Centenary Test, fracturing the Australian's jaw?

What's in a Name?

1 How many players with the surname Darling have played in Ashes Tests?

2 Who is the last alphabetically-listed player to have taken part in Ashes Tests?

3 Which two England captains shared the same surnames with Australian off-spinners?

4 England fast bowler Bob Willis adopted an additional middle name, after which folk singer?

5 What was 'Gubby' Allen's christian name?

6 What is the most common surname to represent Australia in Ashes Tests?

7 Which member of Australia's 1993 touring party shared the same surname with an Australian Ashes player of the 1950s?

8 Who is the only player with a surname starting with 'Q' to play in Australia–England Tests?

9 Five Smiths have played for England in Tests against Australia. Name three of them.

10 Who is the first alphabetically-listed Australian to play in Ashes Tests?

11 Which two England fast bowlers of the 1970s shared the same surname?

12 Name four of the six O' . . . 's who have played for Australia in Tests against England.

13 Which player was born with the surname Durtanovich, but played in Ashes Tests under a different name?

14 The longest surname of an England player in an Ashes Test runs to 14 letters. The owner played just one Test but went on to become president of the MCC. Who was it?

15 The longest surname for an Australian in Ashes Tests also runs to 14 letters. Whose name was it?

Wicketkeepers

1 Which wicketkeeper came into the Australian side to replace the injured Bert Oldfield for the Fourth Test of the Bodyline series in 1932–33?

2 Rod Marsh made 355 dismissals in his 96 Tests . . . how many of them were stumped?

3 Greg Dyer was Australia's wicketkeeper in the Bicentenary Test in 1988, but left the field late in England's innings after being struck on the nose. Who kept wicket in his place?

4 Each of the 11 England players at The Oval in 1884 were called on to bowl, with the wicketkeeper finishing with the best figures of 4/19. What was his name?

5 Which England wicketkeeper of the 1960s played 10 Ashes Tests, but had made his England debut a decade earlier as a specialist batsman?

6 Who was Australia's first-choice wicketkeeper on the 1985 tour?

7 Which player, in the 1930s, became the first wicketkeeper to score an Ashes Test century?

8 Godfrey Evans missed two Tests in the 1958–59 series, enabling which player to make the only Test appearances of his career?

9 With Rod Marsh and Alan Knott at World Series Cricket, who were the two wicketkeepers new to Ashes Tests at the start of the 1978–79 series?

10 Name one of the wicketkeepers in the first Test match back in March, 1877.

11 Who's the only Australian wicketkeeper to score his maiden first-class century in an Ashes Test?

12 Which England champion had an inglorious end to his Test career, conceding a world record 37 byes when he filled in as wicketkeeper after Les Ames was injured during an Ashes Test in the 1930s?

13 England's wicketkeeper in the 1980 Centenary Test at Lord's played only one Ashes Test. Who was he?

14 Australia chose a new wicketkeeper for the last two Tests of 1978–79. Who was he?

15 Which keeper holds the record of 28 dismissals in an Ashes rubber?

The Batsmen

1 Who was the Queenslander who was preferred to Don Bradman after Bradman's maiden Test appearance?

2 Who was the England left-hander who scored 185—his only Test century—in Sydney in 1965–66, sharing a double-century partnership with Geoff Boycott?

3 Which Australian batsmen became the first pair to bat throughout a full day of an Ashes Test in England?

4 Who are the two players who have scored more than 900 runs in an Ashes rubber?

5 What was the name of the England batsman who, in Sydney in 1903–04, scored 287 on his Test debut?

6 In the 1978–79 series, Australia used a total of four opening batsmen, with each of them run out at least once. Who were they?

7 Who were the three teenagers to have scored Ashes Test centuries?

8 The first instance of brothers scoring centuries in the same Ashes Test came from:
a) The Gregorys
b) The Graces
c) The Chappells
d) The Waughs

9 Which England opener figured in 16 first-wicket century partnerships against Australia?

10 Who's the only England batsman to carry his bat through a completed innings without reaching a century—finishing 99 not out?

11 Four batsmen have scored triple-centuries in Ashes Tests. Who were they?

12 Don Bradman's average in the 1930 series was:
a) 118.94
b) 139.14
c) 148.73
d) 164.22

13 Who was the first England player to score a century in his first Ashes Test?

14 Which English player scored four Test double-centuries against Australia?

15 How many Test centuries did Allan Border score against England?

The Bowlers

1 Who was the England seamer who played just two Tests over a 12-year period—recalled at 40 for the Headingley Test in 1961?

2 What was the record tally of wickets shared by Australia's spinners, Shane Warne and Tim May, in England in 1993?
a) 47
b) 55
c) 57
d) 61

3 In the same match back in the 1894–95 series, England's Johnny Briggs and Australia's . . . became the first players to take 100 Test wickets.

4 With what type of delivery did Eric Hollies deceive Don Bradman in the Australian's final Test innings?

5 Who was the Australian slow-bowler who was known to make birdcalls as he was running into bowl?

6 No-one has ever taken more wickets in a day's play than this Yorkshire spinner, who claimed 14/80 on the third day of a Test at Lords, with 15/104 overall. Who was he?

7 The only player to capture two hat-tricks in Ashes Tests went on to become secretary of the Melbourne Cricket Club. Who was he?

8 Who was the record-breaking slow-bowler who played at first-class level for three teams before being chosen for Australia?

9 Which Australian off-spinner had one season of fame— taking 21 wickets at 15.23 in a five-Test series that represented his entire Test career?

10 At Old Trafford in 1981, an England bowler claimed his 100th wicket against Australia, while an Australian claimed his 150th against England. Who were the two bowlers?

11 When Bob Massie took 16/137 on debut at Lord's in 1972, who took the other four England wickets?

12 Seven England bowlers have taken more than 100 Test wickets against Australia. Name four of them.

13 Who has the best strike-rate among these Australian bowlers in Ashes Tests?
a) Dennis Lillee
b) Clarrie Grimmett
c) Terry Alderman
d) Ray Lindwall

14 Which England bowler took only one wicket in the 1932–33 Bodyline series—dismissing Don Bradman first ball.

15 Who were the two Australian bowlers who captured 19 of the 20 England wickets in the First Test of 1934?

Absolute Trivia

1 Which Australian bowler greeted Derek Randall with a rubber snake as he went to the wicket during the Sixth Test of 1978–79?

2 Don Bradman took only one wicket in his 37 Ashes Tests. Who was the batsman?

3 Which England captain's courage was acknowledged by a Sydney barrow boy's cry of: 'FINE LETTUCES! FINE LETTUCES! HEARTS LIKE . . . 'S!'?

4 What was Roy Park's wife doing when he was bowled first ball in his only Test match?

5 Who was the Queensland Sheffield Shield player who took two catches while fielding as a substitute at the Gabba in 1990–91?

6 What is the common thread in centuries scored by Ken Barrington (Adelaide, 1962–63), Barrington (Melbourne, 1965–66), Ian Botham (Old Trafford, 1981), Joe Darling (Adelaide, 1897–98), Doug Walters (Perth, 1974–75) and Rick McCosker (Trent Bridge, 1977)?

7 Six sets of brothers have represented Australia together in Ashes Tests. Who were they?

8 Who was the first batsman given out by video evidence in an Ashes Test?

9 Who was the bowler involved in Dennis Lillee's 'Aluminium Bat Affair' in the Perth Test of 1979–80?

10 For which club in Lancashire's Northern League was Mike Whitney playing when he won a surprise Australian call-up in 1981?

11 Who was the Australian captain who demonstrated his boredom at an impending draw by reading a newspaper in the outfield?

12 Who was Tony Greig's first wicket in Test cricket?

13 Which Australian batsman grabbed a souvenir stump and ran from the field at Trent Bridge in 1948—only to find out Australia still required an extra run for victory?

14 Before the 1896 Test at The Oval, five England players threatened to strike over match payments. How much were the professionals being paid?

15 The great grandfather of Australian batsman Paul Sheahan also played Tests against England. What was his name?

ANSWERS *Specialist Categories*

THE CAPTAINS

1 They led England to defeat
2 Tom Graveney (1968)
3 Archie MacLaren
4 The three are Jack Blackham, Billy Murdoch and Barry Jarman
5 Mike Brearley
6 Bob Wyatt
7 Warwick Armstrong
8 Allan Lamb
9 b) Don Bradman
10 FS Jackson (England) and Joe Darling (Australia)
11 The four are Mike Gatting, Percy Chapman, Len Hutton and Mike Brearley
12 The three are Hugh Trumble (two from two), Hugh Massie (one from one) and Neil Harvey (one from one)
13 Percy Chapman and Bill Woodfull
14 Graham Gooch
15 Billy Murdoch, Bob Simpson and Allan Border

WHERE WERE THEY BORN

1 Mike Denness
2 'Gubby' Allen
3 Andy Caddick (England) and Brendon Julian (Australia)
4 Colin Cowdrey
5 Dominica
6 Northern Ireland
7 Tom Horan
8 Tony Dell
9 England
10 Peter Such
11 Archie Jackson
12 Ted Dexter

13 New Zealand
14 Freddie Brown
15 India

THE VENUES

1 The Oval
2 Adelaide Oval (with a 52 per cent winning rate . . . 13 from 25)
3 13
4 Headingley
5 Lord's
6 The Exhibition Ground
7 b) Melbourne Cricket Ground (Third Test, 1936–37)
8 Edgbaston
9 Melbourne Cricket Ground
10 Headingley
11 Old Trafford (1884)
12 Bramall Lane, Sheffield
13 Sydney Cricket Ground
14 Adelaide Oval (First Test, 1884–85)
15 Bramall Lane (Australia) and The Exhibition Ground (England)

OTHER SPORTS

1 Laurie Nash
2 Mike Smith
3 Brian Booth
4 Patsy Hendren
5 Soccer and tennis
6 Tennis
7 CB Fry
8 Ray Lindwall
9 Melbourne
10 Greg Chappell
11 Norm O'Neill
12 Victor Trumper

13 Boxing
14 Victor Richardson
15 Arthur Milton

INJURIES & ILLNESSES

1 Adelaide
2 Terry Jenner
3 Denis Compton
4 Geoff Boycott
5 Martin Kent
6 Sid Barnes
7 He'd been involved in a car accident during the match
8 John Emburey
9 Graeme Watson
10 Colin Cowdrey
11 Phil Newport
12 Heat exhaustion
13 Victor Richardson
14 Hon Lionel Tennyson
15 Bob Willis

WHAT'S IN A NAME

1 Three (Len, Joe and Rick)
2 Tim Zoehrer (Australia)
3 Peter May (and Tim) and Norman Yardley (and Bruce)
4 Bob Dylan
5 George
6 Gregory (Dave, Ned, Jack, Syd and Ross)
7 Michael Slater (and Keith)
8 Willie Quaife (England)
9 The five Smiths are Robin, Mike, Peter, Alan (or AC) and Ernest (or 'Tiger')
10 Ted a'Beckett
11 Peter and John Lever
12 The six are Leo O'Brien, John O'Connor, Simon O'Donnell, Kerry O'Keeffe, Norm O'Neill and Bill O'Reilly

13 Len Pascoe
14 Stanley Christopherson
15 'Chuck' Fleetwood-Smith

WICKETKEEPERS

1 Hammy Love
2 12
3 Mike Veletta
4 Hon Alfred Lyttelton
5 Jim Parks
6 Wayne Phillips
7 Les Ames (England)
8 Roy Swetman
9 John Maclean (Australia) and Bob Taylor (England)
10 The two were Jack Blackham (Australia) and John Selby (England)
11 Ian Healy
12 Frank Woolley
13 David Bairstow
14 Kevin Wright
15 Rod Marsh

THE BATSMEN

1 Otto Nothling
2 Bob Barber
3 Geoff Marsh and Mark Taylor (1989)
4 Don Bradman and Walter Hammond
5 Reginald 'Tip' Foster
6 Graeme Wood, Gary Cosier, Rick Darling and Andrew Hilditch
7 Archie Jackson, Neil Harvey and Doug Walters
8 c) The Chappells (1972)
9 Jack Hobbs
10 Geoff Boycott (1979–80)
11 Don Bradman (twice), Bob Simpson, Bob Cowper and Len Hutton

12 b) 139.14
13 WG Grace
14 Walter Hammond
15 Eight

THE BOWLERS

1 Les Jackson
2 b) 55
3 Charlie 'The Terror' Turner
4 A googly
5 'Chuck' Fleetwood-Smith
6 Hedley Verity (1934)
7 Hugh Trumble
8 Clarrie Grimmett (Wellington, Victoria, South Australia)
9 Jack Iverson (1950–51)
10 Bob Willis (England) and Dennis Lillee (Australia)
11 Dennis Lillee
12 The seven are Ian Botham, Bob Willis, Wilfred Rhodes, SF Barnes, Derek Underwood, Alec Bedser and Bobby Peel
13 c) Terry Alderman (one wicket every 47.17 balls)
14 Bill Bowes
15 Bill O'Reilly and Clarrie Grimmett

ABSOLUTE TRIVIA

1 Rodney Hogg
2 Walter Hammond (1932–33)
3 Freddie Brown
4 She was picking up her knitting wool, and missed her husband's entire Test career!
5 Peter Cantrell
6 They all reached their centuries with a six

7 Charles and Alec Bannerman, Ned and Dave Gregory, George and Walter Giffen, Albert and Harry Trott, Ian and Greg Chappell, and Steve and Mark Waugh
8 Robin Smith (1993)
9 Ian Botham
10 Fleetwood
11 Warwick Armstrong (1921)
12 Ian Chappell (for a duck)
13 Sid Barnes
14 10 pounds
15 William Cooper

PHOTO ANSWERS

1 a) Victor Trumper (Australia)
   b) Geoff Boycott (England)
   c) Charlie Macartney (Australia)
   d) Len Hutton (England)
2 Centenary Test, 1977
3 a) Australia
   b) 1934
   c) Bill Woodfull
   d) Australia won 2–1
4 a) Brian Statham (England)
   b) Fred Spofforth (Australia)
   c) Arthur Mailey (Australia)
   d) Harold Larwood (England)
5 a) John Snow
   b) 7th Test 1970–71, Sydney
   c) Snow had hit Terry Jenner on the head with a bouncer
   d) Ray Illingworth led the England team off the field
6 a) Chris Old
   b) 40
7 a) Marsh
   b) Marsh
   c) Knott
   d) Knott

8 a) Ian Johnson (Australia)
and Peter May (England),
opposing captains in 1956
b) Lindsay Hassett (Australia)
and Freddie Brown (England),
opposing captains in 1950–51

9 a) Jack Russell (England)
b) Trevor Hohns (Australia)
c) Mark Taylor (Australia)

10 a) The pitch had been
vandalised
b) Headingley, Leeds
c) 1975

11 Tom Graveney (England) and
Barry Jarman (Australia) both
captained their countries in
only one Test. Coincidentally,
it was in the same match ...
fourth Test, Headingley, 1968

12 Ernie Jones

13 a) Lindsay Hassett (Australia)
b) Godfrey Evans (England)
c) Len Hutton (England)

14 Hans Ebeling, who was the
chief organiser of the 1977
Centenary Test

15 Greg Chappell

16 a) Allan Lamb (England)
b) Bruce Yardley (Australia)
c) Greg Chappell (Australia)
d) Rod Marsh (Australia)

17 a) Ian Chappell
b) Neil Hawke